OCR

AS

Critical Thinking

Jo Lally | Ruth Matthews | Alison Rowe | Jacquie Thwaites

www.heinemann.co.uk

✓ Free online support
✓ Useful weblinks
✓ 24 hour online ordering

01865 888118

OCR

ECOGNISING ACHIEVEMENT

Heinemann

Official Publisher Partnership

Contents

What is Critical Thinking?

Critical Thinking is a skill that involves understanding and evaluating reasoning. 'Reasoning' is often defined as 'the act or process of drawing conclusions from facts, evidence, etc.' In Critical Thinking, the word 'critical' is used to mean assessing strengths as well as weaknesses, rather than 'being critical' in the everyday sense.

This may sound remote from everyday life. In reality, we are reasoning every time we think about why, whether and how to do something, or whether to believe what someone is telling us. You may feel that your previous study along with your own abilities already enable you to think critically without you needing to study it further. However, practising Critical Thinking skills is like preparing for a sports event or training as a musician: however strong your natural ability, the right practice will enable you to perform better.

Critical Thinking is not a new subject. The ideas and concepts that make up its study were developed from philosophy and education. It has been part of university courses such as psychology, law and business studies (although not necessarily under the label of 'Critical Thinking') for many years. In the last five years, tens of thousands of students worldwide have taken A Level Critical Thinking.

Why study Critical Thinking?

- Because it is interesting.
- Because it is useful.
- Because it is fun.

Studying Critical Thinking will enable you to:

- understand and analyse what other people say and write
- decide whether other people's reasoning is strong or weak
- assert your own point of view and argue convincingly.

This will help in your other studies and your life to:

- make rational decisions
- give reasons for your own beliefs and actions
- write logical, structured essays.

What is the best way to prepare for a Critical Thinking examination?

This book is designed to prepare you for the OCR AS Critical Thinking examination. By the time you have worked through it you should have developed skills in analysis, evaluation and writing your own cogent, structured arguments.

Working through the materials and activities in this book will help you to prepare for the examination. However, you can apply your Critical Thinking skills every time you write an essay or a report for the other subjects you are studying. It is also one subject you can practise when you read a newspaper or magazine, when you argue with your family and friends, and even when you watch a television 'soap'.

OCR AS Critical Thinking

The OCR AS Level in Critical Thinking asks you to apply your skills in logical reasoning to evidence and arguments taken from a wide variety of sources and contexts.

The examination is modular. There are two units at AS Level that can be taken in the January and/or May examination sessions:

Unit 1   Introduction to Critical Thinking: a written examination of 1 hour 30 minutes
Unit 2   Assessing and Developing Argument: a written examination of 1 hour 30 minutes.

There is no coursework – the subject is assessed by examination only.

What does the examination assess?

The three Assessment Objectives are the criteria against which your answers will be marked in each unit. They coincide with the three skills identified as being central to the study of Critical Thinking.

AO 1   **Analyse** argument
'Analyse critically the use of different kinds of reasoning in a wide range of contexts.'

AO 2   **Evaluate** argument
'Evaluate critically the use of different kinds of reasoning in a wide range of contexts.'

AO 3   **Develop** own arguments
'Develop and communicate relevant and coherent arguments clearly and accurately in a concise and logical manner.'

Unit 1 represents 50% of the AS Level, and 25% of the A Level.
Unit 2 represents 50% of the AS Level, and 25% of the A Level.

You can use the AS Level to progress to an Advanced Level (A2) in Critical Thinking. This also has two units:

Unit 3   Ethical Reasoning and Decision-making (represents 25% of the A Level)
Unit 4   Critical Reasoning (represents 25% of the A Level).

You can find full details in the OCR specification, available at www.ocr.org.uk. There is a Heinemann textbook covering the A2 units.

Student Book

Units 1 and 2

Your AS Critical Thinking course is divided into two units. This Student Book provides an exact match to the OCR specification and as well as teaching material it includes activities, examiner tips and extension opportunities.

Exam Café

In our unique Exam Café you'll find lots of ideas to help you prepare for your Unit 1 and Unit 2 exams. You'll see the Exam Café at the end of Unit 1 and again at the end of Unit 2. You can **Relax** because there's handy advice on getting started on your AS Critical Thinking course, **Refresh your Memory** with summaries and checklists of the key ideas you need to revise and **Get the Result** through practising exam-style questions, accompanied by hints and tips from the examiners.

Student CD-ROM

LiveText

On the CD you will find an electronic version of the Student Book, powered by LiveText. As well as the Student Book and the LiveText tools there are:

- guidance to the activities – indicated by this icon

- interactive activities to help develop your Critical Thinking skills further – indicated by this icon.

Within the electronic version of the Student Book, you will also find the interactive Exam Café.

Exam Café

Immerse yourself in our contemporary interactive Exam Café environment! With a click of your mouse you can visit three separate areas in the café to **Relax**, **Refresh your Memory** or **Get the Result**. You'll find a wealth of material including the following.

- Revision Tips from students, Key Concepts, Common Mistakes and Examiner's Tips.

- Language of the Exam (an interactive activity).

- Revision Flashcards, Revision Checklists and The Basics.

- Sample Exam Questions (which you can try) with student answers and examiner comments.

Introduction to Unit 1

Learning to be a critical thinker is about developing the ability to structure and connect one's own thoughts and ideas logically and present them persuasively. The AS Critical Thinking course will help you acquire the skills necessary to be an effective critical thinker. The foundation for the whole AS and A Level Critical Thinking course is formed through the skills that are introduced in Unit 1.

The first part of the book covers Unit 1 and is itself split into two sections, which follow the format of the examination paper. Section 1 introduces the basic skills needed to analyse reasoning, that is to break arguments down into their component parts (reasons, conclusion, evidence, examples) and to describe how the elements relate to each other and to the argument as a whole. Section 1 also introduces some of the techniques used in evaluating reasoning, that is in judging whether the reasoning is strong or weak: identifying and assessing assumptions and evidence, etc.

In Section 2 of Unit 1 you will learn how to assess the credibility of sources, whether they are people, organisations or documents, by applying benchmarks, known as credibility criteria. Assessing credibility is a technique for deciding if something can be believed, but it does not tell you if something is true. Section 2 covers assessing the relative credibility of people or organisations. Together with the evaluation of evidence and information, this provides a means of reaching a judgement within a given context.

The skills needed for the Unit 1 examination will also help you to begin constructing your own structured arguments. This will be developed further in the part of this book covering Unit 2 of the AS qualification. In Unit 1 you will not be asked to identify flaws in reasoning or to assess the strengths and weaknesses of complete arguments. Those skills will be introduced in Unit 2.

Page 3 listed the three Assessment Objectives, or criteria, which are tested in AS Critical Thinking: analysing argument, evaluating argument and developing one's own arguments. In Unit 1 the marks are divided approximately equally between all three of the Assessment Objectives.

Learning objectives

- Understand the meaning of the key terms: argument, conclusion and reason.
- Identify simple arguments.
- Identify reasons and conclusions in simple arguments.
- Identify and use argument indicators.
- Understand that accuracy is important in Critical Thinking.

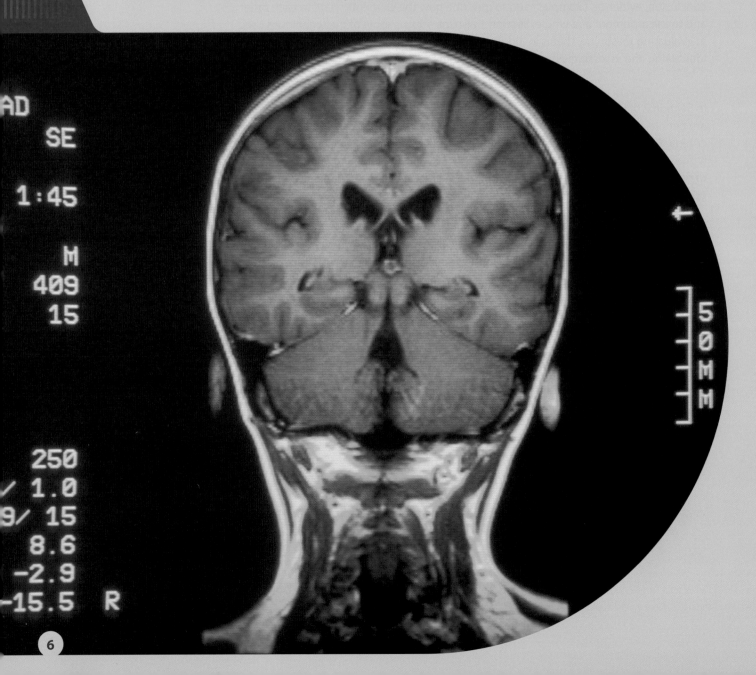

The meaning of 'argument'

> **REMEMBER**
>
> This chapter will focus on AO 1: Analyse argument, which requires you to analyse critically the use of different kinds of reasoning in a wide range of contexts.

In everyday usage the word 'argument' means a quarrel, dispute or exchange of views. In Critical Thinking '**argument**' has a very specific meaning. A Critical Thinking argument always includes:

- one or more reasons and a conclusion
- an attempt by the writer (or speaker) to persuade the reader (or listener) of something.

(You will notice in this book that we talk about the writer, or the author, and the reader of the written material we are considering. Exactly the same principles apply to thinking critically about reasoning in spoken language.)

Here is a very simple argument:

> The weather is very cold today. Therefore you should put on a warm coat.

The **reason** (for accepting the conclusion) is: 'The weather is very cold today.' The **conclusion** is: 'You should put on a warm coat.'

In terms of meaning, the conclusion comes last. However, when the argument is written (or said), its conclusion does not have to come at the end. It can be put at the beginning, the end, or (in longer arguments) anywhere, for example:

> You should put on a warm coat because the weather is very cold today.

Conclusions

A conclusion is often a statement of a point of view which the writer (or speaker) wants to persuade the reader (or listener) to accept. It is usually:

- something that we might (or might not) do
- something we might (or might not) believe, accept or support.

Reasons

Reasons are the basis for persuading you that the conclusion is true. You will find that there are very many different ways in which a writer tries to persuade the reader to accept the conclusion, but for the moment we will look at simple reasons.

Elements of argument

The reason (or reasons) and the conclusion are known as **elements** of argument. In later chapters you will learn about more elements of argument.

Argument

An attempt to persuade a reader (or listener) to accept something. An argument must have a conclusion and at least one reason.

Conclusion

The *conclusion of an argument* is a statement of something that the writer (or speaker) wants the reader (or listener) to accept based on the reasons given.

Reason

A statement that aims to persuade the reader to accept a conclusion.

ACTIVITY 1

Look back at the Key Terms definitions of 'conclusion' and 'reason'. Identify the reason(s) and conclusion in each of the following arguments.

A You enjoy dealing with different people. You should look for a career that involves dealing with people.

B The bus service on this route is useless. We ought to complain to the bus company.

C We are short of money this week. Beans on toast is cheap. We had better have beans on toast for tea today.

D The sun is very strong today and you are going to lie on the beach. You should put on plenty of sun cream.

E Heavy snow is forecast later on. The police have advised everyone to stay at home. You should stay home and not go to work.

F You are allergic to dog hair. The friends you are going to visit have a dog. You ought to take some medication to reduce your allergic reaction.

Identify an argument in source material

We have seen that an argument is an attempt to persuade through the use of reasoning – an appeal to rational thinking processes. However, language is used for many purposes. These are some of the main ones:

- giving an account of an event
- expressing an opinion
- explaining something
- asking questions
- imparting information
- giving instructions
- expressing humour
- telling stories
- rhetoric.

You need to be able to tell the difference between other uses of language and argument.

PAUSE FOR THOUGHT

What other uses of language can you think of?

■ Making others laugh – a vital use of language.

Sometimes written material may appear, at first glance, to be an argument, especially if it is a statement of something the writer believes, for example:

> ■ Manchester United is the best football team in the world.
> ■ Destroying the rainforest would be an environmental disaster.
> ■ Anyone who is more than 70 years old should not be allowed to drive a car.
> ■ Taxes are too high in this country.

Each of these statements is like the conclusion of an argument. But without a reason to support the statement, there is no argument. In Critical Thinking such statements are known as '**claims**', and they can be turned into an argument when one, or more, supporting reasons is added.

KEY TERM

Claim ●

A statement or judgement that can be challenged.

ACTIVITY 2

Turn each of the claims in the previous box into an argument by adding one, or more, relevant reasons. Pick a team and sport of your choice for the first opinion.

Sometimes there is a number of claims which together describe something that has taken place, without any attempt to persuade the reader, for example:

The jury took just 45 minutes to find Smith guilty. He was sentenced to five years in prison. The judge told him: 'You are a menace to society.'

The writer does not attempt to persuade anyone of anything about Smith, and therefore it is not an argument.

If you are unsure whether a piece of text is an argument (or not), check whether there is an attempt to persuade the reader to accept something.

ACTIVITY 3

Decide whether each of the following is an argument or not. If it is an argument, identify the conclusion and reason(s).

A It is obvious that longer prison sentences cut crime.

B The government should spend more on building new prisons. Other ways of punishing criminals are less effective than locking them up.

C We had a nice apartment with a balcony overlooking the bay. There were plenty of bars and nightclubs in the town. It was a really good holiday.

D I want to go on holiday after my exams. I find being by the sea is very relaxing and I will definitely need a rest after all that hard work. I ought to book a holiday at the seaside.

E People ignore the fact that we have animal impulses, because we are supposed to be civilised, but our basic nature is that of the jungle.

F The Prime Minister said that western nations had a duty to address global poverty. After the conference he visited a project to bring medical care to remote villages.

G Democracy is the worst form of government except all those other forms that have been tried from time to time. (Sir Winston Churchill, 1947)

- 'Our basic nature is that of the jungle.'

ACTIVITY 4

For each of the passages below, state whether it is an argument or not. If it is an argument add *one* more reason in support of the conclusion.

A The train has not arrived at the station. This is because a tree has fallen and blocked the line.

B The traffic is always heavy on Monday mornings. It is very important that you get to college on time. You should catch an earlier bus than usual.

C A family with small children wanting a pet should get a dog rather than a cat. Cats can scratch small children when they are picked up and children will always want to pick up a cat. Dogs are too big to pick up and like children more than cats do.

D I think I have caught a cold. My nose feels snuffly, my throat is sore and my head aches.

E The fire which destroyed the company's offices started in the canteen during the night. It spread very quickly through the office buildings because the company had not fitted smoke detectors.

Argument indicators

Being able to identify whether something is an argument, or another use of language, is a very important skill in Critical Thinking. So far we have looked at simple arguments, where it is quite easy to spot the conclusion. In longer arguments the conclusion may come before the reasons, in the middle, or at the end. The writer may not have stated the conclusion explicitly or clearly, or the passage may contain information that is not strictly part of the argument.

Where this is the case there are other clues we can use to help identify whether or not something is an argument. Arguments often contain useful words, known as **argument indicators**, that signal what elements of argument we are looking at and help us to sort out the sense of the argument.

> **Examples of argument indicators**
>
> Indicating a reason
> *because, as, since, due to, such as*
>
> Indicating a conclusion
> *therefore, so, thus, it follows that, consequently, should ..., ought ...*

Sometimes conclusion indicators can have uses other than showing that what follows is a conclusion, so you need to be careful to check that you really have found the conclusion.

PAUSE FOR THOUGHT

Read the comment and editorial pages in the newspaper. Look out for reason and conclusion indicators. What other argument indicators can you find that are not listed above?

REMEMBER

The words in the box above are only indicators, and do not show conclusively that the passage contains an argument. You need to find the conclusion and one or more reasons to be certain you have identified an argument.

ACTIVITY 5

a) **Identify the argument indicator words in this passage. State whether they indicate a reason or the conclusion.**

We should all try to recycle more of our kitchen waste, since this would reduce the amount of waste taken to landfill sites, and also because kitchen waste can be turned into useful compost.

b) **Arguments A–C below do not include argument indicators. Rewrite them with the words 'because' or 'therefore' in the right place to help show the reasons and the conclusion. (Take a look at the Pause for Thought box if you need some help.)**

A Trains are a better way to travel than a car. You can read during the journey and you do not need to worry about breakdowns or traffic jams.

B Football is not as exciting as commentators suggest. Many games end 0–0 and results matter only for the teams at the top or bottom of a table.

C The most popular meal in the UK is now chicken tikka masala. Spaghetti bolognese has replaced sausages and mash as a staple family meal. We should re-think our view of what constitutes classic British food.

c) **Look back at the arguments in Activity 1 (page 8). Insert suitable argument indicator words in each to show the reason(s) and conclusions.**

PAUSE FOR THOUGHT

Example D from Activity 3 (page 10) should help to show you what to do for Task b) (Activity 5).

This can be re-written as:
Because I want to go on holiday after my exams,
because I find being by the sea is very relaxing, and
because I will definitely need a rest after all that hard work,
therefore I ought to book a holiday at the seaside.

Re-write arguments A–C in Activity 5 b) in the same way.

EXAM TIP

Being able to identify an argument, as well as the component parts of an argument, is a very important skill in Unit 1.

Using argument indicators to help analyse the structure of an argument

In the same way as you have used 'because' and 'therefore' to make clear which parts of a passage are reasons and which part is the conclusion, you can use argument indicators to help check whether you have correctly identified these elements of an argument. For example:

■ the *because test* – insert 'because' to check for reasons

■ the *therefore test* – insert 'therefore' to check for the conclusion.

If you have put these words in the right places, then the text should still make sense and you have correctly identified the elements of an argument.

To see how this can work, look again at Argument C in Activity 5 about classic British food. When 'because' and 'therefore' were correctly inserted, it read as follows.

> *Because* the most popular meal in the UK is now chicken tikka masala and *because* spaghetti bolognese has replaced sausages and mash as a staple family meal, *therefore* we should re-think our view of what constitutes classic British food.

See what happens when you put 'because' and 'therefore' in the wrong places.

> *Because* we should re-think our view of what constitutes classic British food, *therefore* the most popular meal in the UK is now chicken tikka masala; *and therefore* spaghetti bolognese has replaced sausages and mash as a staple family meal.

This doesn't make sense, which confirms that the first version shows the argument structure correctly.

The importance of precision and accuracy in Critical Thinking

In this chapter you have studied the key fundamentals of Critical Thinking – identifying arguments, reasons and conclusions. You have also begun to analyse simple arguments.

In the examination, you will be asked to identify the reasons, the conclusion and other argument elements. It is extremely important to be very precise and accurate when you write down your answers. Look again at Argument B from Activity 5 on page 13.

> Football is not as exciting as commentators suggest. Many games end 0–0 and results matter only for the teams at the top or bottom of a table.

If you were asked to write down the conclusion, you might be tempted to put:

> Football is not exciting.

However, the writer is not saying that football is not exciting. He says it is not as exciting as commentators suggest. He implies that he finds it quite exciting, but not to the extent that some people do.

In the examination the answer 'Football is not exciting' would not have been awarded full marks because it is not accurate enough.

If you were asked to identify one of the reasons you might have written:

> Results don't matter for most teams.

Again, this answer would have been too vague to have achieved full marks: the argument specifically says *results matter only for the teams at the top or bottom of a table*.

You also need to make sure that, when you use technical Critical Thinking terms, you can use them accurately and write them down correctly. In the examination marks are available for the quality of written communication; incorrectly spelling key words such as 'reason' and 'argument' is likely to mean that you cannot be awarded all the available marks.

Here's a final (football) example to show the importance of precision when you use quotations.

> In our interview with Sir Jack Hayward, the chairman of Wolverhampton Wanderers, we mistakenly attributed to him the following comment: 'Our team was the worst in the First Division and I'm sure it will be the worst in the Premier League.' Sir Jack had just declined the offer of a hot drink. What he actually said was: 'Our tea was the worst in the First Division and I'm sure it will be worst in the Premier League.' Profuse apologies.
>
> *The Guardian*, 12 August 2003

Summary

You should now be able to:

- identify simple arguments
- analyse the structure of simple arguments
- use argument indicators
- understand the need for accuracy and precision in Critical Thinking

EXAM TIP

Identifying the elements of argument simply means matching the element label to the right section of the text.

Counter-assertions, counter-arguments, hypothetical reasoning and assumptions

Learning objectives

- Use common notation for the component parts of an argument.
- Understand and use counter-assertions and counter-arguments.
- Understand the nature of different claims.
- Recognise simple hypothetical reasoning.
- Understand the meaning of the term 'assumptions'.
- Identify assumptions in arguments.
- Phrase assumptions with precision.

Using common notation for the elements of an argument

You are probably used to using symbols and abbreviations in other subjects such as science and mathematics. In the same way, Critical Thinking makes use of a form of shorthand, sometimes called argument notation. It can help you to show argument structure more clearly and save time.

- **R** represents a reason.
- **C** represents a conclusion.

If there are several reasons, these can be shown as R1, R2, R3 and so on.

We will use this shorthand throughout this book and, in later chapters, we will use some more forms of notation for more complex elements of argument. When you write your own arguments, this notation is very useful in helping you to see the structure of what you have written. In the text that follows we will practise using it in simple arguments.

Using this shorthand, Argument D in Activity 3 (page 10) looks like this.

R1	(*because*) I want to go on holiday after my exams.
R2	(*because*) I find being by the sea is very relaxing.
R3	(*because*) I will definitely need a rest after all that hard work.
C	(*therefore*) I ought to book a holiday at the seaside.

Argument notation will be used throughout this book to help make the structure of arguments clear. You will find that if you start using it now, it will become very easy to use by the time you get to the exam.

Try this yourself with this short argument:

Animal experiments cause a great deal of suffering. The results of animal experiments are rarely applicable to humans. The continued use of animals in experiments cannot be justified.

This can be represented as shown below.

R1	Animal experiments cause a great deal of suffering.
R2	The results of animal experiments are rarely applicable to humans.
C	The continued use of animals in experiments cannot be justified.

In the examination you will not be tested on the use of argument notation, but it is a useful tool to help you work out an argument's structure and write down the structure clearly.

ACTIVITY 6

In each of the following arguments, there are two reasons and a conclusion. Identify these three elements using the appropriate notation.

A   Gas is an inexpensive way to heat your home. Gas heating boilers are small and neat. You should install gas central heating to heat your home.

B   Spending long periods in front of a computer screen can cause eye strain. You've been working on the computer for several hours. You should have a break from the computer.

C   Hair dye can ruin the condition of hair. You have had your hair dyed several times recently. You would be wise to use conditioner to improve the condition of your hair.

D   We need a new television. We ought to buy a Pentang. Pentang televisions have the latest technology.

E   This company has gained extra business in the last six months. People with up-to-date IT skills will be needed to help develop the new computer system. The company should recruit young people who have just left college.

F   The same old work and study routine gets very boring. Lack of exercise is making you feel unhealthy. You should try Soaks, the new and different fitness centre.

G   The government's campaign to get us to eat more healthily is doomed to fail to reduce obesity. Increasing exercise and reducing calorie intake works in very few cases. The government should direct money towards researching the causes of obesity instead.

Developing your own arguments

In the Unit 1 examination you will not be asked to produce your own structured arguments, but it is a skill that you will need as you prepare for later units of the course. Practice at constructing and expressing your own arguments will help you to understand and analyse other people's reasoning.

When you have drafted your argument, take time to review it and decide whether it really is an argument. Does it contain the essential elements of argument (reason(s) and conclusion)? Does it aim to persuade the reader of something?

REMEMBER

Being an effective Critical Thinker means you can apply Critical Thinking skills to your own work. Precision and accuracy are as important when you write your own arguments as when you are identifying the elements in someone else's argument.

TAKE IT FURTHER

Write four of your own arguments using two reasons and a conclusion. Some possible conclusions have been given to you. Alternatively, you could write your own.

Conclusion 1   Therefore, you should buy me a coffee.

Conclusion 2   Therefore, you should give me a pay rise.

Conclusion 3   Therefore, my mobile phone is one of the best on the market.

Conclusion 4   Therefore, I (do not) need to eat more healthily.

Conclusion 5   Therefore, the local council should provide football/skateboarding/some other leisure facilities for young people.

Conclusion 6   Therefore, you should (not) stay in a job if you are unhappy.

Conclusion 7   Therefore, people aged over 70 should not be allowed to drive a car.

Conclusion 8   Therefore, marriage is (not) an outdated institution.

Conclusion 9   Therefore, the Royal Family should (not) be scrapped.

Counter-argument and counter-assertion

So far we have looked at very short arguments. Longer passages, especially where they are discussing contentious issues, frequently contain a **counter-argument**. Here the author includes an opposing argument in order to dismiss it, or show its weaknesses, and therefore support their own argument. The counter-argument may be a single counter-claim (known as a **counter-assertion**), but it may also be a short argument with one or more reasons and an explicit conclusion.

By advancing a counter-argument, the writer also creates the impression that the issue has been considered in a balanced way because an opposing view has been taken into account. Politicians and newspaper columnists often use this technique.

Here is an example of an argument that contains a counter-argument.

> The proposal to allow 16- and 17-year-olds to vote, like the pressure to sexualise them, is yet another attempt to turn young people prematurely into adults. It is claimed that *they should be able to participate fully in society because at this age they can already pay taxes, leave home, marry, fight for their country and so on.* All of these are irrelevant. Few teenagers do these things. Quite rightly they are busy enjoying themselves. Once they have developed emotionally and intellectually, and learnt from some mistakes, there will be time enough for them to vote.

The author is arguing that the proposal to allow 16- and 17-year-olds to vote is an attempt to turn young people prematurely into adults. The counter-argument in italic type (that young people should be able to participate fully in society because they can pay taxes, etc.) is advanced only so it can be dismissed as irrelevant.

KEY TERMS

Counter-argument ●

An additional argument that is against, or counter to, what the conclusion seeks to establish. The writer normally presents the counter-argument in order to dismiss it.

Counter-assertion ●

If the writer presents a reason that would support an opponent's argument, rather than a counter-argument, then the writer is making a counter-assertion/claim.

Here is an example of an argument that contains a counter-assertion.

> We would be better off without modern gadgets. We waste a huge amount of money on them. It is commonly thought that they save time and labour, but we spend so much time choosing them, shopping for them and fixing them, that we actually spend more time and effort on the gadgets than we would have spent on the tasks they do.

Using argument indicator notation, CA stands for counter-assertion or counter-argument. So this argument could be written as follows.

C	We would be better off without modern gadgets.
R1	We waste a huge amount of money on them.
CA	*It is commonly thought that they save time and labour,* but
R2	we spend so much time choosing them, shopping for them and fixing them, that we actually spend more time and effort on the gadgets than we would have spent on the tasks they do.

The part of the argument in italics puts forward a point of view which disagrees with the conclusion. The author then says why it is wrong. This makes it a counter-assertion.

■ Might we be better off without so many modern gadgets?

Words and phrases that indicate there may be a counter-argument or counter-assertion in a passage include the following.

although, despite this, however, it has been said, it has been suggested that, contrary to this, on the other hand, some may argue

REMEMBER

Some of the indicator words above lead into the writer's point of view; some of them lead into the argument or assertion that is being dismissed.

PAUSE FOR THOUGHT

What other counter-argument indicator words and phrases can you think of, or find in news articles?

ACTIVITY 7

Identify the counter-argument or counter-assertion in the following arguments.

A It is commonly taken for granted that the introduction of GM crops should be strictly regulated. Opponents claim that they will be unsafe for human consumption and take over the countryside. However, humankind has been genetically modifying plants and animals for generations through selective breeding programmes. GM crops are no more to be feared than eating a Golden Delicious apple or an egg from a hen.

B Local pubs used to be full of people playing pool and darts, or just enjoying a drink in a convivial atmosphere. Since the ban on smoking in pubs, they have been practically empty. Even at weekends there are just two or three customers in the bar. Supposedly, the smoking ban was going to protect the health of workers and customers. But the smokers are still puffing away, out in the cold, and the non-smokers are sat outside with their smoking friends. The object of the ban has been defeated.

C The council is yet again showing its complete contempt for local residents by closing libraries. Officials argue that people are using the library service less because nowadays cut-price books can be bought in supermarkets. This is not the point: public libraries were one of the great social innovations which made educational opportunities available to the poor. Libraries continue to be used when they introduce new services, such as reading clubs for children or free computer facilities. That is the solution the council should be adopting.

TAKE IT FURTHER

Below are two short arguments. For each, turn the material given into a counter-argument by using a counter-argument indicator. Then write an argument saying why it is wrong. (The example that follows the arguments shows how to do this.)

A Honey could help counter the effects of ageing. A study of rats fed a diet of 10% honey showed that they had lower levels of anxiety and better spatial memory, compared with rats fed on sucrose. We should replace the sugar in our diet with honey.

B The legal age for driving should be raised to 18. After all, we are not allowed to vote until 18. These are both very responsible acts and the age limit should be the same for both.

Example argument

There are very high costs involved in staging major international events like the Olympics. Many cities remain in debt for many years afterwards. It is therefore regrettable that London won the 2012 Olympic Games.

Re-written argument

It has been suggested [counter-argument indicator] that it is regrettable that London won the 2012 Olympics, because the very high costs involved in staging major international events mean many cities remain in debt for several years afterwards. However, the UK will benefit in the long term from the raised profile of the capital city. We should look forward to the Olympics taking place in London.

Hypothetical reasoning

Claims

Any part of an argument can be referred to as a **claim**. Almost everything that is said or written, other than questions, exclamations and instructions, is a claim. A claim might be a fact ('Christmas day is on 25 December'), an opinion ('The Christmas holiday is far too long') or a statement of a principle ('It is wrong to kill animals'). Reasons and conclusions are claims. A claim is therefore something that is stated, and that can be challenged.

The use of the word 'claim' suggests to us that we should not believe it until it is verified or supported with reasons or evidence. However, it is important to remember that in Critical Thinking most of the time we focus on how an argument works if we take its claims to be true.

You will learn more about assessing claims in Chapter 5.

Hypothetical claims

As we have seen, a claim is any statement that can be challenged. A **hypothetical claim** is a statement in the form: 'If this happens, then that will happen.' Here's an example.

If we don't keep hospitals clean, then more people will catch nasty bugs like MRSA.

Hypothetical claims, therefore, predict what will happen, if something else happens.

You need to take care when you identify a statement as a hypothetical claim. First, the 'then' is not necessarily stated. We could write the previous example as: 'If we don't keep hospitals clean, more people will catch nasty bugs like MRSA.'

Second, some statements look similar to hypothetical claims, but are not. For example, 'I want a winter suntan even if I get skin cancer from the sunbed' is not a hypothetical claim, but a statement about what I want. However, 'If you use a sunbed too often, then you may get skin cancer' is a hypothetical claim, because it makes a prediction.

• Animal rights protesters proclaim their principles.

ACTIVITY 8

Read the following sentences and decide whether each is a hypothetical claim.

A Children don't get enough exercise.

B I intend to visit France this summer, even if I can only afford it by stopping going out with friends.

C If you visit France, you will find the way of life is far more relaxed than in this country.

D You ought to go to Professor Bloxwich's lecture, provided you have nothing else planned for today.

EXAM TIP

It is the 'if … then …' form of the statement, and its status as a prediction, which makes it hypothetical.

Simple hypothetical reasoning

A hypothetical claim may be used as a reason or as a conclusion. When you see 'if' within a passage you should think about whether it is a reason or a conclusion – but remember it may be neither. It is the whole claim – the 'if' part together with the 'then' part – that forms a single component of the argument. As we saw earlier, a hypothetical claim looks at the consequences that might occur if something were the case. This can help us to make decisions about how to act, depending on what happens. In this example, **hypothetical reasoning** uses a hypothetical claim as a reason to support a conclusion.

> If it rains, we will get wet. The children hate getting wet, so we should stay at home.

We cannot conclude that we will definitely get wet, because we do not know for definite whether it will rain. The rain is a hypothetical, uncertain event – an unfulfilled condition. But we can predict logical consequences and consider what will or would happen if it did rain. We can make plans for the future on the basis of this reasoning – and either take a waterproof coat or stay at home.

REMEMBER

A hypothetical claim within an argument may be a reason or a conclusion.

ACTIVITY 9

Identify the hypothetical reasoning in the following passages.

A Analysis by one police force of local crime figures has shown an unexpected pattern: crime increases when there is a full moon. If the government seriously wants to cut crime, then it should impose a curfew on known criminals every 28 days when the moon is full.

B The science of profiling people according to their postcode has become so accurate that it provides information about everything from our income and marital status, to our choice of car or soft drink. Call centres apparently now use sophisticated software to decide what order to deal with callers' queries. If this is the case, then it explains why I'm always kept waiting 15 minutes before my call is answered by a bored operative: I live in an area with the wrong postcode.

C A tidal wave of *schadenfreude* will engulf the World Cup should France end up playing New Zealand in the quarter-final in Cardiff instead of Scotland or Italy in Paris. It will happen if Argentina keeps winning and would serve the French right for doling out matches to the Celts in return for the votes to beat England's bid.

Daily Mail, 13 September 2007

> **TAKE IT FURTHER**
>
> **Consider the possible consequences of the following hypothetical events. Discuss in groups how likely these consequences are.**
>
> **A** If the government detains terrorist suspects without trial …
>
> **B** If Britain leaves the European Union …
>
> **C** If we spend December in New Zealand …
>
> **D** If I have unprotected sex …
>
> **E** If the people in this group survive a plane crash in the jungle, uninjured, but miles from help …

- How would any survivors cope?

Assumptions

We have looked at a number of elements of argument – reasons, conclusions, hypothetical reasoning – that can be identified from reading a passage. The next element of argument we will consider is sometimes called a missing step in the reasoning: an **assumption**.

What are assumptions?

'Assumption' is a word with a meaning in everyday usage and a different, more precise, meaning in Critical Thinking. For example, using 'assume' in its usual sense, you might say something like this.

> I assume it will be good fun at university because my older sister really enjoyed her time there.

In this case 'assume' refers to something that may or may not be true – having fun at university.

In Critical Thinking, however, the word 'assumption' is used to refer to part of an argument that is not stated, but is needed in order for the argument to work. Here's an example.

> The office safe has been forced open. Ethan has not turned up this morning. Therefore, Ethan stole the money.

The first assumption is that the money was in the safe. Another is that Ethan has not just overslept or is late for some other reason.

PAUSE FOR THOUGHT

How many more assumptions can you think of in the example about Ethan?

Here is another example.

This argument rests on the assumption that the reader wants to combat skin ageing by making his wrinkly skin look better. The argument could be written as follows.

> **R1** Phwoire is formulated by skin care specialists who fully understand the needs of men.
>
> **R2** Phwoire contains the latest anti-ageing bio-technology – octopeptide liposomes.
>
> **R3** You want to combat skin ageing by making your wrinkly skin look better.
>
> **C** Therefore, you should trust Phwoire to combat skin ageing.

Here is another example.

> Young people are not very interested in politics and tend not to vote. Most people who do vote are older and well-off. Governments tend to represent the interests of those who have voted for them. Elected governments do not represent all sections of society. Politicians should change their approach to ensure that more young people vote.

This argument rests on the idea – the assumption – that governments *should* represent all sections of society. (After all, if the writer believed the current situation was acceptable, they would not want politicians to change it.)

Although it is not stated, an assumption is part of the structure of an argument. Assumptions are a missing step, a missing reason that is needed to support the conclusion. Writing out the structure of the argument shows this more clearly.

> **R1** Young people are not very interested in politics and tend not to vote.
>
> **R2** Most people who do vote are older and well-off.
>
> **R3** Governments tend to represent the interests of those who have voted for them.
>
> **R4** Elected governments do not represent all sections of society.
>
> **R5** (*assumption*) Governments should represent all sections of society.
>
> **C** Politicians should change their approach to ensure that more young people vote.

The assumption acts as the fifth, unstated, reason.

Finding assumptions is a very important Critical Thinking skill. You can expect to be asked to identify assumptions in the exam, so it is worth taking time to practise this particular skill.

EXAM TIP

Remember that assumptions are not stated in the passage.

PAUSE FOR THOUGHT

Before you attempt Activity 10, think about the assumptions in this argument.

Using biofuel is a cheap way to run a car. It is easy to convert an ordinary car engine to run on biofuel. You should have your car engine converted to biofuel.

The author must assume that:

- biofuel is readily available locally
- the cost of fuel is a problem for the car's owner
- the owner can afford the cost of converting the car engine
- it is possible to convert the car.

ACTIVITY

Identify an assumption in each of the following arguments. (Take a look at the Pause for Thought box for an example.)

A Raj wants to audition for a local band. He plays guitar but is also a good drummer. The band plays gigs all over the city and therefore Raj would need a car to transport his drumkit around with him to gigs. Raj does not have enough money to buy a car and consequently it might be better if he auditioned on guitar.

B The traffic is always heavy on Monday mornings. It is very important that you get to college on time. You should catch an earlier bus than usual.

Finding assumptions in more complex passages

Read the following short argument and write down the assumption.

> Graduates from Oxford and Cambridge are often found in senior positions in major British institutions. What is less well-known is that their salaries are often higher than graduates from other universities who have jobs of equivalent status and responsibility. So, whether it is fair or not, a place on an Oxford or Cambridge degree course is still a good guarantee of better earnings after university.

The argument suggests that a degree from Oxford or Cambridge in itself is enough to lead to a higher salary – not because these graduates work harder, are better at their jobs or are more talented, but because of where they went to university.

You should therefore have written the following.

> The author assumes that graduates from Oxford and Cambridge earn more only because of the fact they went to Oxford or Cambridge.

In this example the word 'only' is important. In some contexts, the use of the word 'only' could be too strong, but here it fits precisely.

Techniques for answering questions about assumptions

In the examination you will be asked to find assumptions in a passage which is longer than those we have looked at so far. By now you should understand that you need to find the missing step in the argument. In the examination, to be awarded full marks on the assumption questions, you need to be able to express the assumption very precisely. (We'll look at this in more detail on pages 32–33.)

Look for the assumption(s) in the passage below.

> If the Met Office's powerful computers cannot make correct weather forecasts four days ahead, how can we trust computer projections that global warming will result in a disaster in two centuries' time? The hurricane of 1987, which was missed by the Met Office forecasters only hours before it hit Britain, is a prime example of their inability to forecast the weather accurately.
>
> Adapted from OCR's January 2003 question paper

■ Devastation following the hurricane of 1987.

The writer moves from the failure of the Met Office's computers to forecast weather accurately to a point about computer projections on global warming. The example given (the hurricane of 1987) is some time in the past. The failure on that occasion does not mean that computers used by other organisations cannot now forecast the weather correctly.

For the argument to work, it needs this assumption.

> The Met Office's computers are typical of/similar to other weather forecasting computers.

In the exam you would need to write:

> The author must assume that the Met Office's computers are typical of other weather forecasting computers.

REMEMBER

An assumption is necessary for the argument to work, but is a missing step. There may also be more than one assumption in an argument.

ACTIVITY

There is very often more than one assumption underlying an argument. Consider the suggested (possible) assumptions below and decide which really are assumptions needed for the argument about weather forecasting (page 29) and which are not.

A The author must assume that the hurricane of 1987, which was missed by the weather forecasters, shows their inability to forecast the weather accurately.

B The author must assume that the Met Office is not very good at weather forecasting.

C The author must assume that the Met Office consists of a group of people with training in weather and climate who make weather forecasts.

D The author must assume that computers are the only method of forecasting the weather.

E The author must assume that there are no better or more powerful weather forecasting computers than those used by the Met Office.

F The author must assume that the failure to forecast the hurricane was typical of weather forecasters' failure to forecast the weather accurately.

G The author must assume that the hurricane in 1987 was not much more difficult to forecast than normal weather patterns.

Answers to Activity 11

Possible assumptions A–D are not correct. E–G are assumptions. We shall look at A–D in turn to see why they do not work.

> **A** The author must assume that the hurricane of 1987, which was missed by the weather forecasters, shows their inability to forecast the weather accurately.

This is definitely a reason that supports the argument. However, it is a shortened version of the last sentence of the passage, so it cannot be an assumption, because assumptions are not stated.

> **B** The author must assume that the Met Office is not very good at weather forecasting.

This statement is certainly in a different language from that of the original passage, but it does not say anything new. The author states that the Met Office cannot make accurate forecasts four days ahead; statement B simply re-words that point as a more general comment. It does not add to the argument, and is not an assumption.

> **REMEMBER**
>
> Before you write down your assumption on an exam paper, check that you have not picked something that is in the passage but phrased it differently.

> **C** The author must assume that the Met Office consists of a group of people with training in weather and climate who make weather forecasts.

This is a factual clarification of a term in the passage, and so could help some people to understand the passage. (It is possible that some people do not know what the Met Office is.) However, definitions or clarification are not assumptions.

> **D** The author must assume that computers are the only method of forecasting the weather.

This looks tempting: it is not stated in the passage and you may think that there are other, and better, methods of forecasting the weather than computer models. However, the author does not need to assume this. The author is only arguing about the accuracy of *computer* forecasts of global warming disaster, not about any other methods of forecasting.

ACTIVITY 12

Read the passage below and the four statements that follow. Decide whether each statement is, or is not, an assumption needed by the argument in the passage.

For many years now, Britain has suffered a 'brain drain' of scientists attracted by the rewards of working in other countries. The government has announced that it is investing one billion pounds in science to raise scientific salaries to internationally competitive levels. It is also increasing the grant to postgraduate students. This will stop the brain drain and ensure scientists stay in this country.

A The best British scientists have gone abroad to work.

B The financial incentive is sufficient to persuade scientists to return to Britain.

C The most important incentive to go to another country is financial.

D Only scientists have been attracted by high financial rewards in other countries.

Adapted from OCR's January 2002 question paper

EXAM TIP

Phrasing the assumption clearly and precisely is vital to getting it right (and getting full marks in the exam).

Formulating assumptions

Once you have found an assumption, it is important that you word it carefully to ensure it is clear and accurate. In the examination students very often cannot be awarded full marks for questions about assumptions because they either make the assumption too strong or they make it too weak.

Consider this argument.

Loud music, lawn mowers and aircraft noise can all damage tiny cells in our ears and leave us with premature hearing loss. This can be a particular problem for young people because of the very high noise levels at rock concerts. Not surprising then that the number of Americans under 18 with some form of hearing loss has reached 1.3 million. It seems unlikely that rock musicians will turn down the volume, so the least that we can do is to advise young people to use simple, cheap ear plugs when they attend rock concerts.

Adapted from OCR's January 2007 question paper

The conclusion of the argument is:

The least we can do is to advise young people to use simple, cheap ear plugs when they attend rock concerts.

- Loud music can cause premature hearing loss.

What must the author assume in order to argue this? Below are just three possible ways you could phrase the assumption. (Since the assumption is quite complex, there are many more ways it could be worded.)

> The 1.3 million American under-18s with hearing loss have regularly attended loud rock concerts.

This is too strong: the passage says 1.3 million American under-18s have some form of hearing loss, but there is no implication that all forms of hearing loss are linked to attending rock concerts.

> Some American under-18s with hearing loss could have attended loud rock concerts.

This is too weak: the passage talks about a form of hearing loss linked to loud noise being a particular problem for young people because of high noise levels at rock concerts.

> A significant percentage of the 1.3 million American under-18s with hearing loss have regularly attended loud rock concerts.

This precisely expresses the assumption needed to support the conclusion. It includes all the key information.

ACTIVITY 13

Find one assumption in each of the following passages. Try to make your answers as clear and precise as possible – not too strong, nor too weak.

A Smoking is a major cause of illness and a considerable drain on the health service's resources. Recent figures show that the number of people giving up smoking has increased, so there will be less strain on the health service. The money saved can be used to improve preventive treatments.

B There appear to be growing concerns about the number of 6- and 7-year-olds who are unable to read. However, there is no reason for this to be a problem. Every child has to go to school and is taught by a qualified teacher. Even if this does not work – and apparently it does not always – there are many libraries in our cities, with specialist advisers running after-school reading clubs and book groups, all designed to help young children read.

C Rugby is a much more exciting game to watch than football. Unlike football, it has complex rules and tactics that create many more possibilities, both in attack and defence. Football has much simpler rules and tactics and will never be anything other than boring to watch.

KEY TERM

● **Reverse test**

A strategy for checking whether an assumption is needed by an argument, by asking yourself if the argument would work with the assumption reversed.

Checking assumptions: the 'reverse' test

One useful way of checking whether an assumption really is necessary for an argument is to use the **reverse test**.

This means working out the exact opposite of the assumption you have formulated and seeing how that relates to the argument. If you have the right assumption, then putting its exact reverse into the argument should mean that the argument does *not* work.

Have another look at the argument about graduates from Oxford and Cambridge, which you first met on page 28.

Graduates from Oxford and Cambridge are often found in senior positions in major British institutions. What is less well-known is that their salaries are often higher than graduates from other universities who have jobs of equivalent status and responsibility. So, whether it is fair or not, a place on an Oxford or Cambridge degree course is still a good guarantee of better earnings after university.

The assumption was:

Graduates from Oxford and Cambridge earn more only because of the fact that they went to Oxford or Cambridge.

The reverse of the assumption would be:

> Graduates from Oxford and Cambridge *do not* earn more (only) because of the fact that they went to Oxford or Cambridge.

If this is inserted in the argument, it no longer works. The argument now suggests that Oxford and Cambridge graduates earn more money through working harder or being more skilled or talented. So reversing the assumption, and showing that the argument no longer works, gives a very strong indication that the original assumption was correct.

ACTIVITY

Identify the conclusion and an assumption in each of the following passages. Use the reverse test to check your assumption.

A Hookworm infections are most common in the poorest countries of the world and there are now several programmes aiming to eradicate the problem. This is not surprising because serious hookworm infections are associated with diarrhoea and growth problems in children. However, mild hookworm infections have also been found to be of help to allergy sufferers because they reduce the body's immune response. The countries where hookworm is common are also the ones with limited access to other medication to treat allergies. This means that we may be unwise in trying to eradicate hookworm infections in these countries.

B It is very fashionable to try to remember and seek meaning in our dreams. However, science has suggested that dreams may be random brain activity that helps remove useless information stored in our brains. This process keeps the nervous system working effectively and helps us to be in a good mood the next day. If this is the case, remembering and analysing our dreams will certainly be bad for us. We might be wise to base our approach to our dreams on the science of the brain rather than fashion.

C A survey in an accident and emergency department in Wales has shown that attendances for injuries related to assaults increased on days when the national football or rugby team was playing. Not surprisingly, over-consumption of alcohol has been suggested as a possible cause as fans tend to drink more on big match days, leading to more violence. There is also evidence that the result of matches affects the level of violence. Given the pressures on emergency departments, maybe we should all start hoping our national teams lose big matches, as this is bound to reduce the amount of violence surrounding the matches.

Question A adapted from OCR's January 2007 question paper
Questions B and C adapted from OCR's June 2006 question paper

EXAM TIPS

An assumption is a missing step. Don't just write down something that is not stated in the passage but is vaguely related to it.

An assumption is necessary to support the conclusion.

Check that what you have written is not already stated in the passage, but in different words.

Check that what you have written is not just a definition or clarification of a word or idea, in the passage.

Check very carefully the wording of the assumption you have written down. Precision is especially important to get full marks in identifying assumptions.

...then the car turned into an enormous bear which chased me down Oxford Street and around Piccadilly Circus...

- Is it always a good idea to analyse our dreams?

REMEMBER

An assumption is never ever stated in the passage, but it is a reason that is needed to make the argument work.

REMEMBER

Finding an assumption is simply finding the bit that is missing from the argument.

> **REMEMBER**
>
> Longer passages usually rely on several assumptions. There is generally not one single answer that you have to work out, but several possible assumptions to find.

> **REMEMBER**
>
> Use the reverse test to check if you have correctly found an assumption.

EXAM TIPS

Take care not to phrase the assumption too strongly.

Take care not to phrase the assumption too vaguely.

Summary

You should now be able to:

- use argument notation

- understand the nature of different claims

- recognise and use counter-assertions, counter-arguments, simple hypothetical reasoning and assumptions

- understand the importance of precision and clarity when you phrase assumptions.

Learning objectives

- Understand what is meant by evidence.
- Understand the purpose of evidence in reasoning.
- Identify different forms of evidence.
- Understand the purpose of numerical data and statistical representations in argument.
- Identify where further clarification of evidence is needed.

Factual claims

So far in this book we have looked at fairly simple arguments and we have seen that a reason gives support to a conclusion. In a simple argument it is relatively easy to identify the reasons, as the example below shows.

> Ahmad's old car is dangerously rusty and it breaks down almost every day. He has got a well-paid summer job at the local solicitors' office. Ahmad should get a new car.

Here everything that is not the conclusion is a reason. We can analyse the argument as follows.

> **R1** Ahmad's old car is dangerously rusty.
> **R2** It breaks down almost every day.
> **R3** He has got a well-paid summer job at the local solicitors' office.
> **C**   Ahmad should get a new car.

In this example, all three reasons are **facts**. A fact is information that can be verified, and which is held to be true. **Factual claims** in an argument, therefore, consist of information that can be verified. We treat them as true, but our acceptance of their truth is suspended until we check the facts. (We could check whether the rust on Ahmed's car really is dangerous and how often it does break down.)

In this chapter we will look at the use of factual claims to support reasoning and the ways that this type of information may be presented.

Evidence

One of the key ways in which people try to support their arguments is by including facts (or what they think are facts). Sometimes such facts stand as reasons in their own right, as we have seen in earlier examples ('Ahmad's old car is dangerously rusty' and 'I am also asthmatic').

Often factual information is presented numerically or as statistical data in order to support a reason, which in turn supports the conclusion. In this case the supporting facts are known as **evidence**.

In Chapter 2, page 32, you met this argument.

> Loud music, lawn mowers and aircraft noise can all damage tiny cells in our ear and leave us with premature hearing loss. This can be a particular problem for young people because of the very high noise levels at rock concerts. Not surprising then that *the number of Americans under 18 with some form of hearing loss has reached 1.3 million.* It seems unlikely that rock musicians will turn down the volume, so the least that we can do is to advise young people to use simple, cheap ear plugs when they attend rock concerts.
>
> Adapted from OCR's January 2007 question paper

KEY TERMS

Fact
Information that can be verified and that is held to be true.

Factual claim
A statement or judgement based on information that can be verified and that is held to be true.

Evidence
Something that is used to develop or support a reason. Evidence is often in the form of numerical data, an estimate or a factual claim.

The words in italics provide evidence to support the claim that premature hearing loss is a particular problem for young people because of noise levels at rock concerts.

Evidence can be in the form of:

- an example
- statistical or numerical data
- an estimate
- a factual claim
- a personal observation
- a statement from a source or witness.

Evidence indicator words are: *for example, for instance, such as.*

In this chapter, we will look at different forms of evidence and ways of assessing evidence used to support reasons.

Examples

Examples are one form of evidence that provide a way of developing a reason. They illustrate the reason, giving a specific situation in which the reason holds. The purpose of examples, therefore, is to back up the reason, so that it provides good support for the conclusion.

There are two main ways of using an example to illustrate a reason. First, the author may give a list of specific examples – as in the following example.

Fruit that can be grown in the UK, such as apples, pears, raspberries, gooseberries and strawberries, has many advantages. It doesn't need to be transported around the world. It tastes superior. In short, it is by far the best choice.

The examples strengthen the reason by providing an image or concrete situation to develop it, rather than logical support. The example does not count as part of the reason, even when it is written in the middle of it as in this short argument. Identifying the reason precisely means leaving out examples and perhaps re-wording it. Here the reason is:

Fruit that can be grown in the UK has many advantages.

The second common use of examples is where the author illustrates a general idea through a more developed example.

You don't need a large garden to grow your own food. Many kinds of fruit and vegetables can be grown in containers, which will fit even on a small balcony. For example, Uncle Brian grows potatoes in a dustbin, and tomatoes, peas, beans and strawberries, all in pots on the patio.

- Fruit from the UK doesn't travel thousands of air miles.

Here, Uncle Brian is an example that supports the reason by demonstrating that the general statement is not just an abstract idea, but has instances in the real world.

ACTIVITY 15

Identify the evidence and the examples in the following short argument.

Research carried out by the University of Hertfordshire involved interviewing 100 people aged between 22 and 45 who had been speed-dating. Chat-up lines that are questions rather than statements were found to be more successful. 'I have a PhD in computing', is off-putting but 'What is your favourite pizza topping?' evokes a positive response. So, if you want to chat someone up successfully, you should give them the chance to respond in a light-hearted way.

Numerical and statistical data as evidence

Statistics is about making sense of what is happening. Similarly, evidence is often presented numerically or as statistical data to make it clearer and easier to understand. For example, if you were choosing where to study, you would not necessarily want to read what every student at a local college thought of it: the statistic that 93% of students would recommend their college would be enough.

In the Unit 1 examination you may be asked to evaluate evidence presented in different forms. The way in which evidence is simplified, or summarised, or converted into numerical form, can present problems. In this chapter, we will therefore look at some common ways of collecting and presenting numerical evidence: surveys or research data, percentages and proportions, and averages. You may meet any of these in the examination.

Evidence in the form of surveys or research data

In choosing where to study, you might look at information on a number of colleges to help make a decision. You might want to look into the colleges' IT facilities, the range of courses and subjects offered, the different sports clubs, the social activities, the canteen, the support available for students with academic or personal problems and students' opinions.

In finding out about what local colleges offer, you are carrying out research. The characteristics that you are investigating (the colleges' IT facilities, range of courses, subjects, sports clubs, etc.) can be identified. Once you have collected information on these characteristics, you have the information (known collectively as data) that could be represented numerically and, if you wished, analysed using statistical techniques.

Data is usually numerical, but could be descriptive. For example, you might want to describe the colleges' canteen facilities as good, adequate or poor. Here are some more examples from everyday life that show the use of data.

> On average I spend roughly £15 a week on travel.

You probably do not need to do careful calculations to have a fairly good idea of how much you spend on travel each week, but you are using numerical techniques when you estimate it.

> It's always curry on the menu in the canteen on Thursday.

Here the observations in the canteen in previous weeks have led to a factual statement about the food on offer every Thursday.

Research data can be collected by different methods. In the example of finding a suitable college, you would probably ask questions of staff and other students, and read the colleges' brochures and publicity material. More formal methods of collecting research data include:

- taking measurements, e.g. recording weight and blood pressure of patients visiting the local health centre
- observation, e.g. watching and recording information about the behaviour of animals in the wild
- asking questions through questionnaires, e.g. asking customers about the customer service they receive at the supermarket.

When specialist researchers carry out their work, it is common to collect data based on a sample rather than investigating every possible case. Take the example of the supermarket chain that wants to find out customers' views on the service at their local supermarket. In one week, each supermarket in a large chain would have tens of thousands of customers. It would be impractical to ask every customer their opinions, so the company would probably arrange to interview (or survey) only a sample.

If the research is conducted properly, the sample will be typical of all the customer types (e.g. old people, young parents with families, single people, etc.) and be large enough to give an accurate picture of the opinions of the range of customers.

- Research data on animal behaviour can be collected through observation.

PAUSE FOR THOUGHT

What problems might there be in using a sample to find out about students' opinions of the college where they study?

Problems with evidence based on surveys and sampling

In using evidence to support an argument, many writers interpret, or use selectively, the outcomes of research or surveys. Sometimes the methods used to carry out the research itself are flawed. When you evaluate survey evidence in the examination, you need to think carefully about whether the evidence really tells us what the writer is claiming and whether the research methods might, or might not, be reliable.

Suppose we survey a class of 30 children and find that twelve of them are blonde, six have brown hair, six have red hair and six black hair. We can calculate that 40% of the class are blonde, and 20% respectively brown, red and black-haired. We cannot, however, extend this to the whole population. After all, if we surveyed a similar class of 30 children we would be very likely to get significantly different results. So whenever we look at evidence, we should ask whether the group it is based on is typical – or representative – of the wider group it is being applied to.

The converse is that we must also be careful about applying a statistic that represents the population as a whole to a small group. Suppose we knew that 60% of the UK population had brown eyes. We could not then conclude that exactly 60% of the children in one class have brown eyes.

What questions might we ask about the following evidence before drawing conclusions from it?

> Researchers who worked with families and day care centres have found that children who are cared for at home by a parent until the age of $2\frac{1}{2}$ achieve higher levels in standard tests when they are 7 than children who attended day care centres.

We might want to ask these questions.

- Who funded the research? A specialist university department or a company that sells early learning packs designed for parents to use with their children?

- How many children were sampled? Two, 20 or 2000?

- Were the day care centres in similar social areas to the children who were observed at home?

- How well educated were the parents and the day care staff?

- How did the researchers get access to the children? Probably they could work only with parents who were willing to take part in the survey. These perhaps were parents who were happy with their role at home.

The answers to these and similar questions could show that the sample was unrepresentative, even if the survey was otherwise properly designed and carried out. For example, if the researchers worked only with parents willing to take part in the survey because they were happy to be at home, then we could conclude that it is academically advantageous for young children to be at home with a parent who is happy to be at home, not that it benefits all young children.

PAUSE FOR THOUGHT

Look again at Activity 15. What questions might you ask to help you assess the evidence about chat-up lines?

Percentages and proportions

Percentages can be a valuable tool for presenting data. The results of research surveys are often presented as percentages. However, percentages are often presented in ways that are misleading or provide no useful information. Consider this example.

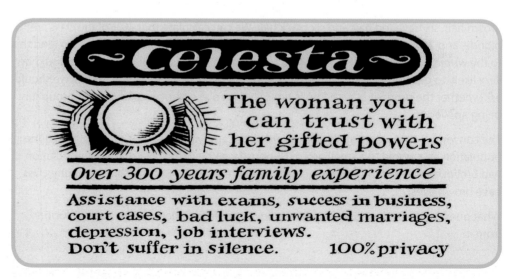

We probably think we know what is meant by 'Over 300 years' family experience' – generations of Celesta's family going back 300 years have used similar powers. But what about '100% privacy'? Do similar services provide only 75% privacy?

As we can see, percentages often provide no useful information. The 100% privacy offered by Celesta is not an unusual example. Look at the next example.

> Gleem washing-up liquid is 50% more effective.

We need to ask 'More effective than *what*?' and 'How has the effectiveness of Gleem been tested?'

ACTIVITY 16

Identify the evidence in the following short arguments and state what form(s) the evidence takes. (You may need to look back at the list of different forms of evidence on page 40.)

A A survey reveals that while 40% of teenagers have no religious faith, the level of unbelievers drops to a mere 8% in the over-65 age group. The closer we get to the Pearly Gates, the more we hedge our bets.

   Peter Rhodes, *Wolverhampton Express and Star*, 13 September 2007

B One major chain store has a new method of encouraging recycling: the UK's first coat hanger amnesty will be held by Marks & Spencer. Research shows there are currently 530 million unused coat hangers stored in UK homes. This would equate to 17,000 tonnes of plastic that could either be reused or recycled. Customers can bring unwanted hangers into stores on the days of the amnesty and place them in the recycling boxes. This is a useful way to reduce waste dumped in landfill, but it would be far better if shops were to stop handing out coat hangers altogether.

C More than 3.5 million people in Britain – 6% of the population – belong to a gym or fitness club, presumably thinking that exercise improves their quality of life. However, growing numbers of scientists accept that punishing workouts are unnatural for the human body and may ultimately impair physical fitness, as demonstrated when Jim Fixx, the American pioneer of jogging, collapsed and died at the age of 52. In order to maintain good health, people should cancel their fitness club subscription and adopt a healthier lifestyle.

D The increase in numbers of a wild bird in Scotland despite its declining numbers in the rest of Europe has mystified experts. RSPB Scotland said it was delighted but it was a mystery as to why red-throated divers had done so well. Their numbers have risen from 935 to 1255 breeding pairs in twelve years. However, in Shetland the population has dropped from 700 pairs to 407. Dr Mark Eaton, an RSPB scientist, said: 'We feared the numbers of red-throated divers might drop because the warming of the North Sea seems to be reducing stocks of the fish they feed on'. Projections about the disastrous effects of global warming on wildlife clearly need revising.

   Adapted from www.birdguides.com/webzine/article.asp?a=110%

The 'average' or mean

The term 'average' is often used carelessly. Look at this example.

> In recent school tests of 11-year-olds, 49% of children failed to reach the average reading level for their age group.

Of course they failed to reach the average reading level for their age group! There was something badly wrong with the tests if they produced any result but children of below-average ability achieving below-average results, children of average ability achieving the average results, and children of above-average ability achieving above-average results.

Let's look at another example.

> The average amount spent on lottery tickets is about £3 a week. This represents only 0.65% of the average income in Britain. Such a small amount completely undermines the idea that expenditure on the lottery is at the expense of more important and essential items such as nutritious food.

The 'average amount' in this example misleads in several ways. First, some people earn more than average; others earn far less. If a poor person spends the average £3 each week on lottery tickets, that may be a greater proportion of their family's income than it is for someone who earns more. Second, 'about £3' is deceptively vague: it could be as little as £2.51 or as much as £3.49. We simply do not know. Third, we do not know how this 'average' was calculated.

▪ The average amount spent on lottery tickets is about £3 a week.

The mean

Nine students took a test, and their results were as follows:

| 40% | 99% | 45% | 49% | 52% | 45% | 53% | 59% | 45% |

If asked to find the average, most of us would add up all nine marks, divide the total by nine, and say: 'The average mark is 54%.' This is not wrong, but it would be more accurate to say: 'The mean mark was 54%.' The mean is a very useful statistical representation. You will not be asked to do calculations in the exam (or need to remember how to find the mean value). You just need to understand that the term 'average' will refer to the mean value.

Numerical and statistical evidence presented as graphs, diagrams or images

Very often it is easier to understand information if it is presented in visual form than if it is simply explained in text. Here is an example taken from a scientific article about the deep sea.

It is now known that there are areas in the deep sea that have high biodiversity, including cold-water coral reefs, seamounts (mountains on the seabed) and areas with a high proportion of unique species, such as hydrothermal vents (see Fig. 1).

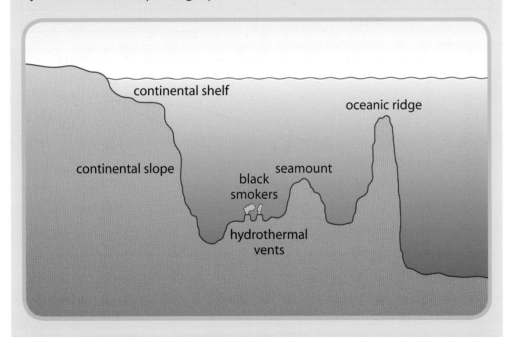

■ Figure 1. Seabed features to depths >2000 metres.

Source: *New Industries in the Deep Sea*, The Parliamentary Office of Science and Technology, www.parliament.uk/parliamentary_offices/post/pubs2007.cfm

For many people the picture helps them understand what the article is about better than the textual information. Here is another example where some very complex information about Alzheimer's disease and dementia is presented first in text, then in a table and a graph.

Read the text below about dementia and then consider the information in the table and the graph.

Dementia in an ageing population

The risk of developing dementia is strongly associated with ageing, although inheritable early-onset dementia does occur very rarely in people under 65 years. Population studies show that the prevalence (number of cases) roughly doubles every five years over the age of 60 (Table 1). The UK population is projected to increase to 69.3 million in 2051 from 60.5 million in 2001. Should prevalence rates remain unchanged over the next few decades, and as the population ages, the total number of dementia cases could more than double, from 750,000 in 2006, to 1.8 million in 2051 (Fig. 1).

Table 1. Prevalence rates of dementia by age.

Age group (years)	Prevalence of dementia (%)
60–64	0.9
65–69	1.5
70–74	3.6
75–79	6.0
80–84	12.2
≥85	24.8

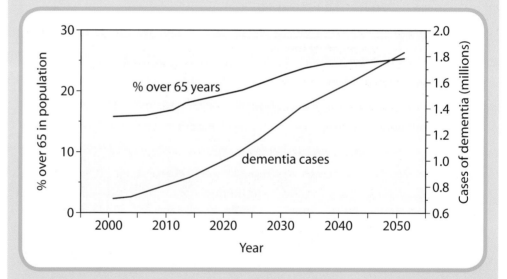

- Figure 1. Projected percentage of UK population over 65 years old, and estimated total cases of dementia.

Source: *Alzheimer's & Dementia*, The Parliamentary Office of Science and Technology, www.parliament.uk/parliamentary_offices/post/ pubs2007.cfm

You can see how it is often far more helpful if information is presented as an image, table, graph or pie chart, than when it is put into words. In the examination you will not be asked to analyse information that is as complex as in the example above, but you may be asked to interpret images, tables, graphs and pie charts which relate to evidence given in the passage.

The use of images will be considered in Chapter 6 when we look at ways of assessing the credibility of documents.

Evaluating evidence

While reasons are normally general statements used to support a conclusion in an argument, evidence, on the other hand, is used to support, illustrate or develop a reason. Evidence may be facts that cannot be disputed (e.g. 'Galileo claimed that the Earth moved round the Sun') but often it takes the form of information, statistics or scientific data.

In the Unit 1 examination you do not need to dispute whether the evidence is true or not. What you do need to consider is whether the evidence itself is reliable and relevant.

Reliable evidence should come from a source that is reputable, authoritative (or expert), and without a motive to mislead. (We will look at ways of judging the reliability of sources in Chapters 5 and 6.)

Statistics and other numerical evidence can mislead even if there is no motive involved. Often such evidence is simply misused. We need to question what is being hidden by the evidence, what is not being said, what is being twisted or manipulated, and what has been omitted because it did not fit the aim of the writer.

If we are told that 'many people', or 'the majority', support a particular measure, it is worth asking for the precise figures. It may turn out that 39% of people asked said they did agree, 38% disagreed, and the rest did not know or care. The writer is not necessarily dishonest, but is not giving the whole picture either.

Evidence and examples need to be relevant. Look at this argument.

> It no longer makes economic sense for families to grow their own vegetables. The modern-day supermarket offers vegetables at a price that undercuts the cost of growing them yourself. Marina Kiblitskaya found that people in Russia spent considerably more money growing their own vegetables than if they had purchased them in local markets.
>
> Adapted from OCR's May 2003 question paper

In this passage the evidence relates to Russia and compares local market costs with home-grown produce. That is not a relevant example to support an argument about the relative costs of UK supermarket food and home-grown food.

EXAM TIP

Mathematical skills will not be tested in the exam. You should focus on evaluating the evidence and assessing how well it supports the reasons and the conclusion.

ACTIVITY 17

a) **Evaluate the evidence given to support the claims in the examples below.**

A People were asked to name their favourite National Trust coastline in a survey. The white cliffs of Dover were runaway winners with 22% of the votes.

B

b) **Look again at the arguments in Activity 16. Evaluate the evidence in them.**

TAKE IT FURTHER

Evaluate the evidence to support the claims in the example below.

More money needed for gambling addicts

More money is needed to help gambling addicts. The Responsibility in Gambling Trust needs its funding increased from £4 million to £10 million, so that it can set up Britain's first dedicated gambling addiction clinic. The Gambling Trust's counselling helpline for problem gamblers took more than 30,000 calls last year, a rise of 34% on the previous year. The number of gambling addicts has risen to about 2% of the population, or about 800,000.

REMEMBER

When you are evaluating evidence and examples, you may need to ask these questions.

- Is this evidence meaningful?
- Who funded the survey or research?
- What was the size of any sample?
- Was the sample representative?
- How was any survey conducted?
- When was the survey carried out?
- Are examples typical and relevant?
- Are research findings clear-cut or ambiguous?

Personal observations and statements from sources or witnesses

As we saw on page 40, evidence may also be in the form of a personal observation or a statement from a source. In Chapters 5 and 6, when we learn about credibility of evidence, we will look in greater detail at these forms of evidence.

PAUSE FOR THOUGHT

As a group, look at a variety of newspapers (local and national), popular magazines and more serious magazines. Find examples of each of the following forms of evidence:

- an example
- statistical data (including graphs or tables)
- an estimate
- a factual claim
- a personal observation
- a statement from a source or witness.

Decide whether or not you think the evidence supports the reasoning in the article.

Summary

You should now be able to:

- identify evidence and examples in argument
- explain the purpose of evidence and examples in an argument
- assess evidence from research or surveys by considering the questions that could be asked to clarify that evidence.

4 Analysing and evaluating reasoning

Learning objectives

● Analyse the structure of longer arguments.

● Understand the link between reasons and conclusions.

● Evaluate how well reasons support conclusions.

Using the Critical Thinking skills

In Chapters 1–3, we have learnt to identify the key elements of argument and begun to analyse simple arguments. We also learnt to recognise assumptions, hypothetical reasoning and different forms of evidence. In this chapter we will practise bringing together the skills learnt so far in order to analyse the structure of longer, and more complex, arguments.

The best way to prepare for the Unit 1 exam is to practise the Critical Thinking skills. In this chapter you will tackle activities which will help you to develop the skills. We will also begin to tackle the types of question that you can expect to meet in the first section of the examination.

Analysing the structure of longer arguments

First things first: finding the conclusion and the reasons that support it

When you start to analyse the structure of any argument, always begin by looking out for the conclusion while you read through the passage. Don't forget that the conclusion indicator words ('therefore', 'so', etc.) can help you to spot the conclusion. You might expect to find the conclusion at the end the passage, but often it is in the first paragraph. However, it could be anywhere in the argument.

Look at this short argument, which we first met in Chapter 1 (page 10). Here the conclusion is at the end.

> I want to go on holiday after my exams. I find being by the sea is very relaxing and I will definitely need a rest after all that hard work. I ought to book a holiday at the seaside.

We can see below that this would work just as well with the conclusion in the middle.

> I want to go on holiday after my exams. I ought to book a holiday at the seaside. I find being by the sea is very relaxing and I will definitely need a rest after all that hard work.

It would also work with the conclusion at the beginning.

> I ought to book a holiday at the seaside. I want to go on holiday after my exams. I find being by the sea is very relaxing and I will definitely need a rest after all that hard work.

PAUSE FOR THOUGHT

Try this yourself with this short argument, which you first met in Activity 5, page 13. Does it work?

The most popular meal in the UK is now chicken tikka masala. Spaghetti bolognese has replaced sausages and mash as a staple family meal. We should re-think our view of what constitutes classic British food.

Having found the conclusion of the argument you should look next for the reasons that support the conclusion. Sometimes arguments are presented neatly with one reason in each paragraph, but never assume that this is the case.

Distinguishing between reasons and evidence and examples

In Chapter 3, we looked at a number of forms of evidence and examples. In the exam, you need to be able to distinguish between reasons and evidence. This means separating a reason from the evidence and examples that support it. Look at this argument.

> 'Infomania' can seriously interfere with your performance at work. Research carried out by the Institute of Psychiatry says that distractions caused by emails and telephone calls result in a ten point IQ drop in the average worker. So, if you want to work at your best, don't constantly check your emails, text and phone messages.

You probably spotted that the evidence (notated as 'Ev', as in the box below) was in the second sentence and that the argument could be analysed as follows.

> **Ev** Research carried out by the Institute of Psychiatry says that distractions caused by emails and telephone calls result in a ten point IQ drop in the average worker.
>
> **R** 'Infomania' can seriously interfere with your performance at work.
>
> **C** So, if you want to work at your best, don't constantly check your emails, text and phone messages.

Real life articles often cannot be analysed as neatly as the short passages you have met so far in this book, but in the exam it may help you to mark up the passage using argument notation in this way.

Read the passage below and identify the conclusion, reason(s) and evidence.

> Researchers have established that blonde females are discriminated against when applying for jobs. They found that a blonde woman and a dark-haired woman with the same qualifications, who applied for the same job, were treated differently. The blonde was offered lower pay and grading than the other woman. Therefore, outdated prejudices are still operating in the workplace.

In this passage the conclusion comes neatly at the end, flagged up by the argument indicator 'therefore'.

> Outdated prejudices are still operating in the workplace.

It may have been a bit trickier to separate out the reasons and evidence. Using argument notation the structure is as follows.

R1	Researchers have established that blonde females are discriminated against when applying for jobs.
Ev	They found that a blonde woman and a dark-haired woman with the same qualifications, who applied for the same job, were treated differently. The blonde was offered lower pay and grading than the other woman.
C	Therefore, outdated prejudices are still operating in the workplace.

Evaluating how well reasons support conclusions

Up to now we have concentrated on breaking down arguments into their component parts (or elements). This is known as *analysing* argument. In the examination marks are awarded for *evaluating* reasoning as well as for analysing it – about the same number of marks for each of these skills.

Evaluating argument means asking: 'Do the reasons support the conclusion?' More simply you might ask: 'How well does this argument work?' In deciding how far a reason supports the conclusion, it helps to ask the following questions.

- Is the reason relevant to the conclusion?
- If the reason is relevant, does it make a difference to the conclusion?
- Would other evidence (not in the argument) make a difference to the conclusion?

Try applying these questions to this argument.

> A recent survey has shown that the majority of people fear becoming a victim of violent crime. They avoid certain places – underpasses, train stations, city centres – as a result. The government should put more police officers back on the beat in order to prevent crime.

The conclusion here is that:

> The government should put more police officers back on the beat in order to prevent crime.

The reasons (that the majority of people fear becoming the victim of crime, and that they avoid certain places) have some relevance to the conclusion in that they all relate to crime. However, the reasons do not support the conclusion well. People's fear of crime is not the same as actual crime. Putting more police officers on the beat does not ensure that the places people avoid would be made safer.

REMEMBER

It helps to ask some questions when you are assessing evidence.

- Is it relevant?
- Is it representative?
- Is it reliable?
- Are the findings of any research ambiguous?
- Could the evidence be interpreted differently?

ACTIVITY 18

The passage below is from an article in a local council's newsletter, which claims that the authority is recycling more rubbish than ever before and that recycling is beneficial. Assess the evidence used to support the claim in the article.

Looking after the environment

With the support of people in the borough, we now recycle more of our household rubbish than ever. In 2006/7, over 34% of your rubbish was recycled or composted – up from 30% the previous year.

This is great news, as it means more of you are recycling and more recyclable bits and pieces are being put to good use rather than thrown in the bin.

This is important because the waste that ends up in your wheelie bins goes to landfill sites, which create methane gas and contribute to global warming. Also nobody wants to live near to a huge pile of rubbish, so by recycling you're helping to protect your environment.

An Audit Commission survey also showed that litter in the borough is at a very low level in 2006/07, making it one of the cleanest places in the country.

Adapted from Telford & Wrekin Council's *Insight*, 22 July 2007

Identifying hypothetical reasoning and counter-argument in longer arguments

The exam questions may help you to identify these argument elements, by telling you which paragraph to find them in. Even if the question does not help you in this way, remember that argument indicator words and phrases may give you pointers.

REMEMBER —————————————————————————————

If the 'if' can be followed by a 'then', *then* hypothetical reasoning is present.

REMEMBER —————————————————————————————

Some argument indicators lead into the writer's point of view. Some lead into a counter-assertion or counter-argument that is being dismissed.

Assessing the reasonableness of assumptions

In Chapter 2 we looked at ways of identifying the assumptions (unstated reasons) that are necessary to make an argument work and how you can check whether the assumption you have identified really is correct.

In the examination you may be asked to assess the reasonableness of an assumption you have identified in an argument. To see how this is done let's have another look at the Pause for Thought example about biofuel on page 28.

R1	Using biofuel is a cheap way to run a car.
R2	It is easy to convert an ordinary car engine to run on biofuel.
Assumption	Biofuel is readily available locally.
C	You should have your car engine converted to biofuel.

'Biofuel is readily available locally' is necessary for the argument to work, but it would not be a reasonable assumption, since there are very few biofuel outlets in the UK (450 registered suppliers at the time of writing this book).

You are not expected to provide this type of factual detail in your responses to questions about the reasonableness of assumption (although it is not wrong either). It would have been enough to write the following.

> This is not a reasonable assumption to make, since proper biofuel is not currently available in as many places as you can get petrol or diesel.

Here is another example to try. Identify some assumptions which underpin this short argument and decide if each is reasonable or not:

> You should train to be an accountant when you have finished your A Levels. All businesses need accountants and they earn good salaries.

Some possible assumptions follow.

■ Assumption 1: Earning a good salary is more important to you than other considerations.

This is a reasonable assumption to make about many young people, but not true of all.

■ Assumption 2: There will be suitable vacancies for trainee accountants when you have finished your A Levels.

This a fairly reasonable assumption because many accounting firms recruit lots of trainees, but it is not a very reasonable assumption, as there is a lot of competition for such vacancies and companies can be very selective when they make their appointments.

■ Assumption 3: You have the right skills and qualifications to complete the training necessary to become an accountant.

Only you know whether or not this would be a reasonable assumption: trainee accountants come with many different A Level subjects, but need to be numerate. It also helps to be a logical thinker, so perhaps it is a very reasonable assumption after all.

ACTIVITY

Read the passage below. Then answer the questions that follow it.

The use of speed cameras is justified on the grounds that, since 'speed kills', anything that will discourage drivers from speeding must be a good thing.

The speed cameras do not deter people from speeding. In 2001, there were 1 million offenders caught on camera; in 2002, 1.5 million; in 2003, 2 million; and these figures have continued to rise. However, the belief that speed in itself is a significant problem needs examination. Excessive speed is found to be a contributory cause in only 10% of accidents.

Speed cameras do not even lead to a reduction in road deaths. From 1950 to 1993, there was a steady reduction in road deaths. But from 1994, there has not been this annual reduction despite the introduction of speed cameras.

The only police chief in the country who has opposed the use of speed cameras is in County Durham. His force uses traffic patrols instead. The accident rate in County Durham is 34% below the national average. There is an important issue here. Speed cameras do not record incidents of dangerous driving; they do not catch drink-drivers. Traffic patrols do. For the sake of road safety, speed cameras should be removed.

Adapted from OCR's June 2004 question paper

a) Identify the conclusion of the argument in paragraph 4.

b) What element of argument is paragraph 1?

c) Identify the reason in paragraph 2 that supports the conclusion of the argument.

d) Identify the reason in paragraph 3 that supports the conclusion of the argument.

e) In paragraph 2 the author uses evidence of the number of offenders caught by speed cameras to claim that the cameras do not deter people from speeding. Identify the assumption underlying this use of evidence.

REMEMBER

Assumptions are unstated parts of an argument. This means that they are not written down. If you are copying something from the passage, it is not an assumption.

EXAM TIPS

Take great care when you identify elements of an argument. Try not to paraphrase, or re-word, what is written in the passage. If you have to re-word, then check what you have written.

Concentrate on being precise about small, common words; you are more likely to misunderstand or lose marks if you don't pay attention to words like 'some', 'all', 'only', 'always' and 'never' than if you don't know what a long word means.

REMEMBER

When you analyse an argument (that is when you break it down into reasons, conclusions, evidence and other elements) you should follow these steps.

- Always identify the conclusion of the argument first.
- Then look for the reasons – those parts of the argument that support the main conclusion by giving you information that helps you to believe, accept or agree with the conclusion.
- The reasons may be supported by evidence – probably statistics – or examples.
- The meaning of any unfamiliar technical words can probably be guessed from the context and will not prevent you analysing the argument.
- You must pay attention to the small words – 'some', 'all', 'only', 'always' and 'never'.

- F1 drivers are multitaskers.

ACTIVITY 20

Analyse this argument.

Students concerned for their long-term health should avoid American football, as it is the sport most likely to cause neck injury in the USA. Researchers combined hospital admission numbers with sport participation figures across the USA in the 1990s. For every 10,000 participants, they found overall neck injuries in 5.85 football players. That's more than the 2.8 hockey players and 1.67 soccer players combined.

ACTIVITY 21

Read the passage below. Then answer the questions that follow it.

Driving skill is an obvious but essential quality in an F1 driver. To achieve the fastest lap times, F1 cars are driven to the limits of safety. Drivers must have split second reaction times to avoid a devastating crash. To maximise speed, they must also place the car centimetre perfect lap after lap.

F1 drivers need cardiovascular fitness. A typical F1 race can last an hour and a half. They also need the strength to deal with turning corners fast. As Jensen Button turns into the flat right-hander at Silverstone's Copse Corner, his neck muscles will be straining to support a weight equivalent to 30 bags of sugar. F1 drivers have to be among the very fittest athletes in the world to cope with the incredible strains that full throttle racing can place on the human body.

Drivers need to be competent engineers as well. They have to interpret the complex data beamed back to the pits, maintain a conversation with the engineer during the race and make adjustments to the car's brakes, fuel mixture and other settings.

The right mental approach is critical. Drivers need to be self-motivated, have the desire to win, and be able to control their aggression. They have to perform under intense pressure in qualifying and during races. F1 drivers also have to shrug off the real possibility of death or injury.

Because drivers have to perform all these amazing feats at the same time, at 200mph, they must surely count among the elite of multitaskers.

Adapted from an article in *Focus* no. 152, July 2005

a) Identify the *conclusion* of the argument presented in the final paragraph of the passage.

b) Write down the *reasons* (one in each paragraph) the author uses to support their conclusion.

c) From paragraph 2, write down the *evidence* the author gives to support the reason.

d) From paragraph 2, write down the *example* the author uses to illustrate the reason.

ACTIVITY 22

Read the following passage carefully. Then answer the questions that follow it.

There is a widespread belief that medical science has been responsible for the increased life expectancy and better health of people in western societies during the last 150 years. However, medical science has made little contribution to this improvement.

Figures from Chicago show that the key decline in infant mortality rates in Chicago was between 1870 and 1900. The chance of reaching the age of 5 increased from 50% to 75% in this period. These improvements were due to better sanitation and water supply. The vast majority of the population could not afford to visit the doctor. Medical science therefore had little to do with the drop in infant mortality.

In Britain, vaccination programmes became widespread only in the middle of the twentieth century, long after key improvements in life expectancy and health had been achieved. The main factor in these improvements was the action to improve the living conditions of the poor.

Clearly there have been great advances in surgical techniques in recent years, but they have not resulted in the dramatic improvements in life expectancy that resulted from public health improvements in the late nineteenth and early twentieth centuries. For example, in Chicago infant mortality fell by 122 per 1000 between 1890 and 1920, but by only 7 per 1000 between 1960 and 1990.

Adapted from OCR's January 2003 question paper

a) Identify the main conclusion, the reasons and the counter-assertion.

b) Identify the evidence and examples precisely.

c) Is the author's use of evidence reasonable? Explain your answer with reference to the material in the passage.

▪ Some people over the age of 70 are still working.

ACTIVITY 23

Read the passage below. Then answer the questions that follow it.

The price of living longer

People are living longer and longer lives. Our concept of the age when people retire from work should be revised. There are a number of reasons why this will be essential.

Not only are people living longer, but the birth rate is also decreasing and this will result in a significant age imbalance in the population. Employers will have to recruit people in the 65-plus age group to compensate for the shortage of younger workers.

The concept of an age when one should 'retire' is a recent one. Figures from the 1921 UK census show that 53% of men in the age group 70–74 were still working in spite of pensions being available at the age of 70. This shows they chose to be economically active and not to isolate themselves from mainstream life.

Pensions experts have warned that, unless the retirement age is raised, the level of pensions must be reduced. The idea of a long autumn in your life while you are still biologically young is attractive, but if you are biologically young you should still be working.

Adapted from OCR's January 2002 question paper

a) Identify the conclusion of the argument presented in the first paragraph of the passage.

b) Write down the reasons (one in each paragraph) the author uses to support their conclusion.

c) From paragraph 3, write down the evidence the author gives to support the reason.

d) What must the author assume to argue as they do in paragraph 3? Explain whether this is a reasonable assumption to make. Refer to material in the passage in your answer.

e) Identify the hypothetical reasoning in the passage.

EXAM TIP ●

When looking at a long passage, break it down into shorter arguments and look for the missing steps. Keep asking yourself if there is anything else you have to agree to between the stated parts of the argument. Be precise; work through the text statement by statement, paragraph by paragraph, looking for the missing links.

Summary

You should now be able to:

■ analyse the structure of shorter and longer passages, identifying reasons, examples, evidence, counter-argument, intermediate conclusion and the main conclusion

■ assess the extent and reasonableness of assumptions

■ evaluate how well reasons support conclusions

■ tackle exam-style questions.

Section 2   Credibility
The credibility criteria

Learning objectives

- Understand what is meant by the term 'credibility'.
- Assess the plausibility and extent of claims.
- Understand and apply criteria for judging credibility.
- Explain how credibility criteria strengthen or weaken claims.

What is credibility?

In Chapter 3 we looked at different forms in which evidence may be presented. In Chapter 4 we looked at ways of assessing whether evidence supports reasoning – e.g. by considering whether or not the evidence is likely to be reliable.

In this chapter we will look at ways of deciding whether evidence is *credible* – that is, whether it can be *believed*.

> **REMEMBER**
>
> 'Evidence' has two slightly different meanings, both of which are important in assessing **credibility**.
>
> - The available facts and circumstances that support a reason or conclusion, which are often in the form of numerical or statistical data.
> - Claims quoted from a source, e.g. a person, organisation, document, journal or website.

Claims

In Chapter 2 we saw that any part of an argument can be referred to as a claim. Almost everything that is said or written, other than questions, exclamations and instructions, is a claim. A claim might be a fact or an opinion. Reasons and conclusions are claims. A claim is therefore something that is stated, and that can be challenged.

In deciding whether something is credible (believable), it makes sense to start by working out whether it is a *plausible* claim – that is, whether it is *reasonable*.

A claim which is both *plausible* and *credible* may or may not be true.

For example, a government minister at the centre of a scandal might be quoted saying: 'I have given the Prime Minister my resignation in order to spend more time with my family'. The claim is plausible. Some people – who believe what politicians say – might find it also credible. However, if the minister has been sacked, then his claim is not true.

> **REMEMBER**
>
> In Critical Thinking, asking 'Is this credible?' is similar to asking 'Can I believe this?'

> **REMEMBER**
>
> A claim is a statement or judgement that can be challenged.

Later in this chapter we will look at Critical Thinking techniques for judging credibility of claims, but first try assessing the content of different claims.

In other words, do the claims in Activity 24 stand up on their own, or do they fail because they conflict with your own observations and knowledge?

KEY TERMS

Credibility
Whether someone's claims or evidence can be believed.

Plausibility
Whether or not a claim or piece of evidence is reasonable.

EXAM TIP

To remember the difference between **plausibility** and **credibility**, use a mnemonic, e.g. **C**harlie **B**rown *credibly believed* he **R**aised *reasonably plausible* **P**umpkins.

ACTIVITY

The quotations below are different claims. Decide whether you can accept the content of each claim or not. Explain why (why not).

A The likelihood is that somewhere in the universe the conditions are right for the existence of life as we know it.

B Aliens have landed in Manchester.

C According to the Organisation of Economic Co-operation and Development (OECD), earnings for graduates are on average 58% higher than those who have only completed secondary education.

D The [National Minimum Wage] main rate for workers aged 22 and over increased on 1 October 2006 to £5.35 an hour.

E There is 'not only climate change but humanity is responsible for that'.

F Shrewsbury Town FC is set to do well this season.

G Scientists have unveiled the world's first invisibility cloak.

You probably decided that you could accept the content of claims A, C, D and E, but not B, and that it was difficult to know for certain about quotations F and G. Quotation B ('Aliens have landed in Manchester') sounds completely absurd. What about quotation G ('Scientists have unveiled the world's first invisibility cloak')? On the face of it, this sounds nearly as unlikely as aliens having landed in Manchester. We will look at this claim again later in this chapter.

Where you decided you could accept the content of the claim, it was probably because it did not conflict with what you had previously observed, or with what you think you know to be fact. Sometimes this is referred to as the claim 'having merit'. Most of us carry out this sort of initial assessment of information many times a day, but without being aware we are doing it. This is how we know not to believe adverts like Celesta's which we met on page 44.

Assessing the plausibility and extent of claims

In Activity 24, it was probably the *nature of the claim* itself that led you to decide that claim B, 'Aliens have landed in Manchester', was not plausible. In this section we will look at ways in which you can assess the plausibility and extent of claims.

Supporting evidence and further clarification

Calling something a 'claim' does not mean it cannot be accepted. For example:

> Galileo claimed that the Earth moved round the Sun.

Galileo found himself in a lot of trouble when he made this claim, but it is now long established. However, it may be necessary to consider how to interpret a claim. Look again at claim F, which was made by John Black, a lifetime Shrewsbury Town FC supporter:

> Shrewsbury Town FC is set to do well this season.

▪ Shrewsbury Town FC in action.

When challenged, John Black, the supporter, could provide the following evidence to support his claim.

- There are good, new, young players in the team.
- A lot of money has been invested in the club.
- The club has a new stadium and the team no longer plays on a pitch which floods when it rains.
- The team did so badly last season, it can't do any worse.

So how might the claim – especially the words 'set to do well' – be interpreted? If John Black clarified the claim, we might find that he means any of these.

Shrewsbury Town will win some matches.
or
Shrewsbury Town will be promoted at the end of the season.
or
Shrewsbury Town will be more successful than last season.

The performance of Shrewsbury Town will be affected by many factors, but these claims would be regarded as plausible by most people – except perhaps rival supporters.

REMEMBER

In Critical Thinking, asking 'Is this plausible?' is asking 'Is this reasonable?'

Plausibility of evidence

In Chapter 3 we learnt that we can decide whether or not to accept a claim in an argument based on how well it is verified by, or supported with, reasons or evidence. In Chapter 3, we looked mainly at evidence in the form of examples, statistical or numerical data, estimates and factual claims.

However, evidence may be presented as personal observations or as statements from sources or witnesses. For example, this is part of the statement by a **witness** to a robbery:

KEY TERM

Witness

A person who saw (or heard) an event.

> At around 10.15am I was walking along the high street past the Central England Bank, when a large car pulled up and two men wearing balaclavas got out and ran inside the bank.

Let us look again at claim B in Activity 24 (page 66).

> Aliens have landed in Manchester.

Evidence in support of the claim might be personal observation:

> I was driving home after an evening out with friends, when I saw a strange glow in the sky towards the south of the city. The light moved towards the ground, hovered for a few minutes, then landed. There were no houses or any other lights in the area.

This evidence in itself is reasonable, but does not persuade that aliens have landed. The witness's observation might have been influenced by poor weather or other factors. The statement just tells us what the witness believes she saw.

PAUSE FOR THOUGHT

What other explanations might there be for the statement in support of claim B, Activity 24, that aliens have landed in Manchester?

REMEMBER

The plausibility of the claim itself is one of the first things to consider in assessing credibility. You need to ask the following questions.

- ■ Is it reasonable? What are the reasons why it is not plausible?
- ■ Does it need interpreting?
- ■ Does it need supporting with evidence?

ACTIVITY 25

a) **Working as a group, consider the nature of the following claims and decide whether each is plausible or not. Give reasons why the claim may (or may not) be plausible. (Take a look at the Pause for Thought box below, which shows how you could answer the questions for claim A.)**

A You must see this film – plot, screenplay and acting are absolutely superb.

B Waists are back: this season's essential fashion item is a wide belt.

C There is no real health hazard in drinking several cups of coffee a day. Research suggests that long-term coffee drinkers are less likely to develop dementia in old age than those who have drunk little or no coffee.

D 43% of divorced people will have another partner within five years.

E Channelling white light into your home will clear it of negative energies and bring it back into balance and harmony.

F Every person in the UK uses on average ten aerosol cans per person or 27 cans per household, including aerosols for food/personal hygiene and do-it-yourself jobs.

Telford & Wrekin Council's Insight, 22 July 2007, page 5

b) **Below are some newspaper headlines. What evidence might support each claim? What evidence could undermine it?**

A Less than 50% of teachers have a degree in the subject they teach.

B After Jamie Oliver, children lose their appetite for lunch.

C Bugs are the best weathermen.

D Pumpkins could help diabetics.

Adapted from The Times, 9 July 2007

PAUSE FOR THOUGHT

Look back at claim A in Activity 25. Here's how you could answer the questions for that claim.

Claim A is fairly plausible. It is a subjective and perhaps exaggerated opinion that plot, screenplay and acting are absolutely superb, but this type of recommendation often encourages people to see a film. However, the reader may not be interested in the type of film referred to, so the claim that they 'must' see it is too strongly worded to be entirely plausible.

- Bugs are the best weathermen.

Assessing the credibility of individuals and organisations

Witnesses and sources

When assessing evidence, it is important to consider the **source** of the evidence, and in particular the credibility of that source. The source may be a person giving oral testimony (e.g. in a court of law) or an account of events, which is written or spoken. Researchers, such as historians, use documentary evidence and regard some sources as more reliable than others. Sometimes, in the absence of other conclusive evidence, court cases have to be decided on the basis of which **witness** is the more believable, or credible.

In the examination you will be asked to assess the credibility of individuals or organisations. Assessing credibility does not tell you whether someone is telling the truth or not, but it does help you to decide whether someone is reliable and likely to be telling the truth. In Critical Thinking the term 'source' is used to refer to the person whose credibility you are considering. 'Source' can also refer to an organisation or a document.

We will look at how **criteria** for assessing credibility can be used to help decide whether individual people are reliable sources or not, but first you should try the Pause for Thought box overleaf.

KEY TERMS

Source ■

A person, organisation or document providing information or evidence.

Witness statement ■

A report by someone who has actually seen (or heard) an event.

Criteria ■

Standards, measures, or benchmarks, against which something can be measured.

71

PAUSE FOR THOUGHT

The report below about Andrew Atkins will be used as a starting point for considering how the credibility criteria can be applied. If you are familiar with the article you will be able to understand the credibility criteria better when these are explained next.

Read the local newspaper report below. Working as a group decide whether you would believe Andrew Atkins if he tried to sell you 'a quality car which will give years of trouble-free motoring'.

Probation for garage owner who sold 'lethal' cars

Local businessman Andrew Atkins, 55, yesterday pleaded guilty before city magistrates to two specimen charges of selling a vehicle in an unsafe condition from his garage, Atkins Quality Motors.

Magistrates heard evidence from two customers who both became suspicious when vehicles they had purchased developed faults within a few days of purchase. Suzy Thomson, the city council's senior consumer protection officer, told the court: 'These customers bought cars in good faith. Both showed serious faults within days of purchase.'

Customer Ethel Blake told the court: 'Mr Atkins told me that the car was low mileage and would be reliable. But the day I drove it home I had difficulty stopping and so I asked my cousin's advice.'

Miss Blake's cousin, retired car mechanic William Blake, told magistrates: 'I spent 40 years in the motor trade and did not have to look at the car. I knew immediately from what my cousin said that the brakes needed fixing.'

Vehicle safety engineer Tim Harris stated: 'My inspection showed that the car sold to Miss Blake had dangerously faulty brakes, which would soon have failed completely.'

Catherine Lee, solicitor for Atkins, explained that her client had become depressed after he split up with his girlfriend and his business ran into difficulties. He had been selling cars for more than 20 years and had no previous convictions. He denied that the brakes on Miss Blake's car were dangerous, but agreed that the car had not been properly serviced before she collected it. Atkins was well known locally for his charity fundraising work for the Retired Greyhounds Rehoming Centre.

Atkins asked for sixteen similar offences to be taken into account. Magistrate Gurvinder Gosal told Atkins that he would not face a jail sentence, in the light of evidence of his previous good character from his business partner Colin Davis. Atkins was sentenced to six months' probation and ordered to pay compensation to the customers.

Credibility criteria

In a situation where you need to decide between conflicting information from two (or more) people, then assessing their relative credibility can help you to decide who to believe.

There are several criteria that can be used to help decide whether a person, and therefore their claim or evidence, is credible or not:

■ ability to perceive

■ corroboration

■ consistency and inconsistency

■ bias

■ neutrality

■ vested interest

■ expertise or experience of source

■ reputation (negative or positive).

We will look at each of these in turn below.

> **REMEMBER**
>
> ■ If you are applying a single standard, use the term (one) *criterion*.
> ■ If you are applying more than one criterion, use the term *criteria*.

Ability to perceive

Ability to perceive includes 'ability to see', 'ability to hear' or using any of the senses. This is sometimes called ability to observe.

The source's ability to see or hear what actually happened may be a key criterion in deciding whether or not their evidence is credible.

It is important to remember that the criterion 'ability to perceive' relates to the credibility of an **eye-witness** to an event. You may have heard it said that '**hearsay** is not evidence'. Hearsay is an account which is not based on personal knowledge, but on information from other people, which could be rumour or gossip.

Factors that affect the ability to perceive an event

In assessing an eye-witness's ability to perceive events, it helps to ask these questions.

■ Did the witness see, or hear, the whole event? If not, which part did the witness see or hear?

■ Does the witness have any medical condition or disability that might affect their ability to observe (and recall) the event accurately?

■ Was the witness under emotional or other stress?

■ Was the witness under the influence of alcohol or drugs (including prescription medicine)?

■ Was the witness distracted by other things that were going on at the same time?

KEY TERMS

● **Ability to perceive**

A source's ability to use any of the five senses to assess an event or situation.

● **Eye-witness**

Someone who provides evidence based on first-hand experience.

● **Hearsay**

Evidence based on secondhand information from another source, who may have interpreted it.

▪ Poor visibility can affect our observation.

Activity 26 a) highlights some of the factors that may affect how well an eye-witness could observe what was happening.

REMEMBER ─────────────────────────

Ability to perceive can involve any of the five senses: sight, hearing, touch, taste and smell.

ACTIVITY **26** ─────────────────

a) What might make it difficult for potential witnesses to perceive what happened in the following events?

A   A woman's handbag is stolen inside a night club.

B   A fight takes place at a pensioners' Christmas party.

C   A car accident occurs in fog.

D   An anti-war demonstration ends in a riot?

b) Look again at the witness's account of the alien landing in Manchester (page 69). Asses the credibility of her evidence by using the criterion ability to perceive.

c) Refer to the newspaper report about Andrew Atkins. Explain whether the criterion ability to perceive strengthens or weakens the evidence of William Blake.

TAKE IT FURTHER ───────────────────

Working in groups, use newspapers (local and national) to find two reports of incidents where it may be difficult to learn what exactly happened from eye-witness accounts. Use the five questions opposite to help explain why.

Corroboration

Law courts place a lot of importance on whether the evidence from a witness is **corroborated** by other witnesses' accounts. In other words, the court considers whether the evidence of one witness agrees with that of other witnesses.

REMEMBER

Corroboration normally confirms the reliability of evidence, unless there is reason to think that any of the sources may have reason to be untruthful or misleading.

If the account, or evidence, from two sources does not agree, but is contradictory, then there is *conflicting* evidence. Sometimes the main parts of the account are corroborated, but there is conflict in the detail. Then you need to decide how important those details are.

ACTIVITY 27

Refer to the newspaper report about Andrew Atkins. Identify, where witnesses' evidence is *corroborated*. (You should use the wording in the article in your answer.)

Consistency and inconsistency

Corroboration (or conflict) refers to whether the accounts of different witnesses, or sources, agree with each other. Looking for consistency (or inconsistency) within one person's account of events is a means of judging the credibility of the evidence itself.

ACTIVITY 28

Refer to the newspaper report about Andrew Atkins. Identify any *consistencies* or *inconsistencies* in individual witnesses' evidence. (You should use the wording in the article where possible in your answers.)

REMEMBER

Later in the course, when we start to consider the ways of assessing the effectiveness of an argument it will be useful to see if there is consistency or **inconsistency** within it.

Do not confuse a counter-argument (which we looked at in Chapter 4, page 57) with inconsistency within an argument. A counter-argument is an intentional device by the writer to strengthen the argument, whereas inconsistency weakens it.

Bias

Bias means a prejudice in favour of one side rather than another. It may well not be conscious, or intentional, but subconscious beliefs may lead to someone having a tendency to support a particular point of view. Bias may originate in religious or political beliefs, or from being a member of a group or even family. However, the person who is biased may have nothing to gain personally from the outcome of the situation.

KEY TERM

Bias

Tendency to be prejudiced against, or in favour of, certain beliefs, or people who engage in particular activities. This gives a **motive** or subconscious reason to lie, misrepresent or distort information or evidence, e.g. by being selective in what is reported in order to blame someone else or support strongly held beliefs.

PAUSE FOR THOUGHT —————————————————————

Sometimes it is said that everyone has some form of unconscious bias. Read the letters page in a local or national paper. Identify where the writer is showing bias and try to work out what they are biased towards or against.

ACTIVITY 29 —————————————————————

a) Refer to the newspaper report about Andrew Atkins. Identify the people whose evidence may be weakened by bias.

b) What might be a source of unconscious bias for the individuals in the situations described below?

A Doreen Henderson's car has been vandalised. She has seen two groups of young people in the street. Louise Long, who lives next door, was with other A Level students from the specialist technology school. Mohammed Hussain was with friends he works with at the burger bar.

B Annabel Waterworth owns a very successful business. She suspects that one of the employees in the accounts department has been 'fiddling the books'. The likely culprit could be Patrick O'Flanaghan, who has been trying to recruit other workers to a trade union. It might also be Tracy Biggs, who is leaving to join a competitor.

KEY TERMS

- **Neutrality**

  Being impartial; having no reason to favour either side in a dispute or difference of opinion.

- **Vested interest**

  Personal interest, usually financial, in a state of affairs or in an organisation leading to the expectation of personal gain from a favourable outcome.

- **Motive**

  Factor that may cause a person to act in a particular way.

Neutrality

Someone who is neutral in a dispute has no connection to any of the parties involved in the dispute. A witness who is neutral has no motive or reason to lie, or distort their account of events or is someone who gives a balanced account (to some extent) of the various options.

People in many professions are expected to be neutral when doing their job, for example journalists and social workers.

REMEMBER !

Bias is the counterpart of neutrality – someone who is neutral has no reason to give a misleading or untrue account of events.

ACTIVITY 30

a) Refer to the newspaper report about Andrew Atkins. Identify the people who should be neutral.

b) Identify *five* jobs (other than those already mentioned) where you would expect the person to be professionally neutral.

Vested interest

Vested interest provides a **motive** to say one thing rather than another, to lie or distort what is said, because the witness has a personal interest in a situation. The difference between vested interest and bias is that the person with a vested interest will gain personally from the outcome of the situation. Bias leads to a *desire* to believe one interpretation or explanation of events; vested interest provides an *incentive* to present one interpretation.

In the case of Andrew Atkins (see page 72), it could be argued that the customer, Ethel Blake, stood to gain compensation if Atkins were found guilty.

Vested interest giving a motive to tell the truth

We usually expect a vested interest to give a motive for misrepresenting evidence. Sometimes it may provide a motive for giving an accurate account of events. People whose job depends on maintaining their professional independence – e.g. accountants, doctors, or health and safety inspectors – can be expected to have a motive to give an accurate account of events. Failing to do so may damage their professional *reputation*.

ACTIVITY 31

Refer to the newspaper report about Andrew Atkins. Identify the sources who have a vested interest. Explain whether their vested interest strengthens or weakens any claims made.

┌─ **PAUSE FOR THOUGHT** ─────────────────────────────

The BBC is financed by a licence fee, which is indirectly controlled by the government. The BBC has always been proud of its reputation for independent, accurate reporting. However, reporters may gain individually from producing a sensational news report. Does a BBC reporter have a vested interest in the safeguarding of the BBC's reputation, even if the report would seriously embarrass the government?

- How far is the media independent?

Expertise or experience of source

Having specialist **expertise**, training or experience may suggest that someone is a reliable source or witness particularly as regards interpreting a situation. Law courts often rely on specialist witnesses such as forensic experts, pathologists, psychiatrists and medical experts.

Relevant expertise generally strengthens the credibility of evidence given by that person because their training, skills and knowledge should enable them to provide accurate evidence. However, real court cases sometimes go back to the courts on appeal, because fresh evidence has cast doubt on the specialist evidence given at the original trial. People often question specialist advice that is given out by government departments, because they believe there may be a vested interest which gives a motive to present a view of the situation which puts the government in a good light.

KEY TERM

Expertise

Skills, experience and training that give someone specialist knowledge and judgement.

ACTIVITY 32

a) In each of the examples below, explain whether the source has expertise that is relevant or irrelevant to the claim they have made.

- State the nature of the source's expertise.
- Explain what expertise would be relevant to the claim.
- Explain whether the source's expertise is relevant in this case.

(Take a look at the Pause for Thought box on page 81, which shows how you could answer the questions for example A.)

A A former top athlete recommends a breakfast cereal in an advertising campaign on the basis that it helps keep his heart healthy.

B The local police force advises people not to travel because the Meteorological Office has forecast severe flooding in the area.

C A plumber advises a customer that the electrics in his house need rewiring.

D A politician, who is a former lawyer, tells a meeting of business managers that the economic situation will improve in the next 12 months.

b) Refer to the newspaper report about Andrew Atkins. Identify the sources who have specialist expertise and the area of their expertise. Explain whether the source's expertise is relevant to any claims made.

- A meeting of politicians and business managers.

PAUSE FOR THOUGHT

Look back at example A in Activity 32 a). Here's how you could answer the questions for that claim.

The former athlete would have expertise in his own field of sport, but this would not be relevant to the claim that the cereal keeps his heart healthy. The relevant expertise would be in diet/nutrition or in heart disease. In this case the source's expertise is not relevant.

TAKE IT FURTHER

Use the Internet to find out about a current, contentious issue where specialist expertise has been challenged. What conclusions can you draw about reliance on specialists? (If you can't think of a current issue, you could research the inquest into Princess Diana's death, the case of Dr David Kelly and the Iraq weapons dossier, or the case of Professor Southall.)

Reputation (negative or positive)

We often make decisions on whether to believe what someone tells us because we know whether or not we have found that person to be truthful in the past.

Reputation is based on what we know about someone's past performance, behaviour and character. These may be supported by qualifications or specialist expertise in a particular field. Some people and organisations have a positive reputation, such as the BBC, which is widely seen as presenting news accurately and independently. Others have a negative reputation, such as the former American President, Richard Nixon who was forced to resign after a political scandal in which he was implicated. The reputation of some organisations such as governments and businesses changes over time.

When assessing someone's credibility based on their reputation, you are working on the basis that their past performance is a guide to how they will perform in a particular situation. However, past performance is not necessarily a reliable guide.

Fortunately for many people, court cases are not decided on the basis of reputation, but on other evidence. Reputation, after all, may have originated in hearsay not fact. It may also not be relevant to the issue being decided. For example, a top surgeon's reputation in his field would be irrelevant if he was accused of fraud.

KEY TERM

Reputation

What is generally said or believed about the character of a person or an organisation.

EXAM TIP

You may be asked to assess a real document on the exam paper.

ACTIVITY 33

a) **Refer to the newspaper report about Andrew Atkins. Explain how far the credibility of Andrew Atkins is strengthened by his reputation.**

b) **Working in groups, examine a variety of newspaper articles.**

A Identify the claims that are based on someone's expertise.

B Identify the claims that are based on an appraisal of reputation, whether positive or negative.

C Assess the claims you have identified.

REMEMBER

Reputation might weaken or strengthen credibility based on past experience, but this may not relate to the present situation.

▪ Would you buy a used car from Atkins Quality Motors?

ACTIVITY 34

Refer again to the newspaper report about Andrew Atkins (page 72). In Activities 26, 27 and 29–33 you have applied credibility criteria to the sources in the senario. Use your answers to help you to:

- ▓ assess the claims made by each source (the first one has been done to help you)
- ▓ explain which person is the most credible (apart from the magistrate Gurvinder Gosal).

Sample answer

Andrew Atkins, owner of Atkins Quality Motors, claimed through his solicitor the following.

- ▓ That he had become depressed after he split up with his girlfriend and his business ran into difficulties.

- ▓ That he had been selling cars for 20 years and had no previous convictions. All these claims are both plausible and credible, but are not corroborated and there is no evidence to support them. They are made through his solicitor, who is not neutral as she is acting on Atkins' behalf. She would therefore tell the court what Atkins wants her to tell them. However, solicitors need to maintain their professional reputation, and would be unlikely to deliberately mislead the court.

- ▓ That although the car had not been serviced properly before Miss Blake collected it, the brakes were not dangerous. It is entirely plausible and credible that the car had not been serviced properly as Atkins would be unlikely to own up to something he was not responsible for. He may feel that it would help his position to admit a lesser matter than the charge against him. His claim that the brakes were not dangerous is contradicted by the expert evidence from the vehicle safety engineer whose inspection showed the car had dangerously faulty brakes. It is also contradicted by the evidence of the customer, who had difficulty stopping it on the day she drove it home and by the evidence of her cousin, the retired mechanic. Atkins' claim the brakes were not dangerous is inconsistent with his own plea of guilty to two charges of selling a vehicle in an unsafe condition.

The other sources to consider are:

- ▓ Suzy Thomson, city council senior consumer protection officer
- ▓ Ethel Blake, customer
- ▓ William Blake, retired car mechanic
- ▓ Tim Harris, vehicle safety engineer
- ▓ Catherine Lee, solicitor for Atkins
- ▓ Colin Davis, partner in business with Andrew Atkins.

ACTIVITY 35

Read the article below. Then answer the questions that follow it.

Scientists at the University in Trondheim have now claimed that because of their burping and farting, moose are contributing massively to global warming. An adult moose expels – from both ends – the methane equivalent of 2,100 kg of carbon dioxide emissions, which has a similar environmental impact to the emissions caused by 8000 miles of car travel. The biologist Reidar Andersen has said: 'Shoot a moose and you have saved the equivalent of two long-haul flights.'

While researchers in Scotland and Wales have been examining how the feeding of dairy cows could be changed to cut back their gaseous belching, such work has not been possible on the 120,000 wild moose in Norway.

The moose's eating habits have already been altered by climate change with the result that they are now part of a vicious circle of increasing gas emissions, which began when snows started to recede in Norway. 'Moose normally eat branches in the winter, a not particularly nutritious diet,' said Erling Solberg, of the Norwegian Institute for Nature Research. 'But since snow has become so much rarer they have access to wild blueberries.'

The result has been fatter moose that are more likely to break wind. Moreover, better-fed moose have started to reproduce more quickly and herds are swelling.

Last winter there were reports of moose straying into towns in search of food – eating Christmas decorations and even smashing shop windows to reach displayed vegetables.

Norwegians are therefore pleading for higher hunt quotas to keep moose numbers down and the gas emissions under control. In the 2007 hunting season the authorities allowed a kill-quota of 35,000.

Professor Andersen, who hunts moose as well as studying them, said: 'Remove a moose from the world and you have saved the equivalent of 36 flights between Oslo and Trondheim.'

The Kyoto protocol counts a tonne of expelled methane as the equivalent of 21 tonnes of carbon dioxide.

Ruminant livestock worldwide produce 80 million tonnes of methane annually.

Adapted from Roger Boyes, 'Moose with wind are worse than gas guzzlers', *The Times*, 23 August 2007

a) Assess the credibility of Reidar Andersen. You should refer to credibility criteria in your answer and explain how these may strengthen or weaken his credibility.

b) What else would you need to know in order to reach a judgement about the credibility of the researchers in Scotland and Wales?

c) Professor Andersen claims: 'Remove a moose from the world and you have saved the equivalent of 36 flights between Oslo and Trondheim.' Identify the evidence that supports this claim.

ACTIVITY 36

In Activity 24 you considered whether claims A–G were plausible. The sources of the claims are given below. Explain whether each claim is credible or not.

A The likelihood is that somewhere in the universe the conditions are right for the existence of life as we know it.

A scientist

B Aliens have landed in Manchester.

Aliens R Us website

C According to the Organisation of Economic Co-operation and Development (OECD), earnings for graduates are on average 58% higher than those who have only completed secondary education.

Education Guardian.co.uk, 12 September 2006

D The [National Minimum Wage] main rate for workers aged 22 and over increased on 1 October 2006 to £5.35 an hour.

Department for Business Enterprise and Regulatory Reform

E There is 'not only climate change but humanity is responsible for that'.

David Attenborough

F Shrewsbury Town FC is set to do well this season.

John Black, lifetime supporter of the club

G Scientists have unveiled the world's first invisibility cloak.

Science reporter

Summary

You should now be able to:

▪ understand what is meant by key terms such as 'plausibility', 'credibility', 'evidence', etc.

▪ assess the plausibility, extent and credibility of claims

▪ understand the credibility criteria

▪ apply the credibility criteria to sources in a straightforward scenario.

Learning objectives

- Assess the credibility of documents and organisations.
- Explain what other information is needed to decide about the credibility of a document or source.
- Assess how far the use of images and graphical representations weakens or strengthens the claims within a document.
- Compare and contrast the credibility of people or organisations.
- Make informed judgements about which source is most/least credible and the probable course of events in a given scenario.

Assessing the credibility of documents and organisations

In Chapter 5 we looked at the criteria that can be applied to help assess the credibility of individual people in a scenario. We also considered ways of assessing the credibility and plausibility of the claims made by people. In the context of Critical Thinking, individuals are usually called sources. In the examination, the sources will not necessarily be people. We have seen this already; some of the quotations we considered at the end of Chapter 5 were from organisations.

In the examination, you will also be asked to assess the credibility of organisations and documents. This can be done using the credibility criteria (pages 74–81) in a way that is very similar to assessing the credibility of an individual. Similarly the claims made by organisations, or in documents, can also be assessed in the same way as claims made by individuals.

REMEMBER

Assessing credibility does not tell you if the evidence given is true. It does not tell you whether or not you should believe it. It just helps you to decide if a source is likely to be reliable, and to compare the credibility of different sources.

PAUSE FOR THOUGHT

Many people research their own family history. Family history experts advise that a good starting point is to ask grandparents what they remember about their own parents and grandparents.

After talking to elderly relatives, people often start searching archives for birth, death and marriage certificates, and census records. This often reveals some interesting surprises. Perhaps an ancestor died in prison, not in a war. Or great-grandfather's occupation was recorded as 'farm labourer' not 'mill owner'. Sometimes someone's aunt turns out to be an illegitimate half-sister.

What reasons might there be for these inconsistencies? Should the family history researcher believe the relative, who has always been truthful, or the evidence of archive documents?

What other situations can you think of where you should regard documentary evidence as more reliable than witness evidence?

Assessing the credibility of documents

Historians often consider documentary evidence to be more reliable than oral history (personal recollections) because memories of events may become confused over time. However, the fact that something has been recorded in documentary form does not necessarily make it intrinsically more reliable than other evidence.

In the examination you may be asked to assess how far an article or report is credible. To do this you need to think about:

- the credibility of the writer
- the plausibility of the writer's claims
- how far the article or report reads like a balanced account, which draws on relevant sources, rather than a one-sided report
- the credibility of the source organisation, whether that is a newspaper, journal, or other organisation.

Credibility of the writer

Sometimes we have little or no information about the writer of an article: the article may be anonymous. However, many of us may question whether an article in a newspaper written by a well-known politician is likely to be unbiased. We might, though, accept an article by a well-known journalist, because the writer has a long-standing reputation for independent reporting.

REMEMBER

You can apply all the credibility criteria to the writer of an article and the claims made. The credibility criteria are:

- ability to perceive
- corroboration
- consistency and inconsistency
- bias
- neutrality
- vested interest
- expertise or experience of source
- reputation.

Often we need additional information before we can judge the credibility of the writer of an article. For example, if an article depends on complex scientific information, we might need to know the extent of the author's scientific knowledge before we could judge their credibility when writing on that topic.

- How credible is scientific information?

If you were thinking about buying a new computer you might read reviews of different computers in the computer journals. In deciding which reviews to take seriously, you might want to think about the credibility of the various writers.

Read the short excerpt below (from a magazine article) and identify which criteria would be relevant in assessing the writer's credibility. What other information would you need to know in order to reach a judgement about the claim that the computer is top of the range?

> **Apexus' new top of the range laptops launched**
>
> You may very well think there is nothing to compare between one computer laptop and another. That is, until you try the latest Apexus T2010 and the smaller, lighter Apexus T2011. The 'T' certainly means 'top of the range'. The Apexus T2010's smart black case and keyboard are the product of designer Jason Lansbury. The latest graphics card and the Octium chip mean the Apexus T2010 not only has the appearance of the ultimate games machine, but it has the processing power to deliver what it promises. The Apexus T2011 is definitely a machine for girls: the same massive processing power comes packed in a stylish, fuchsia-pink case.
>
> Duncan Dreyfus, *Computer Chronicle*, May 2008

Ability to perceive would be a relevant criterion for judging the writer's credibility as a reporter on computing. The writer gives some technical information about the two laptops, but this could simply be taken from publicity material. It does not appear that he has actually used either laptop, which makes his report less credible. In this instance consistency or inconsistency are not relevant. Vested interest, expertise and reputation would be appropriate criteria for judging the writer's credibility (and the credibility of *Computer Chronicle* magazine).

In order to reach a judgement as to whether the claim that the computers are 'top of the range' is reasonable, we would need to be certain that the writer, and the *Computer Chronicle* magazine, are completely independent from the computer industry. We would also need to know whether the writer has relevant technical expertise and whether the claim is just the writer's opinion or is shared by other people who have used the computers – for example, other reporters on computing.

If you were asked in the examination to comment on whether the claim is strengthened or weakened by particular credibility criteria, then you might argue the following:

> Relevant expertise and experience of using computers would strengthen the writer's claim that the computer is top of the range, because his experience would enable him to compare the computers with other similar computers and judge their technical specification.

Assessing the plausibility of the writer's claims

In Chapter 5 we looked at a number of claims and considered whether or not they were plausible and credible. Most of us would immediately dismiss some claims ('Aliens have landed in Manchester') without further thought. Likewise, we accept some claims without further thought ('Galileo claimed that the Earth moved round the Sun'). Often, however, we need to think more carefully about whether a particular claim is plausible, and to consider the claim as it stands.

ACTIVITY 37

Read the passage below, which is taken from an article by Michael Portillo, who was Conservative MP for Kensington and Chelsea until 1997. Then answer the questions that follow it.

Michael Portillo for Kensington & Chelsea News
3 March 2005, Chewing Gum & Cyclists

Westminster City Council has proposed a tax on chewing gum to finance the colossal cost for local authorities of cleaning it up. It reminded me that few things disgust me more than finding that I have stepped on a piece of discarded gum and have it stuck firmly to my shoe. Getting gum off is extremely difficult, though nail varnish remover seems to be the most effective remedy. I nearly gag at the smell, and am appalled to think in what diseased mouth it may have been.

Of course Westminster's plan is not a good one, since we ought to be encouraging people to dispose of it responsibly. If they have paid a tax they can argue that they have paid for someone to pick it up. But Westminster is to be congratulated on raising the issue. Bleeding heart liberal that I am, I would be happy for chewing in a public place to be banned, with hideous punishments for non-compliance.

Adapted from http://www.michaelportillo.co.uk/articles/art_kandc/gum.htm

a) Assess the credibility of the writer. In your answer you should indicate whether the writer's credibility is strengthened or weakened by relevant credibility criteria.

b) The writer claims that: 'Westminster's plan is not a good one, since we ought to be encouraging people to dispose of it responsibly.' How far is this a reasonable claim?

Assessing how far the article or report provides a balanced account, or a one-sided report

The person identified as the author of a newspaper article or report has normally written most of it, and incorporated information and evidence from different sources. A balanced report may contain a counter-argument. However, the fact that a document contains a range of information, evidence and counter-argument does not necessarily mean that it provides a balanced report. It is how the author selects and deals with the information and evidence that makes it balanced or not.

Look at these two different letters to a local newspaper on the same topic.

Dear Editor

I am appalled and disgusted by the inconsiderate and ignorant dog owners who allow their dogs to foul public pavements and parks where children play. It is beyond belief that people can do this in a so-called civilised society. People who behave in this way should lose the right to be dog owners. Their dogs should be confiscated and destroyed. People who want to be dog owners should be required to pass an intelligence test to ensure they are suitable and responsible enough.

Josephine Drakeley, Little Fittledean Manor

Dear Editor

The introduction of a compulsory dog licensing scheme, together with the micro-chipping of all dogs and local council dog patrols, is vital to help promote responsible dog ownership. The majority of dog owners are responsible and take care to use poop scoops, but a minority continue to ignore the dangers that dogs can cause. Dog faeces can carry *toxocara canis*, which causes serious illness and even blindness. Young children are particularly vulnerable. It is time the local council took action.

Joan Wykes, The Queen's Head, Aston Fittledean

The first letter is little more than a rant and provides no evidence or reasons in support of the claims made. You may think that the second letter is not a very persuasive argument, but it is more balanced than the first: it acknowledges that only a minority of dog owners are irresponsible, and it provides some evidence of the dangers. The language of the second letter is less angry and emotional: it claims that the suggested initiative will *help promote* responsible dog ownership, whilst the first letter uses phrases like 'beyond belief' and 'so-called civilised society'.

In assessing how far an article provides a balanced account you need to ask the following questions.

■ Is the language, or the use of images, emotive or reasoned?

■ Does the evidence selected demonstrate bias or neutrality?

■ Does the writer consider alternative viewpoints and alternative evidence from different sources, experts or witnesses?

PAUSE FOR THOUGHT

Look again at the article in Activity 37. Use the questions given above to decide if it provides a balanced account.

ACTIVITY

Working in groups, choose a current, controversial issue or news story that interests you. (It does not have to be a serious issue.)

a) Collect as many articles as you can that represent differing perspectives on the issue. You should select the articles from a range of newspapers and Internet news sites.

b) Use the three questions given above to assess how far each article provides a balanced report. Try to order the articles on a scale ranging from 'very biased' to 'neutral'.

c) What can you conclude about the bias, or political stance, of the different websites and newspapers which published the articles you have chosen?

Assessing the credibility of an organisation

In Activity 38 you had the opportunity to see how very different versions of the same news story can be published by different news organisations.

In the examination, you may be asked to assess the credibility of the organisation that published an article, or organisations quoted within the article. In both cases you should use the credibility criteria (see Chapter 5), in the same way as when you assess the credibility of individuals.

Some criteria are more relevant than others when assessing an organisation's credibility. These are bias, expertise and reputation.

Bias

Many national newspapers traditionally support one or other of the major political parties. Although their coverage overall is biased, the paper may still stimulate debate by printing articles from writers with differing viewpoints. You should not assume that, because a particular newspaper has printed it, the article follows the same political line.

Specialist expertise or experience

There is an enormous number of specialist journals publishing on every subject from accountancy to zoology. Organisations also exist to campaign on behalf of environmental or charitable causes. In assessing the credibility of such organisations you need to bear in mind that even though they may have unique specialist expertise, their credibility could be weakened by their bias towards causes they have sympathy with. A charity, which exists to help people who have suffered strokes, could write in support of the government funding rehabilitation centres for victims of brain injury. Their specialist knowledge of strokes makes them very credible, but their bias towards people with this condition may also undermine their credibility.

You also need to think about whether the organisation's specialist expertise is relevant to the issue. The stroke charity probably has a great deal of specialist knowledge about stroke, but not necessarily about the needs of people with other types of brain injury, such as those resulting from accidents.

At the same time as having specialist expertise, the organisation may have a vested interest in the promotion of a particular viewpoint. The stroke charity in our example probably relies on donations; publicising the needs of stroke victims indirectly reminds and encourages people to continue donating to that charity – which then helps keep the charity's employees in their jobs.

Reputation

Some news organisations have a well-established reputation for supporting a certain political point of view. The BBC is an obvious example of a news organisation with a reputation for balanced, unbiased reporting. It can be argued that an organisation like the BBC has a vested interested to ensure its reputation for independence is maintained.

ACTIVITY 39

Read the article below, then answer the questions that follow.

Established in 1891, this beautiful-looking boozer has retained its position in the heart of Brum's theatreland. A front-door blackboard advertising family Sunday roasts proudly says: 'You've tried the rest, now try the best.'

Hmmm. My roast featured two slices of tough beef. They were so strangely ridged the gravy made them resemble aerial shots of a muddy African delta.

The potatoes seemed to have been hanging around, the cabbage and carrots were school dinners revisited. Evening drinkers probably like the Old Fox just as it is, but it has a long way to go to become an essential Sunday roast destination for families.

> Adapted from Graham Young's pub review of The Old Fox, Hurst Street,
> Birmingham in the *Birmingham Mail*, 27 September 2007

a) How far is the article about 'The Old Fox' a credible report?

b) What else would you need to know about the writer to assess the claim that The Old Fox 'has a long way to go to become an essential Sunday roast destination for families'?

Images and graphical representations

In the examination you may be asked to assess the use of an image or a graphical representation in relation to the argument in the article.

In Chapter 3 we saw how graphical representations are often used to present numerical or statistical information so that its significance is more easily understood. If the information in the graph is not relevant, then the use of the graph undermines the credibility of the document. The same applies if the data is selected, or presented, in such a way that it misleads.

Images are frequently used in newspapers and magazines to attract the reader's attention, but they often convey very little hard information. In searching for articles for Activity 38, you may have noticed that tabloid newspapers (for example, *The Sun* and the *Daily Mirror*) look much more lively than the broadsheets (for example, *The Times* and *The Guardian*) because they use more pictures and photographs.

REMEMBER

Images and graphs or charts are simply evidence in visual form. You should assess the use of an image or a graph in the same way as you would assess any other evidence by asking these questions.

- Is this evidence significant?
- Is it relevant?
- (In the case of a graph or chart) is it typical and representative?

PAUSE FOR THOUGHT

Look again at the images and captions on pages 79, 80 and 88. Assess the relevance of the image to the caption.

Making informed judgements

In the examination you will be presented with information which includes two or three different opinions, and information and evidence, about an issue. You may be asked to make reasoned judgements about two things:

■ which source in a given situation is the most or least credible

■ the probable course of events in a given scenario.

Assessing which person, or organisation, is the most or least credible

These are some of the questions to ask when you need to reach a judgement as to which person in a given situation is the most or least credible.

■ How far do the credibility criteria strengthen or weaken each source's credibility?

■ What information is relevant to the decision and what can be put to one side?

■ Which facts are established?

■ Which facts are in dispute?

Look at the article about chocolate below, which is taken from a free daily newspaper, the *Metro*. As you read it, use the questions to help decide which organisation is the more credible.

Why chocolate is 'good for teeth'

Most of us cannot resist the temptation to bite into some. And now a chocolate maker reckons a touch of the dark stuff is actually good for our teeth. Cadbury claims chocolate is 'not as bad' for teeth as people may believe and brushing with it is the perfect way to ensure a gleaming set of gnashers. The natural substances in cocoa help to stave off plaque, it claims. But the British Dental Association dismissed the idea and urged people to stick to using toothpaste. 'While some research claims that cocoa may help prevent tooth decay, the sugar associated with chocolate certainly doesn't,' a spokesman said. 'Sugary food is a major cause of tooth decay.' Cadbury's claims are based on a study which also says chocolate improves circulation and ensures a healthy heart. But the British Heart Foundation says chocolate is more often a cause of heart disease.

Metro, 18 May 2007

■ The information about heart disease is not *relevant* to the claim that chocolate is good for teeth, so this can be discounted.

■ The British Dental Association accepts that *some* substances in cocoa may help prevent plaque, so this is an established fact. The key claim in dispute is whether or not chocolate (not cocoa) is good for teeth.

▨ Chocolate contains sugar as well as cocoa, and therefore cleaning teeth with chocolate would not be beneficial, as claimed by Cadbury, but harmful.

▨ Cadbury is a manufacturer of chocolate and sweets, so has a *vested interest* in promoting its products. It has *specialist expertise* in the manufacture of chocolate, but perhaps not in the health aspects of chocolate. The British Dental Association is a professional body representing dentists and so presumably has *expertise* and *experience* as regards the effect of foods such as chocolate on teeth. It also has a *reputation* as an independent, *neutral*, respected body, which makes its claim stronger than Cadbury's.

▨ The credibility of Cadbury is weakened because we have limited information about the study quoted, e.g. we do not know whether it was independent or funded by Cadbury, how many people were involved, whether it used cocoa or chocolate, and how the researchers measured the effect of the substances in cocoa on tooth decay.

▨ The British Dental Association is the more credible organisation because its expertise and neutrality are more significant than Cadbury's expertise. The British Dental Association has nothing to gain from this research being publicised, but Cadbury does stand to gain.

▪ The perfect way to gleaming gnashers?

Making a reasoned judgement about the probable course of events in a scenario

A judgement is a decision reached by weighing up the available evidence. In many cases in a court of law, the judgement which settles a dispute between two parties is often (but not always) made on the balance of probabilities. 'Black and white' disputes are unusual.

Use the following questions to help you decide what probably happened.

▨ What are the alternative explanations?

▨ What conclusion does the evidence lead towards?

In the examination your judgement about the chocolate issue could be:

Cadbury is using research about substances in cocoa to argue that chocolate is 'not as bad' for teeth as believed. Chocolate, however, also contains lots of sugar which is harmful for teeth. It is therefore probable that Cadbury is interpreting the research for its own purposes (marketing), but that the research does not support Cadbury's position.

The next activity requires you to think about how the criteria can be used to assess the credibility of the different people involved, then make your own judgement about what probably happened.

ACTIVITY 40

The material below is based on archive documents. Read the documents carefully, then answer the questions that follow them. (You may find it helps to read some of the documents aloud in a group.)

A   Special report by Sergeant Alexander Matthews dated 2.30am, Sunday 3 January 1932

At 2.45am on Friday 1 January 1932 in company with Police Constable George Younger I went to Rockside Boarding House, occupied by Mr Kent. I inquired for Mr Fred Larkin as his motor car, along with two others, was standing outside. Larkin had travelled along Roker Terrace earlier in the evening at a rather fast speed. I was desirous of seeing his condition. Mr Kent asked the police constable and myself to come in which we did and saw Larkin dancing and he appeared to be alright. After satisfying ourselves as to his condition, we left the premises and proceeded to Box 33.*

I rang at Box 1 at 2.40am and at Box 33 at 3.15 in company with PC Younger.

---

* Before police officers had radio communication they had to telephone regularly into the police station from police boxes.

B   Report by PC George Younger dated 9pm, 3 January 1932

At 2.45am Friday 1 January 1931 I was standing at the north end of Roker Terrace, on duty, when I saw Sergeant Alexander Matthews approaching from the direction of the police box. At that time there were three motor cars standing outside the house 'Rockside'. Sergeant Matthews recognised one of them as Mr Fred Larkin's and said: 'We will go and see what condition Larkin is in, as I have had a complaint regarding the careless manner in which he has been driving along the road.'

We then went to the door of 'Rockside' and saw Mr Bert Kent, the occupier. Sergeant Matthews asked him if Mr Larkin was inside, and he replied 'Yes.' Sergeant Matthews then said, 'What is his condition?', and Kent replied: 'Alright, I think, come in and see him.' We then entered the house and spoke to Larkin for a few minutes. We then left the house and proceeded to Box 33 and rang in at 3.15am.

C   Report of Occurrences signed by Superintendent G Hook 2 January 1932

On Saturday 2 January 1932 while I was on duty at half time at the football ground Alderman Taylor* said: 'I have reliable information that Sergeant Matthews and Constable Younger went in "Rockside" between 2 and 3am 1 January 1932 and had some drink and also that the Sergeant sang a song.'

D   Interview of Sergeant Matthews by Superintendent Hook

I saw Sergeant Matthews who was on duty at the match and asked him if he was on night duty on New Year's Eve in Roker Terrace and if anything unusual occurred between 2 and 3am. He replied: 'No but I will try and find out and let you know.'

E   Interview of PC Younger by Superintendent Hook

Supt Hook	*Did you go into 'Rockside' between 2 and 3am New Year's morning with Sergeant Matthews?*
PC Younger	*Yes.*
Supt Hook	*What did you go in for?*
PC Younger	*We saw Fred Larkin's car outside and went in to see what condition he was in.*
Supt Hook	*Did you have any drink?*
PC Younger	*No.*

F   Interview of Sergeant Matthews by Superintendent Hook

Supt Hook	*I understand you were in Rockside between 2 and 3am New Year's morning. What did you go in for?*
Sergeant Matthews	*To see Fred Larkin about his car.*
Supt Hook	*Did you have a drink while you were in and sing a song?*
Sergeant Matthews	*No.*

* Alderman: a senior elected member of the city council.

Supt Hook	*Why had you not submitted a report about going into a private house while on duty setting forth your reasons for doing so?*
Sergeant Matthews	*You know what Fred Larkin is for drink and we went in to see if he was alright and fit to drive a car. We found him alright and as it was only a suspected offence I did not report it.*
Supt Hook	*Both you and PC Younger must submit a report on the subject.*
Sergeant Matthews	*Does this mean I am to be reported?*
Supt Hook	*I will submit your reports to the Chief Constable.*

G Interview of Mrs Kent by Superintendent Hook at 6pm at 'Rockside', Roker Terrace

Supt Hook	*Had you a Sergeant and a Constable in your house on New Year's morning?*
Mrs Kent	*Yes.*
Supt Hook	*What did they come for?*
Mrs Kent	*There was a knock at the door, which I answered. The Sergeant said: 'It is not you I want to see, it's your husband.' I sent my husband who took them into my private room. I left them with my husband.*
Supt Hook	*Who was in the house at that time?*
Mrs Kent	*Fred Larkin, Bob Charman, Pickering and his wife, Nancy Tideswell and Kathleen Barton and others. It was a free house. The sideboard was full of drink. My husband is outside. See what he says.*

H Interview of Bert Kent by Superintendent Hook

Bert Kent	*I took the Sergeant and Constable in. When they came to the door they asked if Fred Larkin was in and I said: 'Yes, if you want to see him, you had better come in.' I took them into the room and left them there. The Sergeant said he wanted to see Fred Larkin about his car skidding.*
Supt Hook	*Did you see them have any drink?*
Bert Kent	*No, I left them in the room because just as they came I had to take two girls home in my car.*
Supt Hook	*Have you seen the Sergeant today?*
Bert Kent	*He was waiting outside of my house when I came home from the match and he said to me: 'You remember when I was in your house on New Year's Eve. Well, there's likely to be some trouble. You know that I came to see Fred Larkin about his car. I did not have any drink.' I replied: 'I did not see you have any drink.' The Sergeant said: 'That's all you can say then.'*

I   Interview of Fred Larkin by Superintendent Hook at 10.15pm

Supt Hook   *I am making enquiries respecting the visit of a Sergeant and Constable to 'Rockside'.*

Fred Larkin   *I have already heard about it. Alderman Taylor rang me up.*

Supt Kent   *Did either of the officers speak to you about your car or mention anything about a skid you had had?*

Fred Larkin   *No. I certainly don't remember them saying anything about that.*

Supt Hook   *Did they have anything to drink or did the Sergeant sing a song?*

(Note by Superintendent Hook: Fred Larkin would not make any further statement excepting to say that he was annoyed that the police had suggested that he might not be fit to drive his car.)

J   Misconduct Form dated 14 January 1932

Sergeant A Matthews admits the following charge(s): Neglect of Duty by failing to report a matter it was his duty to report.

Entering a private house 'Rockside', Roker Terrace at 2.45am 1 January 1932 and failing to make a report of his reasons for so doing.

Severely cautioned by me 14 January 1932.

(signed) Chief Constable

I admit the charge of failing to make a report.

(signed) A Matthews

K   From Sergeant Matthews' police record

24 September 1923: commended for judgement and prompt action in a case of cruelty to a horse.

7 July 1930: commended by Chief Constable for his speedy action and manner in rendering first aid to a man who had attempted to commit suicide by gas poisoning.

Sergeant Matthews retired from the Sunderland Police in 1934 having completed 26 years police service, including ten years as a sergeant.

Questions

a)   What difficulties are there in assessing what actually occurred?

b)   Which source is the most credible: Bert Kent, Fred Larkin or Sergeant Matthews, and why?

c)   What do you think probably happened early on the morning of 1 January 1932? In your answer you should identify the claims which are corroborated, and those which are not.

Use relevant credibility criteria to explain your answers to questions b and c.

ACTIVITY 41

Beware of the cowboy bin police!
by Steve Doughty

An army of wardens will enforce the rigorous rules which go with fortnightly rubbish collections. The Bin Police will have powers to slap £100 on-the-spot fines on householders who put out rubbish too early or leave their bin lids open. And they will be set quotas for handing out penalties – raising fears that they will behave like the notorious cowboy car-clamping gangs loathed by motorists.

- On-the-spot fines will be applied to those who litter.

The wardens are the latest development in the drive to wipe out weekly rubbish collections which inspired the *Daily Mail's* Great Bin Revolt.

Yesterday it was revealed that Defra (the government Department for Environment, Food and Rural Affairs) gave councils the go-ahead to set up their own wheelie-bin police in 'guidance on the use of fixed-penalty notices for environmental enforcement' smuggled out last month. The Bin Police will wear uniforms and operate in the same way as traffic wardens – but there are no rules to prevent councils hiring ill-trained and unsuitable individuals for the job.

The Defra guidelines say that bin wardens must be trained in the law and how to deal with uncooperative or violent householders. But a training course set up by the department itself lasts no more than four days.

Defra recommends that wardens should have past criminal records checks. But there are no firm rules to insist that these are made. The guidelines say: 'An authority might want to set targets for the number of fixed-penalty notices that it issues for a particular offence in a given year'. They add that councils can use the money raised from fines to pay their wardens.

The legal basis for bin wardens was laid down in the 2005 Clean Neighbourhoods and Environment Act, which gave councils powers to slap fixed-penalty fines on those who break environmental laws. The Act – brought in to coincide with the abandonment of weekly rubbish collections by nearly 150 councils covering a third of the population – said fines of typically £100 should be applied to those littering, spraying graffiti or allowing their dog to foul the pavement. In law, littering includes putting out household rubbish at the wrong time or place. The £100 on-the-spot fines faced by those breaking the rules are higher than the £80 given to shoplifters.

Hugh McKinney of the National Family Campaign said: 'There are no rules here to stop councils using cowboy bin police. The victims of this proposal will often be families with young children who have more rubbish than anyone else and who will be the easiest to find and pick on'.

Daily Mail, 28th April 2007

1 a) Assess the credibility of the *Daily Mail*.

b) Assess how far the document 'Beware of the cowboy bin police!' is a credible report. In your answer you should make two points, identifying and explaining relevant credibility criteria.

2 Consider the image in the document. How far is this relevant to the article?

3 Assess the credibility of Defra.

4 a) Assess the credibility of Hugh McKinney of the National Family Campaign. In your answer you should refer to credibility criteria and explain how these may strengthen or weaken his credibility.

b) What else would you need to know in order to reach a judgement about the credibility of Hugh McKinney?

c) Hugh McKinney of the National Family Campaign said: 'There are no rules here to stop councils using cowboy bin police'. Assess the reasonableness of this claim.

d) Identify evidence within the passage that contradicts this claim.

Summary

You should now be able to:

- apply credibility criteria and assess the credibility of documents and organisations
- assess how far images and graphical representations strengthen or weaken claims
- compare and contrast the credibility of sources
- assess which source is more credible
- explain what you think probably happened in a scenario.

ExamCafé
Relax, refresh, result!

Relax and prepare

Getting started in Critical Thinking

Study skills to learn

During this course you will learn the skills of **analysis** and **evaluation** of **reasoning**. You will also learn to **develop and communicate your own reasoned arguments**.

We are reasoning every time we think about why, whether and how to do something, or whether to believe what someone is telling us. You may feel that your previous studies, and your own abilities, already enable you to think critically without you needing to study it further.

However, practising Critical Thinking skills is like preparing for a sports event, or training as a musician: however strong your natural ability, the right practice will enable you to perform better.

Refresh your memory

Revision tips

For Unit 1 your revision needs to focus on two topics: **analysis of argument** and **assessing credibility**.

However, overall you cannot revise for Critical Thinking in the same way as for other subjects because it does not have a large body of content. But you can do the following.

1. Use the key terms and the glossary to learn the meaning of the important Critical Thinking terms.
2. Write your own mnemonic (memory aid using the first letter of each word) to help recall the credibility criteria.
3. Read lots of magazines and newspapers, especially tabloids and local newspapers.
4. Use the comment (or editorial) and letters sections to practise the skill of argument analysis.
5. Read articles on topical issues, as these are what you will meet in the exam.
6. Work out how you could counter arguments you read and hear.

Revise by practising

Practise, practise and practise the Critical Thinking skills by doing the following.

1. Look for the reasons and conclusion in other people's arguments.
2. Spot the assumptions in other people's arguments (e.g. experts and politicians talking on television, friends, or anyone who is trying to persuade someone of something).
3. Think about how statistics are used as evidence when you read newspaper or magazine articles.
4. Think about whether the credibility criteria are relevant to people or organisations you read about in news stories.

Get the result !

What is in the AS Unit 1 exam?

The exam is based around two or more passages totalling about 900 words, and some of the material might be presented in the form of diagrams or images.

The question paper is in two sections.

Section A: The Language of Reasoning – which is the analysis of a simple argument through short-answer questions.

Section B: Credibility – where you are assessing the credibility of sources within a scenario, through short- and long-answer questions.

There are 75 marks available from the Unit 1 exam.

What the examiner thinks

General advice

▷ Remember the exam is divided into Section A and Section B and you have 1 hour 30 minutes to complete the whole paper. The maximum number of marks for the whole paper is 75. If you allow time for reading the passages thoroughly, and for checking your work at the end, then you will have to earn marks at a rate of one mark in less than a minute. Use this to help you manage your time as you work through the questions.

▷ Read each passage in the Resource Booklet very carefully before you begin to answer the questions. Sometimes a single word makes a difference to the meaning of a reason or the conclusion.

▷ Write your answers in the spaces on the question paper. Remember that the number of lines, and the marks available, help to show you how much to write in your answer.

▷ If you cannot answer a question, move on to the next one.

▷ Look out for these words: **Identify**, **Explain**, **Analyse**, **Evaluate**. They tell you what you should do in your answer.

▷ It is important that when you use Critical Thinking terminology, you use it correctly.

Section A advice

▷ As you read the Section A passage, try to get a general sense of the argument it contains. Ask yourself, what does the author want me to believe?

▷ While you are reading through the passage, use coloured pens or highlighters (and argument notation if you wish), to mark the following:
  • argument indicator words
  • reasons supporting the argument
  • the main conclusion
  • evidence and examples
  • any counter-argument.

▷ When a question asks you to identify the **main conclusion** of the argument or the **reasons**, use the exact wording in the passage – **not** your own words.

▷ Look for any gaps or jumps in the reasoning to help you identify assumptions. Remember that an assumption is never stated.

Section B advice

▷ It is not enough simply to identify (name) credibility criteria – to get the marks you need to show how the criteria you have named strengthen or weaken the credibility of the sources (people) in the scenario and what they say.

▷ When you are asked to assess the reasonableness of claims, make sure you refer to material in the passage.

▷ You may be asked to compare or contrast sources' credibility — follow the instruction.

▷ When you are asked to make an informed judgement pay close attention to the wording of the question and refer to material in the passage.

Section A – The language of reasoning
Read the passage below, then answer the questions.

Let the punishment fit the crime – baby yobs require baby ASBOs

1   Police statistics for 2006 record that 3000 crimes in England and Wales were committed by children under ten. It is shocking enough that 3000 child criminals are walking around among us, but 66 of the recorded offences were sex offences. Child crime is out of control.

2   It is argued that the majority of these recorded crimes by children are acts of minor criminal damage or petty shoplifting – that is, they are little or nothing worse than normal childhood naughtiness – which do not justify labelling children as criminals. Such incidents, it is said, are recorded only because of the modern-day insistence on collecting statistics. The reality is that women and the elderly never leave their homes after dark for fear of abuse or violent attack.

3   Worse than that, for the people who live in many areas of our towns and cities, life within their own homes is completely miserable because every evening noisy gangs of tiny thugs gather in the street outside, creating a racket until the early hours of the morning. Their favourite forms of entertainment include revving up cars and, during winter evenings, letting off fireworks.

4   Despite jibes that acquiring an ASBO is an achievement, since it is the only qualification some young people will ever gain, ASBOs have proved a useful tool for hard-pressed police struggling to tackle yobbish behaviour. Unfortunately, the police are completely powerless to take action against those below the age of criminal responsibility (when someone can be charged and taken to court) – currently ten years of age. The minimum age for an ASBO at present is also ten years.

5   It is time that the government finally took effective action and reduced the minimum age for ASBOs. Critics have claimed that introducing 'baby ASBOs' for children as young as five years old serves only to label as criminals children who desperately need care and rehabilitation rather than punishment. That is precisely the point: if children behave as criminal thugs, then they should be dealt with as such.

6   Child crime is completely out of control and solutions are needed urgently. Baby yobs should be dealt with by means of baby ASBOs.

Questions

1. Identify the main conclusion of the argument in the passage 'Let the punishment fit the crime – baby yobs require baby ASBOs'. [2]

2a) Identify the evidence in paragraph 1 that is used to support the claim that child crime is out of control. [2]

b) What other interpretations might there be for the evidence used in paragraph 1? [6]

c) Explain one way in which these could be strong pieces of evidence. [3]

d) Explain one way in which these could be weak pieces of evidence. [3]

3. Identify the argument element in paragraph 2. [2]

4a) In paragraph 2 the writer states that 'women and the elderly never leave their homes after dark for fear of abuse or violent attack'.

Identify one assumption needed to support the writer's reasoning. [2]

b) Identify the reason in paragraph 3 that is given to support the main conclusion. [2]

5. In paragraph 3 the writer refers to the gangs' favourite entertainments.

Identify what element of argument these are. [1]

6. Identify two reasons in paragraph 4 used to support the main conclusion. [4]

7. In paragraph 5 the writer states: 'Critics have claimed that introducing "baby ASBOs" for children as young as five years old serves only to label as criminals children who desperately need care and rehabilitation rather than punishment'.

a) Identify what element of the argument this is. [1]

b) Identify the hypothetical reasoning in paragraph 5. [2]

8. Give two reasons that would support an argument against baby ASBOs. [4]

9. In paragraph 5, the writer argues that: 'It is time that the government finally took effective action and reduced the minimum age for ASBOs'.

Does the reasoning in this paragraph support the writer's overall argument? Explain your answer. [6]

[40] marks

Read the passage below, then answer the questions.

Forget moderate exercise, say the health police; get sweaty

1   New guidance from the American health police suggests that the UK government's recommended minimum of 30 minutes of gentle exercise a day is not sufficient to maintain basic fitness.

2   Scientists writing in *Circulation*, the journal of the American Heart Association, including world-leaders in public health and exercise advice from the American College of Sports Medicine, now say that people are not doing enough exercise, and that people should do vigorous exercise as well as moderate activity. Jogging and twice-weekly weight training sessions are needed to reduce the risk of heart disease and obesity.

3   The UK Department of Health currently recommends 30 minutes of moderate physical exercise at least five times a week, which can include walking, mowing the lawn and housework. The new American guidelines for adults, which are likely to be adopted by the UK government, include advice such as the following.

   • Combining days of moderate exercise with other days of vigorous exercise is better for you.

   • Moderate exercise should be in addition to daily activities such as casual walking, shopping or taking out the rubbish.

   • Two weight-training sessions a week.

4   However, David Haslam, chair of the National Obesity Forum, said: 'If you suggested everyone here should do weight-training twice a week they wouldn't do it. They don't have the time or money for the gym, it would be an unrealistic guideline. I'd rather see healthy habits built into daily life – gyms aren't a sustainable habit.'

5   Further concern is caused by a report from Sport England that half the UK population do no sport or active recreation, as revealed by a poll of more than 350,000 people. UK Minister for Sport, Richard Caborn, said the survey showed disappointing levels of participation in sport. He said: 'The government can only do so much. Individuals must start to take responsibility for their health and fitness too.'

KPI 1 - Participation 3x30
The % of the adult population participating in at least 30 minutes of sport and active recreation (including walking and cycling) of at least moderate intensity on at least three occasions a week.

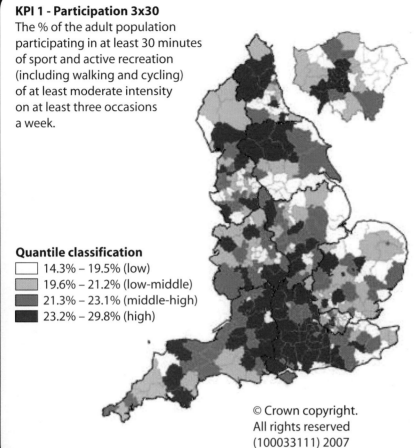

Quantile classification
- ☐ 14.3% – 19.5% (low)
- ☐ 19.6% – 21.2% (low-middle)
- ☐ 21.3% – 23.1% (middle-high)
- ☐ 23.2% – 29.8% (high)

Top ten activities
Walking – 8.1 million
Swimming – 5.6 million
Gym (including exercise bikes and rowing) – 4.7 million
Recreational cycling – 3.2 million
Football – 2.9 million
Jogging/Running – 1.8 million
Golf/pitch and putt/putting – 1.4 million
Badminton – 0.9 million
Tennis – 0.87 million
Aerobics – 0.6 million

Who is doing recommended 30 mins three times per week
24% of men and 18% of women

33% of 16 to 24-year-olds,
25% of 35 to 44-year-olds,
16% of 54 to 64-year-olds and
6% of 75 to 84-year-olds

25% of highest socioeconomic groups and 16% of lowest socioeconomic groups

6 *Daily Mail* columnist, Janet Street-Porter, in a recent article offered an alternative: 'Forget jogging. It's a horrible way to get fit, especially if you live in a town – an opportunity to wreck your knees by pounding up and down on tarmac, wreck your lungs by breathing in clouds of exhaust fumes, and wreck your figure by jiggling your curvy bits about in a really undignified way – and I really don't want to end up with a washboard chest looking like Paula Radcliffe, thanks very much.'

7 Instead, Ms Street-Porter, a prominent member of the Ramblers' Association, advocates country walks: 'The best way to avoid heart disease is walking in the countryside, striding up and down hills at a brisk pace, on footpaths rather than roads, breathing in unpolluted air, enjoying peace and quiet, getting spiritually regenerated by the sights and sounds of nature rather than an arterial road. If you want to see healthy people, check out a group of walkers, straight-backed and firm of limb. Running is full of stress – just another way of avoiding human contact.'

Questions

1. Assess how far the document 'Forget moderate exercise, say the health police; get sweaty', is a credible report.

   In your answer, you should make two points, identifying and explaining relevant credibility criteria. [6]

2. Consider the map and statistics in the box. Explain whether these are relevant to the discussion in Document 2. [4]

3. Assess the credibility of David Haslam, chair of the National Obesity Forum.

   In your answer, you should make two points, referring to credibility criteria and explaining how these may strengthen or weaken his credibility. [6]

4. What else would you need to know in order to reach a judgement about the credibility of David Haslam's statement? [3]

5. Assess the credibility of Janet Street-Porter, the *Daily Mail* columnist.

   In your answer, you should make two points, referring to relevant credibility criteria and explaining how these may strengthen or weaken her credibility. [6]

6. In paragraph 7 Janet Street-Porter claims: 'The best way to avoid heart disease is walking in the countryside'.

   a) Identify one piece of evidence in the article that supports this claim. [1]

   b) Assess the reasonableness of this claim. In your answer you should refer to material within the article. [4]

7. Make an informed judgement on whether *Circulation*, the journal of the American Heart Association, or Janet Street-Porter is more credible. State your judgement. In your answer you should use credibility criteria to compare and contrast the relative credibility of the two sources. [5]

[35] marks

Total [75] marks

Introduction to Unit 2

Unit 2 extends and develops the skills you have learnt in Unit 1. You will need to remember and keep using the skills from Unit 1. The Assessment Objectives are the same as in Unit 1:

AO 1 **Analyse** reasoning
Break reasoning down into its component parts (i.e. reasons, intermediate conclusions, principles, analogies, conclusion, etc.) and label them. Understand the way the parts fit together into a structure. This is being dealt with in Section 3, Chapters 7 and 8.

AO 2 **Evaluate** reasoning
Say how well the reasoning works – or how strong or weak it is – by considering the use of evidence, examples and explanations; appeals; flaws and patterns of reasoning such as analogy, hypothetical reasoning and the use of principles. This is being dealt with in Section 4, Chapters 9–12.

AO 3 **Develop** your own reasoning
Give reasons to support a conclusion; provide evidence, examples or explanations to support a conclusion; give a principle to support a conclusion; write an argument of your own. This is being dealt with in Section 5, Chapters 13–15.

Strength and weakness

Unit 2 includes much more evaluation of reasoning (AO2) than Unit 1. In Critical Thinking we use the words 'strong' and 'weak' to evaluate how well an argument works. A strong argument has reasons which give us good, logical grounds for accepting the conclusion, and uses relevant, reliable evidence to support the reasons. The logical links of support hold together without inconsistency or irrelevance.

A weak argument has reasons which do not give us grounds for accepting the conclusion or uses irrelevant or unreliable evidence. There may be inconsistency, flaws or irrelevance, and the logical links of support do not hold together.

I wish I'd listened to the experts!

We also use the words 'strong' and 'weak' to refer to claims. They have a different meaning in this context. A strong claim is certain, bold, all-embracing. For example, 'Everyone must use sun cream,' is a very strong claim. Strong claims like this need a great deal of support. Whereas it is a good thing if an argument is strong, it can be a bad thing if you make too many strong claims in your reasoning, because they are hard to support well.

A weak claim doesn't state much and may be uncertain or accept limitations. For example, 'Some people with very fair skin who want to spend time in the sun should perhaps consider using sun cream,' is a very weak claim. Weak claims like this need very little support.

Writing arguments

In Unit 2 you will have to write your own arguments. You will focus on giving structure to your reasoning. This is a really important skill, which should improve your written work in other subjects. You will probably find it useful to practise writing arguments all the way through your course.

Unit 2   Assessing and Developing Argument
Section 3   Analysis of Argument

Identifying elements of argument

Learning objectives

- Distinguish between arguments and other types of writing, e.g. explanations and descriptions (accounts).
- Identify main conclusions and intermediate conclusions and understand the difference between them.
- Identify other argument components in shorter passages including reasons, counter-arguments, evidence and examples.
- Draw conclusions from evidence and short pieces of reasoning.

Identifying whether passages are arguments, explanations or descriptions

In Unit 1 you learnt how to recognise an argument. You will remember that the main characteristic of an argument is that there is an attempt to persuade you through the use of reasoning. An argument will always have a conclusion, which will be supported by one or more reasons and may also include evidence, examples, etc. However, there are other forms of language that you will come across that may appear, at first glance, to be arguments, e.g. opinions, explanations and descriptions (accounts).

Opinion

An opinion is a statement of a person's beliefs and ideas. Most of us hold opinions and sometimes we feel that offering our opinion to someone else will be persuasive. However, an opinion is not the same as an argument. An argument has a conclusion which is always supported by relevant reasons, but opinions are not always supported.

> **PAUSE FOR THOUGHT**
>
> Here are some opinions. Can you turn them into arguments by adding one or more relevant reasons?
>
> ■ The voting age should be reduced to 16.
> ■ There should be a tax on aviation fuel.
> ■ Capital punishment is wrong.

Explanation

An explanation is a reason, or reasons, given to show how or why something is the way that it is, but which does not attempt to persuade the reader to accept the conclusion. Instead it explains why something is the way it is. Sometimes, an explanation can at first look like an argument as there seem to be reasons and a conclusion. However, it is not the same as an argument. Telling us how or why something is the case is not the same as giving reasons to persuade us that it is the case. The author is giving you what they believe is the explanation for something but there is no conclusion that they want you to agree with.

> I am late for the lesson today because there was a crash on the motorway. Two lanes were closed while the emergency services dealt with the incident. We were stuck in the queue of traffic.

Although there is an argument indicator word, 'because', in this passage, this alone does not make it an argument. This is an explanation. The writer is giving reasons for an accepted statement of fact: 'I am late for the lesson today'. There is no attempt to persuade us of anything; rather, the author is explaining how this came about.

Description (account)

In a description or account, the author describes something that has taken place or an object. There is no attempt to persuade the reader using reasons to support a conclusion so it is not an argument.

> The shops are getting ready for Christmas. The shop window displays include Father Christmas and his reindeers. Inside there are racks with Christmas cards and stands with food like mince pies and Christmas pudding.

- Christmas display.

This is a description of what the writer has seen. They are not trying to persuade of us anything about Christmas shopping and so this is not an argument.

Claims

In Unit 1, Chapter 2, page 22, you were introduced to the idea that any part of an argument can be referred to as a claim. Reasons, evidence, examples and conclusions can all be called claims. 'Claim' means a sentence that is thought to be true but which might not be.

> **REMEMBER**
>
> A claim is something that is stated, and that can be challenged. Reasons and conclusions are claims.

As you will remember from Unit 1, in Critical Thinking we do not generally check whether claims are true (although in real life it is often useful). In Critical Thinking we are most interested in how some claims give support to other claims, *if* what is claimed is true.

Look at examples A and B that follow. One is an argument (a conclusion supported by relevant reasons) and the other is a series of claims.

A I am tired after a busy day at college. I haven't been sleeping well. Having a bath before I go to bed helps me sleep. I should have a bath before I go to bed.

B Having a bath relaxes me. Drinking hot chocolate helps me go to sleep. Taking sleeping pills means I won't wake up for 8 hours.

In the first passage there are four claims: a recommendation supported by three facts. The conclusion, 'I should have a bath before I go to bed', is supported by three reasons. The second passage is a list of three claims but none of these claims supports any of the others. They are all concerned with helping to get to sleep, but it is not an argument. There is no attempt to persuade us of anything.

ACTIVITY

Decide what each of the following statements is.

A We've always used animals as a means to our own ends. There is no real difference between creating a sheep whose organs can be harvested for use in humans and breeding them for their wool or for their meat.

The passage above is:

  1 an argument
  2 an explanation
  3 a description
  4 an opinion.

B There has been an increase in the number of people who believe in paranormal activity. With all the scientific advances over the past few years, which have led to the average lifetime being extended, people are less accepting that this life is all that there is and so are more willing to believe in some sort of life beyond the grave.

The passage above is:

  1 an argument
  2 an explanation
  3 a description
  4 several unconnected claims.

C Scientists claim that drinking red wine and cooking with olive oil may help us to live longer. A study has found that key ingredients in both substances can significantly increase the lifespan of yeast. Since yeast and humans share many genes, scientists have speculated they may have the same effect in people. The Mediterranean diet may be the secret to living a long and healthy life.

The passage above is:

  1 an argument
  2 an explanation
  3 a description
  4 several unconnected claims.

- Scientists claim that drinking red wine and cooking with olive oil may help us to live longer.

Identifying main conclusions

In Unit 1 you were asked to analyse passages by identifying the main elements of an argument – reason, conclusion and counter-argument. In Unit 2 you will be asked to analyse both shorter and longer passages. The questions on shorter passages will be multiple choice, where you will be given a range of possible answers from which you will have to chose the correct answer. Questions on longer passages will include ones that ask you to identify the main conclusion.

PAUSE FOR THOUGHT

In Unit 1 you were introduced to conclusion indicator words as a good way of identifying the main conclusion. How many conclusion indicator words can you remember?

Whether you are looking at a long argument or a short one, you must always identify the main conclusion first. Ask yourself what the author wants you to agree to. This is important, because your analysis will focus on identifying the reasons that support the conclusion. If you have not identified the conclusion, you are in a poor position to understand how the argument is persuading you to accept it.

> **REMEMBER**
>
> The **conclusion** of an argument is a statement of something that the writer (or speaker) wants the reader (or listener) to accept as true based on the reasons given.
>
> A **reason** is a statement that aims to persuade the reader to accept a conclusion.

> **REMEMBER**
>
> Remember to use conclusion indictor words to help you identify the conclusion. A conclusion indicator is a word or phrase that helps us to identify the conclusion, e.g. *therefore*, *so*, *thus*, *hence*, *it follows*, *consequently*.

Identifying conclusions in shorter passages

In the exam, multiple-choice questions on shorter passages will ask you to identify the conclusion from a range of possible answers, which may include other argument components, e.g. reasons as well as supporting information. You will need to read the passage carefully so you can identify the main conclusion. You should then choose the option that is the main conclusion, or is closest to the main conclusion in the original passage. Look at the following example.

> A high number of fatalities in air crashes are caused by front facing seats. Backward facing seats would be capable of restraining the massive forces created by the human body during impact and would prevent all whiplash and internal injuries caused by seat belts. We are used to backward facing seats on trains and passengers do not seem to object to these seats. Many people would survive aeroplane crashes if they sat in backward facing seats.

Which of the following is the main conclusion of the above argument?

a) A high number of fatalities in air crashes are caused by front facing seats.
b) Many people would survive aeroplane crashes if they sat in backward facing seats.
c) We are used to backward facing seats on trains …
d) Backward facing seats would be capable of restraining the massive forces created by the human body during impact …

OCR Unit 2, January 2007

First, analyse the passage then identify the reasons and main conclusion.

R1 A high number of fatalities in air crashes are caused by front facing seats.

R2 Backward facing seats would be capable of restraining the massive forces created by the human body during impact.

R3 [They] would prevent all whiplash and internal injuries caused by seat belts.

R4 We are used to backward facing seats on trains …

R5 Passengers do not seem to object to these seats.

C Many people would survive aeroplane crashes if they sat in backward facing seats.

Once you have done this it should be clear that the answer is b) as all the other options are reasons which support this conclusion.

ACTIVITY 2

For each of the following passages (1 and 2), identify the main conclusion in each argument.

1 Technology manufacturers would like us to live in digital homes where all appliances and audio-visual equipment are digitally controlled and connected. Even our fridges will tell us when we need milk. However, surveys show that most consumers want to use digital technology for no more than using the Internet or storing their holiday snaps on a computer. This shows that consumers do not want to live in a home with appliances that do everything for them.

A Our fridges will tell us when we need milk.

B Surveys show that most consumers want to use digital technology for no more than using the Internet.

C Consumers do not want to live in a home with appliances that do everything for them.

D Technology manufacturers would like us to live in digital homes.

OCR Unit 2, January 2007

2 Health experts claim that GPs are prescribing far too many anti-depressants. People with only minor symptoms of depression are often given drugs when some form of counselling would be more appropriate and effective. However, the current availability of such counselling services is limited, with anything up to a sixth-month waiting list for NHS treatment. We should provide a much better level of counselling support at GP practices as our GPs must be able to offer the best treatment to patients with symptoms of depression.

A We should provide a much better level of counselling support at GP practices.

B Health experts claim that GPs are prescribing far too many anti-depressants.

C GPs must be able to offer the best treatment to patients with symptoms of depression.

D The current availability of such counselling services is limited.

OCR Unit 2, January 2007

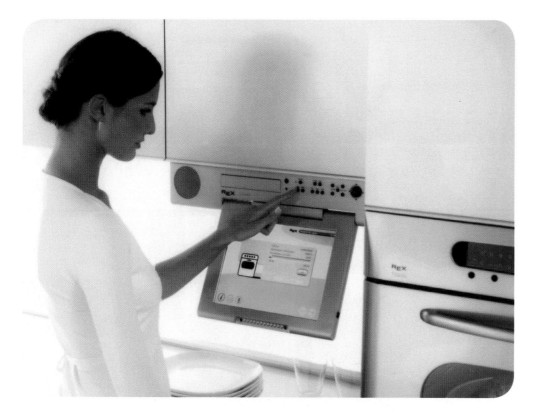

■ What would it be like living in a high-tech home?

Identifying intermediate conclusions

Arguments are often longer and more complicated than the ones we have examined so far in this section. Many longer arguments contain one or more **intermediate conclusions** before the main conclusion.

Have a look at this example.

> Very cold winters lead to high numbers of elderly people needing to be admitted to hospital.
>
> We are expecting a very cold winter.
>
> So we should expect high numbers of elderly people needing to be admitted to hospital.
>
> Therefore, we will need to make sure that we have enough hospital beds to meet demand.

In this example, the third statement is in the form of a conclusion, indicated by the word 'so'. However, the argument continues to a fourth statement. The third statement is therefore an intermediate conclusion, which is supported by the first two statements.

In this example, both the third and fourth statements are conclusions. We can identify them as conclusions as both sentences begin with conclusion indicator words. However, the third statement is not the main conclusion of the passage, but provides support for the fourth statement, which is in fact the main conclusion. The third statement is therefore an intermediate conclusion, which is supported by the first two statements.

KEY TERM

Intermediate conclusion

A conclusion that is formed on the way to the main conclusion. The intermediate conclusion is supported by reasons and gives support to/acts as a reason for the main conclusion.

117

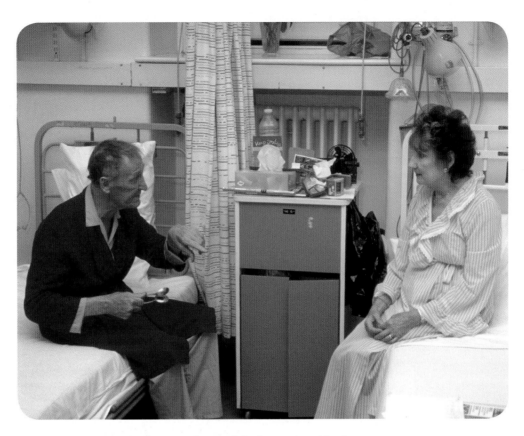

- Hospital beds can be in great demand during very cold winters.

Every intermediate conclusion goes on to act as support for the next stage of the argument – it acts like a reason for the **main** or **overall conclusion**.

We indicate the parts of the above argument like this (note the abbreviation IC for 'intermediate conclusion').

R1	Very cold winters lead to high numbers of elderly people needing to be admitted to hospital.
R2	We are expecting a very cold winter.
IC	So we should expect high numbers of elderly people needing to be admitted to hospital.
C	We will need to make sure that we have enough hospital beds to meet demand.

KEY TERM

Main (or **overall**) **conclusion**

A word or short phrase that helps the reader to identify the components of an argument.

REMEMBER

The **intermediate conclusions** are supported by reasons.

An intermediate conclusion acts as a reason for the main conclusion.

Identifying the difference between an intermediate conclusion and the main conclusion

When you read any Critical Thinking passage, or indeed any argument, the first thing you should do is analyse it and identify the argument components. A longer argument will have a much more complex structure than a short passage.

Each reason should support the main conclusion. But some of the reasons may also support an intermediate conclusion. Several types of exam question will require you to identify and distinguish between intermediate and main conclusions. There are two steps in this process.

Step 1: Identify all the conclusions present by using the 'therefore' approach (see Chapter 1, page 14 in Unit 1) or by looking for other conclusion indicator words. Look at the following example.

- Which to choose?

Raj wants to audition for a local rock band. He plays guitar but is also a good drummer. The band plays gigs all over the city and therefore Raj would need a car to transport his drum kit around with him to gigs. Raj does not have enough money to buy a car and consequently it might be better if he auditioned on guitar.

There are two statements here in the form of conclusions, signalled by *therefore* and *consequently*.

> ■ *Therefore* Raj would need a car to transport his drum kit around with him to gigs.
>
> ■ *Consequently* he might be better to audition on guitar.

Step 2: The next step is to decide which of the statements supports the other. In the above example, the need for a car and the fact that Raj doesn't have enough money to get one clearly suggest a problem in becoming the band's drummer. They give support (jointly) for the *main conclusion* – that he should consider auditioning on guitar. The *intermediate conclusion* is that Raj would need a car to transport his kit around, because this statement lends support to the final conclusion.

Now go back and check that the argument doesn't work the other way around to make sure you've got the right answer. Suggesting that Raj should audition on guitar, and the fact that he does not have enough money to buy a car, would not support a main conclusion that he will need a car to transport his kit around with him.

The intermediate conclusion will always offer support for the main conclusion. Check this by swapping them round and seeing if the argument makes sense. (It shouldn't.)

Finally, then, the argument is as follows.

> **R1** Raj wants to audition for a local rock band.
> **R2** He plays guitar but is also a good drummer.
> **R3** The band plays gigs all over the city.
> **IC** Raj would need a car to transport his drum kit around with him to gigs.
> **R4** Raj does not have enough money to buy a car.
> **C** It might be better if he auditioned on guitar.

This example also shows us that there may be other reasons used, in combination with the intermediate conclusion (IC), to support the main conclusion (C).

REMEMBER

The intermediate conclusion will always offer support to the main conclusion. Swap them round and you should have something that does not make sense.

ACTIVITY

In each of these passages, identify the intermediate conclusion and which is the main conclusion.

- If children cycled to school they would get more exercise.

A Many children live close enough to school to cycle but are dropped off by their parents. If children cycled to school they would get more exercise. This could help to combat the increase in childhood obesity. More children should cycle to school. There isn't any way for pupils to keep their bikes securely at school. The school should build bike sheds for pupils to keep their bikes.

B Passive smoking has negative health effects and is anti-social. Non-smokers are at risk of getting diseases such as lung cancer from the smoke they inhaled passively. Clothes smell stale from being in a smoky atmosphere such as a pub. The government was right to introduce a law banning smoking in public places.

C There should be incentives to encourage people to buy more fruit and vegetables. An Institute of Food Research study has shown that compounds called flavonoids, which are found in onions and apples, reduce some early signs of heart disease. In the UK we are only consuming about two portions of fruit and vegetables per day on average, so this study underlines the importance of getting your five a day to stay healthy throughout life.

REMEMBER

Remember that an intermediate conclusion is a conclusion which is supported by reasons, and which is itself a reason for the main conclusion.

Identifying other elements of argument in shorter passages

We have looked at how to identify the main conclusion and intermediate conclusions in shorter passages. As in Unit 1, you may also get questions asking you to identify other elements of argument, e.g. reasons and counter-assertions.

REMEMBER

Remember to look for **argument indicators** to help you indicate a reason, e.g. *because, as, since, due to, such as*.

A **counter-argument** is an additional argument that is against, or counter to, what the conclusion seeks to establish. The writer normally presents the counter-argument in order to dismiss it.

If no reason is present, then the writer is making a **counter-assertion/ claim**, rather than a counter-argument.

The activity on the next page gives you a good chance to revise skills from Unit 1 on identifying reasons, conclusions and counter-assertions, and practise skills in identifying intermediate conclusions.

■ To stay healthy you should eat five portions of fresh fruit and vegetables each day.

ACTIVITY 4

For each of the following short passages (A-D), identify all the elements of argument: e.g. reasons, counter-assertions, intermediate conclusions and main conclusions.

A Although many people enjoy drinking a coffee late at night, coffee contains caffeine, which is a stimulant. Taking any stimulant before going to bed stops you from sleeping soundly and so drinking coffee before going to bed will stop you from sleeping soundly. A poor night's sleep may lead you to feeling tired in the morning. Therefore drinking coffee before going to bed may cause you to feel tired in the morning.

B Heather and Bill have been living together for five years. They plan to keep their relationship healthy by taking up new activities and interests as well as setting aside time to discuss their relationship. They have in place good strategies to help them in the future. Many experts suggest that happy relationships rely on just these types of strategies. It is therefore likely that Heather and Bill will continue to live together happily.

C To stay healthy you are advised to have five portions of fresh fruit or vegetables each day. You have only had four so far today, so you should have a piece of fruit. We only have apples and oranges and you do not like oranges, so you should have an apple to maintain your good health.

D The grass is very long, so we need to cut it today. We also need to go to town to buy food. It looks like it is going to rain soon and we cannot cut wet grass. Therefore we had better cut the grass before we go out to buy food.

EXAM TIP

When you are asked to identify an argument component in the exam you need to copy it out exactly from the passage. Do not include additional information.

We have just looked at how to identify individual elements of argument, e.g. the main conclusion, intermediate conclusion, reason and counter-assertion. In Unit 2 you will also come across questions which ask you to look for evidence and examples in a passage.

REMEMBER

Evidence is something that is used to develop or support a reason. Evidence is often in the form of numerical data, an estimate or a factual claim.

An **example** is something that is used as evidence because it is characteristic of the same kind of things or because it can serve to illustrate a principle. Examples are one form of evidence that provide a way of developing a reason. They illustrate the reason, giving a specific situation in which the reason holds. The purpose of examples, therefore, is to back-up the reason, so that it provides good support for the conclusion.

We can work through the passage below, identifying the elements of argument.

> Although many magazine adverts promote the advantages of taking vitamin pills, a good diet contains all the vitamins that an average person needs. Even cloudy British days give enough sunlight for our bodies to produce Vitamin D. There isn't any need for most people to take vitamin pills – indeed, high concentrations of some vitamins can positively be bad for us. We should consider imposing some kind of restriction on this type of advertising.
>
> Adapted from OCR Unit 2, June 2007

Look at the argument above and decide which of the following it consists of.

A   A conclusion, two reasons, one example and an intermediate conclusion.
B   A conclusion, a counter-assertion, two reasons, one example.
C   A conclusion, a counter-assertion, three reasons and an intermediate conclusion.
D   A conclusion, a counter-assertion, three reasons and an intermediate conclusion.

First, analyse the passage and identify which argument components are present.

CA	Although many magazine adverts promote the advantages of taking vitamin pills …
R1	A good diet contains all the vitamins that an average person needs.
R2	Even cloudy British days give enough sunlight for our bodies to produce Vitamin D.
IC	There isn't any need for most people to take vitamin pills.
Eg	For example, high concentrations of some vitamins can positively be bad for us.
C	We should consider imposing some kind of restriction on this type of advertising.

From our analysis of the passage we can see that the correct answer is d) – the passage contains a conclusion, a counter-assertion, three reasons and an intermediate conclusion. Let's move on to Activity 5.

• Should fuel taxes be increased?

ACTIVITY 5

Read the following passages, then decide which each consists of.

A Fuel usage is a significant contributor to global warming. Increasing tax on fuel would lead to a decrease in fuel usage. Although the government has suggested that people are not prepared to pay 'green taxes', in fact people are willing to make serious changes to their lifestyles to combat global warming. In a recent study 83% of people said they were prepared to change their lifestyle. Therefore the government should increase tax on fuel in an attempt to lessen the effects of global warming.

Which of the following does passage A consist of?

   a) A conclusion, intermediate conclusion, two reasons, counter-assertion, evidence.
   b) A conclusion, three reasons, counter-assertion, evidence.
   c) A conclusion, four reasons, counter-assertion.
   d) A conclusion, three reasons, intermediate conclusion and evidence.

B The introduction of the National Curriculum in 1988 was praised by many as it ensured that all students received a similar education. However, all children are different. Some excel at traditional academic subjects such as mathematics while others are better focusing on more vocational studies, e.g. construction. The introduction of specialist schools has gone some way to redressing this balance in allowing schools to focus on particular areas. The Education Ministry should continue to allow schools to apply for specialist status.

Which of the following does passage B consist of?

   a) A conclusion, two reasons, two examples, counter-assertion.
   b) A conclusion, three reasons, counter-assertion, one example.
   c) A conclusion, four reasons, counter-assertion, intermediate conclusion.
   d) A conclusion, three reasons, intermediate conclusion and one example.

C The continued high level of divorce means that more people are living on their own. Current statistics show that two in five marriages end in divorce. There has also been an increase in the number of people from Europe coming to live and work in the UK. More houses need to be built to meet this need. However, an increase in house prices means that both buying and renting a house is becoming too expensive for many people. The housing built needs to be affordable.

Which of the following does passage C consist of?

   a) A conclusion, three reasons, counter-assertion, evidence.
   b) A conclusion, four reasons, counter-assertion.
   c) A conclusion, intermediate conclusion, two reasons, counter-assertion, evidence.
   d) A conclusion, three reasons, intermediate conclusion and evidence.

KEY TERM

Infer

To draw a conclusion; to consider what is implied by evidence. To decide what the next step is; what can be supported by the evidence or reasons.

Drawing conclusions

We have seen how evidence and examples support reasons, and how reasons provide support for conclusions. These same skills allow us to look at reasons, evidence and examples and draw conclusions from them – that is, to decide which conclusions can be supported by the reasoning.

In multiple-choice questions on shorter passages, as well as being asked to identify the main conclusion from a range of options you will also be asked what conclusion we can **infer**, or what conclusion can be drawn from the passage, i.e. which conclusion can be supported by the reasoning. Take the following example.

> Rabbits are soft, furry, grey creatures with long ears. Daisy is soft, furry and grey. She has long ears. What can we conclude about Daisy?
>
> **a)** Daisy must be a rabbit.
> **b)** Daisy cannot be a rabbit.
> **c)** Daisy may be a rabbit.

We know that Daisy shares four characteristics with a rabbit. We do not know anything else about her. We know nothing to suggest that she cannot be a rabbit, so we can exclude b) as an answer. On the other hand, extra information may reveal that she brays. So we cannot be sure that she must be a rabbit – other creatures are soft, grey and furry with long ears. Thus we can conclude that Daisy *may* be a rabbit.

Let's look at an example of a multiple-choice question that you would see in the exam.

> Most new car drivers pass their test after a period of intense, rapid learning and practice. Unfortunately, rapid learning can lead to over-confidence and short-lived knowledge. In contrast, learning at a slower pace leads to more secure knowledge and a realistic confidence. In the case of driving, over-confidence can lead to accidents and serious injury.
>
> OCR Unit 2, June 2007

Which of the following is the conclusion that can best be drawn from the above passage?

a) Learner drivers should be required to have lessons over a long period of time before being allowed to take a test.

b) Tighter regulations should be imposed on driving schools to improve driving standards.

c) New drivers should only be allowed to drive the safest types of cars until they are more experienced.

d) All drivers should re-take their tests every few years to ensure that they maintain the required standard.

First, analyse the passage and identify any reasons and intermediate conclusions.

R1	Most new car drivers pass their test after a period of intense, rapid learning and practice.
R2	Unfortunately, rapid learning can lead to over-confidence and short-lived knowledge.
R3	In contrast, learning at a slower pace leads to more secure knowledge and a realistic confidence.
IC	In the case of driving, over-confidence can lead to accidents and serious injury.

Then decide which of the options is the conclusion that can *best* be drawn from the passage. Not all of the options will be possible conclusions, so first narrow it down to claims that could be supported by the reasoning, and then decide which claim is *best* supported by the argument. This is the conclusion, as it is supported by all the reasoning in the passage.

The correct answer is a). The reasoning about rapid learning leading to over-confidence, which in turn can lead to accidents and serious injury, supports this claim.

The incorrect answer is b). There is nothing in the reasoning about driving schools or the need to improve driving standards, so this claim is not supported.

Also incorrect is c). Again this claim is unsupported by the reasoning in the passage. There is no mention of the types of cars new drivers ought to drive.

And d) is also incorrect. Similar to option b) this claim is concerned with driving standards, which is not something covered by the reasoning in the passage and so is not supported.

ACTIVITY 6

What conclusions can you draw from the following?

A I need to wash up and take the dog for a walk. The forecast is for rain later this morning. I do not like walking in the rain.

B Girls aged 13–15 spent an average of £8.50 a week on clothing and footwear in 2007. This was a quarter of their weekly spend and double the £4.25 spent by boys. Girls in this age group spent an average of just £1.10 on games, toys, hobbies and pets, while boys spent £5 on this.

C Between 1971 and 2003 the number of people aged 65 and over rose by 28% while the number of under-16s fell by 18%.

D Many people argue that iPods are the best MP3 players on the market today as they are stylish and can hold many thousands of songs. However, they are also expensive and I also need a new mobile phone as mine has broken.

For E and F, pick the conclusion best supported by the reasoning. Hint: look back to the example on p. 124 to help answer the questions. In the following questions you are presented with a list of reasons and four possible conclusions. You need to decide which one is best supported by the reasons. For some of the options we would need more information than given in the question to draw the conclusion, so this can be discounted.

E Diving requires grace, elegance, strength and courage. Gina has all these qualities.

    Conclusion 1 Gina will be a fantastic diver.
    Conclusion 2 Gina may well have the potential to be a good diver.
    Conclusion 3 Gina should learn to swim.
    Conclusion 4 Gina should join a diving club.

F We have had trouble getting our wireless network to work, even though it was recommended on the website. Dave had trouble getting his wireless network to work, even though he writes computer software. This technology is developing fast.

    Conclusion 1 Current wireless networks are rubbish.
    Conclusion 2 Don't buy a wireless network.
    Conclusion 3 It may be worth waiting for improvements before buying a wireless network.
    Conclusion 4 Wireless networks are unnecessary.

- Diving requires grace, elegance, strength and courage.

Summary

You should now be able to:

- distinguish between passages that are arguments as opposed to explanations or descriptions

- identify the difference between intermediate and main conclusions

- identify other argument components, e.g. reasons, examples, evidence and counter-arguments

- draw conclusions from evidence and short pieces of reasoning.

8 Applying and extending analytical skills

Learning objectives

- Identify analogies.
- Identify principles.
- Identify a range of elements in longer texts.
- Identify inconsistency and contradiction.
- Use technical and semi-technical terms accurately.

Identifying more elements of argument

In this section you will learn how to identify two more elements – analogies and principles. Analogies and principles are slightly different in nature from the other elements, as you will see.

Analogies

Analogies are a form of argument which use parallels between similar situations to persuade the audience to accept a conclusion. The analogy is a special form of comparison which suggests that the situations are significantly similar and work in the same way. So, if we accept a claim about one situation, we should accept the same claim about the other situation. When you identify an analogy, you need to:

◼ identify precisely the situations being compared

◼ identify the conclusion being supported by the analogy.

Here's an example.

> New road building can have a negative social impact. Feeding our addiction to cars (which everyone knows are bad for us) by building new roads must be wrong in the same way that it has been proven that giving alcohol to an alcoholic causes health problems.
>
> OCR Unit 2, June 2007

▪ New road building can have a negative social impact.

Step 1: Identify precisely the situations being compared

The dangers or negative consequences of building roads for car addicts is compared to the dangers or negative consequences of giving alcohol to an alcoholic.

You need to make sure that you are very clear and precise about the situations being compared. It is the whole situation being compared. Let's look at two other possible answers.

Possible answer: 'Car addicts are being compared to drug addicts.'

This answer has identified only part of the situation. It has missed the vital ideas of our response to the addiction and the consequences of this response. In an exam, this response would be unlikely to gain you any marks at all.

Possible answer: 'Giving roads to car addicts is compared with giving alcohol to alcoholics.'

This answer is better, but still misses the key idea of the dangers or negative consequences of this action. In the text it is clear that giving roads to car addicts and giving alcohol to alcoholics are negative things. So your answer needs to make this clear too. This answer would probably gain you some credit in the exam, but not as much as if you had included the idea of danger, risk, problem or negative consequences.

One way of thinking of the analogy is: A is to B as C is to D.

A: Giving roads to car addicts is B: dangerous.
C: Giving alcohol to alcoholics is D: dangerous.

Other analogies may take the form: A leads to or causes B, as C leads to or causes D, for example.

Step 2: Identify the conclusion being supported by the analogy

In the example on page 131, the analogy is used to support the conclusion that new road building can have a negative social impact.

ACTIVITY 7

Identify the analogies in arguments A and B.

> **REMEMBER**
>
> Remember to take the following steps.
>
> Step 1: Identify precisely the situations being compared.
> Step 2: Identify the conclusion being supported by the analogy.

A We cannot expect politicians to be honest in the run-up to a general election. Expecting them to resist the temptation of gaining success by dishonest means is like leaving a very small child alone in a sweetshop and expecting them not to eat the sweets.

B We do not encourage mature, independent adults by continuing to spoonfeed them beyond babyhood. Neither will we encourage the poorest countries in the world to develop to maturity unless we allow them access to the spoon. Aid for developing countries must focus on the development of science and technology.

Analogies in everyday writing are often used without a stated conclusion, leaving the audience to work out which conclusion is implied. However, in your AS exam, it is most likely that the conclusion will be stated and you will have to identify it. If the conclusion is not stated, you could be asked, 'What conclusion can be *drawn* from the analogy?' or 'What conclusion is the analogy *intended* to support?'

General principles

A **principle** is a general, rule-like statement which applies beyond the immediate circumstances and acts as a guide to action. In Unit 2 you will need to identify a principle used in an argument.

A principle is a special kind of argument element which can be a reason, intermediate or main conclusion in an argument. Principles can be identified by their nature as general statements which act as a guide to action. As you learnt in Unit 1, they are often moral guidelines, such as 'We should treat all people equally'. However, they may be everyday recommendations, legal rules or business practices, such as 'Companies should be run as efficiently as possible'. As with all other argument elements, you will need to quote the principle precisely when you are identifying it. Let's look at an example.

> Our lifestyle is not sustainable. We are destroying our world with our emissions, our rubbish and our exploitation of natural resources. We should put the future of the world before our selfish desires. This means we should moderate our lifestyle.

The principle in the above argument is, 'We should put the future of the world before our selfish desires.' Let's analyse the argument into its component parts.

R1 We are destroying our world with our emissions, our rubbish and our exploitation of natural resources.
IC Our lifestyle is not sustainable.
R2 We should put the future of the world before our selfish desires.
C This means we should moderate our lifestyle.

REMEMBER

An **intermediate conclusion** is a claim which is supported by reasons and which gives support to a further conclusion.

We can see that the principle is a reason which works with an intermediate conclusion to support the conclusion. The principle in this argument is not supported – but it could be. For example:

> We are guardians of the world for our children and our children's children. Some of the things we want for ourselves – such as fast cars, electronic gadgets, foreign holidays, cheap food and wear-once clothes – damage the world in ways that conflict with our duty to look after it for our children. So we should put the future of the world before our selfish desires.

If we analyse this argument, we can see that the principle is the conclusion.

R	We are guardians of the world for our children and our children's children.
Ex	Such as fast cars, electronic gadgets, foreign holidays, cheap food and wear-once clothes.
R	Some of the things we want for ourselves damage the world in ways that conflict with our duty to look after it for our children.
C	So we should put the future of the world before our selfish desires.

Principle indicator words

Principles are often expressed using the word 'should', e.g.:

▨ You *should* be kind to other people.

▨ You *should* clear up after yourself.

▨ We *should* consider the needs of others.

However, many specific recommendations and conclusions also use 'should'.

▨ You *should* stop teasing your brother right now because I'll *get cross* if you don't.

▨ You *should* know *that* by now. I've told you often enough.

▨ We *should* go to visit the family this weekend because we haven't been for ages.

▨ We *should* try harder to tolerate our rather badly behaved nieces and nephews because it is a shame not to see much of my brother.

All of the above cases have a specific conclusion which is expressed with 'should' and is not a principle.

There are also other ways of expressing principles.

▨ *It is wrong* to kill.

▨ *It is right* to help those in need.

▨ *It is fair* to share things evenly.

▨ *It is unfair* to let your friends down.

▨ *It is unacceptable* to discriminate on the basis of race, gender or sexual orientation.

▨ Everyone *has the right* to equality of opportunity.

So, when you are identifying principles:

▨ check that it is a general statement which acts as a guide to action

▨ check that it applies to lots of different situations

▨ look for words such as 'should', 'right', 'wrong', 'unfair' – but double check.

You may have come across 'should' as a conclusion indicator. Many conclusions are expressed as recommendations using 'should'. However, 'should' has lots of uses, including that as a principle indicator, so you need to treat it with caution and use your other analytical skills to decide whether an argument component is a principle, a conclusion, both or neither.

ACTIVITY 8

Identify one or more principles in arguments A–C.

A We should all become vegetarians. Animals feel pain and we should not hurt them. Farming and killing them involves hurting them.

B Every year thousands of people inflict damage on themselves. It is not fair that genuinely ill people have to wait for treatment, so people who cause their own problems should not be treated on the NHS.

C You should treat other people as you would want them to treat you. You probably wouldn't want Jemima to hug your boyfriend like that. So you shouldn't hug her boyfriend like that.

▪ Treat other people as you would want them to treat you!

- Common land or new homes?

ACTIVITY

Look at this argument. Which of the following, A–D, is a principle used in the argument.

We absolutely must attend the meeting tonight to protest about the proposal to build 345 new homes on the common. Common land is really important as wide-open space in city centres. It is our only contact with nature, and provides peace, greenery and somewhere for children to play. We should protect our common land.

A   Common land is really important as wide-open space in city centres.

B   It is our only contact with nature, and provides peace, greenery and somewhere for children to play.

C   We absolutely must attend the meeting tonight to protest about the proposal to build 345 new homes on the common.

D   We should protect our common land.

Identifying elements of argument in a longer text

In Unit 1 you learnt how to identify basic elements of argument in a text. In Unit 2 you may be asked to identify any of these elements in a longer text and, in addition, you are likely to have to identify an intermediate conclusion, an analogy and a principle.

If you are asked to identify an intermediate conclusion, you need to make sure that you are choosing and quoting a claim which is supported by several key reasons and which gives support directly to the main conclusion.

You will also need to be aware that an argument may have more than one claim which is supported by reasons and gives support to a further conclusion. That is, there may be more than one intermediate conclusion. You will be looking for the intermediate conclusion which directly supports the main conclusion. Let's look at an example.

> Dom is intelligent and very practical. Electrical engineering requires intelligence and practical skill. So Dom would probably be a good electrical engineer.
>
> There is a shortage of electrical engineers at the moment. So electrical engineers are being very highly paid. Electrical engineering would be a good career choice for Dom so he needs to find out how to train and qualify as an electrical engineer.

If we analyse this argument, we can see that there are three intermediate conclusions, as follows.

EXAM TIP

When you are asked to identify the main conclusion, it can be tempting to go for the intermediate conclusion, because it is often supported by all of the reasons. However, you need to check whether there is another claim which is supported by this intermediate conclusion. Remember that the intermediate conclusion supports the main conclusion but the main conclusion will not support the intermediate conclusion. You can check this by swapping them round.

> **R1** Dom is intelligent and very practical.
> **R2** Electrical engineering requires intelligence and a great deal of practical skill.
> **IC1** So Dom would probably be a good electrical engineer.
> **R3** There is a shortage of electrical engineers at the moment.
> **IC2** So electrical engineers are being paid very highly.
> **IC3** Electrical engineering would be a good career choice for Dom.
> **C** So he needs to find out how to train and qualify as an electrical engineer.

In this argument we can see that IC1 and IC2 give us reason to accept IC3. IC3 directly supports the main conclusion. So, if you were asked to identify 'the intermediate conclusion' of this argument, you would choose and quote IC3, because it is logically closest to the main conclusion.

■ Music has lots of benefits.

ACTIVITY 10

Read the extract below.

a) Identify the main conclusion of the passage.
b) Identify the intermediate conclusion of the passage.
c) Identify a reason given for the main conclusion in paragraph 2.
d) Identify a principle used in the argument.
e) Identify the situations being compared in paragraph 4.

Funding for music lessons in schools is increasingly being squeezed, leaving many children without the opportunity to learn an instrument. This is a disgrace – every child should have this opportunity. Music clearly has a great many benefits.

Because children have to listen carefully to the sounds that they and others are making, and play the right note at the right time, learning a musical instrument can improve their concentration. Research by the Sapphire Primary Music Trust shows that 95% of children who learn an instrument are better focused during other lessons.

Music is based on repeating mathematical patterns. Learning to play an instrument involves a conscious, academic effort to understand these patterns and also an intuitive, emotional, internal understanding of which patterns feel right when played. This improves children's mathematical ability and we should do everything we can to aid children's education.

Because music accesses our deepest emotions, playing an instrument can also provide a valuable emotional outlet. People who are stressed, sad or excited can play through their emotions, turning them into something beautiful, rather than repressing their feelings or taking them out on friends and family. Depriving people of a musical outlet for their feelings would be as bad for their health as depriving them of medication to treat illness.

Being able to play an instrument is also socially useful. Whether strumming the guitar around the camp fire, banging an old piano in gran's living room or playing first violin in an orchestra, a musician can bring joy and focus to any social group. Children can also make new friends and gain confidence and maturity through playing in orchestras, bands and concerts.

Identifying inconsistency and contradiction

You are familiar with the idea that there is a logical link between reasons and a conclusion. In a longer argument you may need to look at the different reasons and pieces of evidence used to support a conclusion. Sometimes you will find that there are logical problems between these elements in the argument. An author may use reasons which cannot both be true, and are inconsistent, or which are completely opposite to each other, and are contradictory.

(In)consistency

In Unit 1, you used the criteria of consistency and **inconsistency** to help you judge whether a source is credible. In Unit 2 you will need to be able to identify parts of an argument which are inconsistent. This may be two pieces of evidence in different paragraphs which cannot both be true, or a reason and a piece of evidence which would support different conclusions.

Let's look at a short example.

- Yoga – better than a manicure?

You cannot achieve inner serenity if your hair, nails and skin are not perfect. Yoga is nothing compared with a good manicure.

Exercise is the best way to improve the way you feel about yourself.

It releases serotonin in the brain which promotes feelings of happiness. So get down to the health centre now!

'Yoga is nothing compared with a good manicure' and 'exercise is the best way to improve the way you feel about yourself' are clearly inconsistent. If the second sentence is right, then the first sentence cannot be true – as a form of exercise, yoga should be better at helping you to achieve inner serenity and improve the way you feel about yourself than a manicure.

ACTIVITY 11

Identify the inconsistency in the following passage.

We should encourage people not to use cosmetics because they are a means of concealing the true personality. A further reason not to use cosmetics is that they increase our exposure to harmful chemicals. It would be better to use natural alternatives such as lemon juice or aloe vera.

Contradiction

Contradiction is a special form of inconsistency. Ideas or facts which are contradictory say exactly the opposite things. For example:

> Children don't watch TV instead of running around; they do it instead of other sedentary activities such as reading. Some children spend up to eight hours a day watching television. It's not surprising they don't run around as much as they used to.

This passage is not just inconsistent, it completely contradicts itself. It starts off by saying that children 'don't watch TV instead of running around' and then says exactly the opposite. Because they watch up to eight hours a day of television, 'it's not surprising they don't run around as much as they used to.'

In a short passage such as this one, contradiction clearly appears to be nonsense. In a longer passage the contradiction may not strike you as quickly, but it is still nonsensical. This weakens an argument.

Language

Language is the means by which we express our ideas. The clarity and precision with which language is used can make the difference between a strong, well-supported argument and a weak one. Clumsy use of a key word can affect the strength of support given to a conclusion.

Ambiguity

Many words have more than one meaning, or a range of meanings. It is important to be clear how a word is being used in a particular argument and to be precise about its meaning, because this can affect the argument. A word or phrase is **ambiguous** if it can have more than one meaning and it is not clear which meaning is intended in a particular context. For example:

> The town centre is an ugly mess of sixties concrete blocks with dull shops, nothing to do and a problem with binge drinking and violence. We would like to improve the town centre. The council intends to improve the town centre. So, because we all want improvement, we should support the council.

KEY TERM

Contradiction ■

This is a special form of inconsistency. Ideas or facts which are contradictory say exactly the opposite things.

KEY TERM

Ambiguous ■

A word or phrase is ambiguous if it can have more than one meaning and it is not clear which meaning is intended in a particular context.

In this argument, we need to be sure that we all have the same understanding of 'improvement'. 'Improvement' here is a vague, ambiguous term. It might mean any of the following: razing to the ground; making more economic; making more attractive; making a dramatic statement; providing more entertainment; providing more variety; increasing policing; making safer. We should support the council only if their idea of improvement agrees with ours.

In Critical Thinking, we are particularly concerned about vague use of language if it means that the words or ideas do not give precise support to the conclusion.

ACTIVITY

Read the text and answer the questions below.

Conviction rates vary between police forces. In Bedfordshire only 51% of cases end in a conviction, whereas in Warwickshire the figure is 93%. So there are victims in Bedfordshire who have been deprived of justice.

a) **What does the word 'justice' mean in this context?**
b) **Discuss any problems raised by the use of the word 'justice' in this way.**

Technical terms

Critical Thinking has its own semi-technical language and there are a number of terms you will need to be familiar with in order to understand and to be able to answer the questions in the Unit 2 exam.

Make sure that you are really familiar with all the names of the argument components, such as reason, assumption, intermediate conclusion, counter-argument, conclusion, etc. Look back at Chapters 1 and 2 from Unit 1 for basic revision, and Chapter 7. It cannot be emphasised enough how important it is to make this vocabulary your own.

ACTIVITY

Read the text and answer the questions below.

a) **Identify the main conclusion.**

b) **Identify the intermediate conclusion of the argument.**

c) **Identify a contradiction in the argument.**

d) **Identify an inconsistency in the argument.**

e) **Identify the situations being compared in the analogy in paragraph 3.**

f) **Identify a principle used in the argument.**

1   We should not expect improving the economy to improve the crime rate because people are generally not responsible for their criminal actions.

2   Young people, especially, are strongly influenced by the behaviour of their parents and friends. Research indicates that children who see their family and friends using guns or stealing are likely to copy this behaviour. We should not blame people for things they cannot affect.

3   Some people are naturally criminal. For example, some genes, combined with an abusive environment and poverty can make it more likely that a person will break the law. Piers Lyon, for example, comes from a good home in Harrogate – his father is a judge and his mother a doctor. Yet Piers was caught shoplifting in Harrods on a family trip to London. We cannot blame Piers for his actions. To do so would be as unreasonable as blaming him for the colour of his eyes.

4   Some people do commit crimes because of poverty. They may steal if they cannot afford food, although that is unlikely in a country where the economy is as strong as it is in Britain. It is more likely that people will commit violent crimes because they feel alienated in a consumer world where others have so much and they have so little.

5   Yet it will not do to blame poverty for the actions of criminals. Each and every one of us is an independent person able to make our own choices. Not every child who comes from a deprived background turns into a criminal. There have even been members of the government who have come from poor backgrounds.

Inference

We have talked a lot about the logical link between reasons and conclusion. The technical term for this link is 'inference'. In Chapter 7 you learnt how to draw a conclusion. Drawing a conclusion is looking at the next logical step in an argument. Inference is just another name for this process of looking at the next logical step. Another word we use here is 'follows'. If you can draw a conclusion from some reasoning, you can say that the conclusion follows from the reasoning.

Opposition

You are familiar with the word 'counter' which means oppose. For example, 'Write an argument to counter the claim that…' You will also come across the word 'challenge' to mean 'oppose' – for example: 'Write your own argument to support or challenge the conclusion.'

There are two other words 'refute' and 'repudiate' which can be very useful when you want to counter someone's argument.

■ 'Refute' means demonstrate to be wrong. So if you refute someone's arguments, you show that their arguments do not work – you highlight the weakness in their arguments, perhaps by showing them to be inconsistent.

■ 'Repudiate' means disown, condemn an opinion, reject as unfounded or inapplicable. Repudiate has a sense of rejecting without showing why.

Necessary and sufficient conditions

A necessary condition is something that must be the case. For example, talent is necessary if you wish to become a professional footballer or musician.

A sufficient condition is something which is enough to ensure that something will be the case. For example, being convicted of murder is a sufficient condition for a stay in prison.

> **PAUSE FOR THOUGHT**
>
> Consider other factors which contribute to sporting or musical success. Are any of them necessary?

Knowledge and belief

You have learnt about several different kinds of claim. Some of these were factual claims, others were opinions, others hypothetical claims and others principles. One further distinction that can be made is between claims to knowledge and claims about beliefs.

■ If we claim to know something, we expect that it is true, and can be objectively checked and confirmed.

■ If we claim to believe something, we accept that it may not be true, or that it may not be possible to confirm it objectively.

Let's look at an example.

> **A** I know the sun is shining outside.
> **B** I believe the sun is shining outside.

WIKIPEDIA

English
The Free Encyclopedia
2 124 000+ articles

Deutsch
Die freie Enzyklopädie
677 000+ Artikel

Français
L'encyclopédie libre
593 000+ articles

Polski
Wolna encyklopedia
449 000+ haseł

日本語
フリー百科事典
445 000+ 記事

Nederlands
De vrije encyclopedie
386 000+ artikelen

Italiano
L'enciclopedia libera
383 000+ voci

Português
A enciclopédia livre
344 000+ artigos

Español
La enciclopedia libre
308 000+ artículos

Svenska
Den fria encyklopedin
264 000+ artiklar

- Where does our knowledge come from?

In claim A, we expect that the speaker has some information – perhaps they have just been outside, or looked out of a window. In claim B, we think that there is some uncertainty, or inability to check. Perhaps the speaker is in a windowless room, but has heard a weather forecast.

In everyday life, we make quite a lot of claims to knowledge. Often, we are just stating what we believe to be the case. We cannot often be sure that we know a fact – that it is certain, and that circumstances in the real world are a true, objective match for our belief. In Critical Thinking we should take a step back and consider how much we really know, and how much we just believe. We also need to consider what we *can* know, and what we can only believe.

PAUSE FOR THOUGHT

Is being certain the same as knowing something?

Can we know that a tree falling in a forest with no people in it makes a noise?

Summary

You should now be able to:

■ identify analogies

■ identify principles

■ identify a range of elements in longer texts

■ identify inconsistency and contradiction

■ use technical and semi-technical terms accurately.

Section 4 Evaluating Argument

9 Evaluating reasoning: the use of evidence, examples and explanations

Learning objectives

● Evaluate the use of evidence in argument.
● Evaluate the use of examples in argument.
● Evaluate the use of explanations in argument.

Evaluating argument

In Unit 1, you learnt how to identify evidence, examples and explanations, and how to evaluate the reliability of evidence based on its source and sample size, etc. In this chapter you will learn how to evaluate the use of these components in an argument. You will ask questions such as these.

- Is this evidence precisely relevant to the author's reason/conclusion?

- Does this evidence support the author's reason/conclusion?

- Are there other conclusions that could be supported by the evidence?

- Is this example typical of the issue the author is talking about?

- Does the example support the author's reasoning?

- Are there alternative, plausible explanations of this evidence?

Evaluating the use of evidence

REMEMBER

Evidence is often in the form of numerical data, an estimate or a factual claim. It is used to develop or support a reason.

In Unit 2 there is some emphasis on evaluating the use of evidence in an argument. The evidence you will come across will usually be facts, statistics, numerical information such as graphs, charts and tables, and references to the results of research or surveys. It will be used to support reasons as part of an argument. You may find it useful to refer back to Chapters 4 and 8 to check that you remember how to distinguish between evidence and reasons. This is a skill you need to master – if you are not sure which part of the text is the evidence and which is the reason, you will struggle to make a judgement about whether the evidence supports the reason.

In most forms of reasoning evidence is really important. Reasons give logical support to a conclusion but evidence can root your argument in the real world. However, just because there is evidence given in an argument, it is not necessarily a strong argument. Frequently in life (and Critical Thinking exams) we are provided with statistical evidence, examples and research evidence that is *supposed* to support an argument. Almost as frequently, the evidence provided is irrelevant, insufficient or misused, so that it actually does not give us grounds to accept the rest of the author's reasoning. The key question to ask yourself is: 'Does this evidence actually give us grounds to accept the author's reasons and conclusion?' And this question can be broken down into three further questions, as follows.

- Is this evidence precisely relevant?

- Is this evidence sufficient?

- Is this evidence used in a strong way?

The key to evaluating the use of evidence is to keep asking questions about the link between the evidence and the reason or conclusion it is supposed to support.

EXAM TIP

In Unit 1 you were asked questions about the evidence itself. In Unit 2 you will be asked about the author's *use of the evidence*. You should not doubt the reliability or truth of the evidence or question the way the author has used it. This is a different task from asking about the reliability of the survey sampling, or the credibility of the source of the evidence, as you did in Unit 1.

Is the evidence relevant?

Relevant evidence is precisely focused on the reason it supports. It must be about precisely the same thing as the reason. It must cover the same timescale, and be about the same area or the same group of people to which the reason is referring. In everyday language we would count information about roughly the same topic as relevant, but in critical thinking, 'relevant' means precise and focused on the reason.

For example, if we are considering what evidence we need to support a claim that 'Hawkwood Towers is an academic school', we might look at:

■ 'Hawkwood Towers is one of four schools in town' and

■ '80% of students achieve at least two A grades at AS Level'.

The first piece of evidence is on the same topic of schools, but it is not precisely relevant to our claim that Hawkwood Towers is an academic school. The second piece of evidence is precisely relevant as it is about the high percentage of students who have achieved the highest grades at AS Level. Therefore it gives some support to the idea that Hawkwood Towers is an academic school.

Let's take another example.

> Lemar collected awards for Best Album and Act of the Year at the Music of Black Origin (MOBO) Awards in 2005. This shows that he is one of the strongest British musicians.

The evidence is about the MOBO awards in one year. It is too limited to tell us that Lemar is now one of the strongest British musicians.

■ *Group*: Lemar may be one of the strongest musicians in Music of Black Origin but this is only one subset of British music, so this evidence cannot be used to support the idea that he is one of the strongest *British* musicians. We don't have information about how he fares against non-MOBO artists. So this evidence is not precisely relevant to the conclusion because the evidence refers to one small part of the whole that the conclusion covers.

■ *Timescale*: The evidence refers only to 2005 but the conclusion says he 'is' now one of the strongest British musicians. So this evidence is not precisely relevant to the conclusion because the evidence refers to a different timescale from the conclusion.

When evaluating whether the author's use of evidence is *relevant*, it is helpful to ask yourself questions such as the following.

■ Is the focus of the evidence the same as the focus of the reason or conclusion it is supporting? For example, is it talking about the same group of people, or the same subject?

■ Does the evidence refer to the same timescale as the reason or conclusion it is supporting?

ACTIVITY 14

Explain a weakness in the way the evidence in the following passage is used to support the conclusion.

The average person gets through 120 aluminium cans in a year, which adds up to 0.2 tonnes of CO_2. If we all reduced our consumption of fizzy drinks, we could make a huge difference to the country's carbon footprint.

- The average person gets through 120 aluminium cans in a year.

Is the evidence sufficient to support the conclusion?

REMEMBER

'Sufficient' means 'enough'.

In Chapter 8 we looked at sufficient conditions. A sufficient condition is something which is enough to ensure that something will be the case. Evidence which is sufficient to support a conclusion is enough, and strong enough, to give support to a conclusion.

Another common problem in the use of evidence is using insufficient evidence to support a fairly strong conclusion. Let's look again at the example of Hawkwood Towers.

> 80% of students achieve at least two A grades at AS Levels.
> So Hawkwood Towers is an academic college.

The evidence is relevant, and does give us grounds to believe that Hawkwood Towers is an academic college. However, it is not sufficient to support the conclusion on its own. We would also need evidence about A Level results, and about other indicators of academic success such as university entrance.

One particular form of insufficiency is the unreasonably selective use of evidence. Of course, there is a great deal of evidence available to us. Whenever we write an argument we will select evidence. The problem is when an author selects only the one or two bits of evidence which support their argument and ignores vast quantities of evidence which would oppose their argument. Let's look at an example.

> **Red wine is good for your health.**
> A study has found that red wine is a rich source of polyphenols, which are linked to long life. They also have an anti-oxidant effect which combats cancer and heart disease. We should clearly ditch the guilt and savour a health-giving glass or two.

This argument has used only the evidence which supports the conclusion. It has ignored evidence about the damage done to our health by the alcohol in red wine. This is common knowledge, but the argument has also omitted information which is not common knowledge. For example, a search on the Internet shows that the study linking red wine to long life talks about small quantities of red wine; the study also suggests that olive oil is just as good; scientists suggest that the polyphenols in red wine lengthen the life of yeast, not people, and the journalists have generalised from the scientific study on yeast to the effects of these chemicals on people. So, when we consider the common knowledge that alcohol is bad for your health, and do a little simple research into the actual evidence, we can see that the author has been overly selective in their use of evidence. This means that we cannot accept their conclusion that red wine is good for your health. We can conclude only that red wine contains substances that have beneficial effects.

In the Unit 2 exam, you may be expected to judge that a passage which ignores evidence in common knowledge is unreasonably selective in its use of evidence. You will not be expected to have specialist knowledge. But you should remember that your Critical Thinking skills can be useful for your other subjects and the way you approach everyday information from the media.

Is this evidence used in a strong way?

If the evidence is precisely relevant, then you can mention this as a strength. If the evidence is sufficient, you can mention this as a strength. Let's look at an example.

> Research over 40 years and hundreds of thousands of people consistently shows that people who smoke are significantly more likely to get lung cancer than non-smokers. We can, therefore, fairly safely conclude that smoking is a contributory cause of lung cancer.

In this example, the evidence is precisely focused on the conclusion, which makes it strong. The conclusion is fairly weak – it suggests only that smoking contributes to getting lung cancer, not that it is the only cause – and the evidence of a pattern of correlation over many years and hundreds of thousands of people provides strong support for this weak conclusion.

ACTIVITY 15

Explain two weaknesses in the use of evidence in each passage below. Consider any strong use of evidence.

A Only four of the eleven driverless, robotic cars entered for the Urban Challenge (a competition held in October 2007 in a simulated suburb outside Los Angeles) finished the course without freezing up or crashing into each other or buildings. This shows that driverless, robotic cars are not likely to be safer than humans soon.

B Many parents would prefer their children to stay in school for their sixth form education. However, evidence from 2004/5 shows that students at Lands End Sixth form College thought that the education they received was of a very high quality, with 85% rating it as good or better. With this in mind, Cornwall education authority should continue to close school sixth forms in favour of colleges.

C A recent poll suggested that 55% of the population (based on a sample of more than 10,000) supported the use of the death penalty for convicted murderers. Previous votes in the Houses of Parliament have consistently opposed the use of the death penalty. Members of Parliament should represent the views of the British people. The current views of the people are clearly not being represented by our MPs so we should lobby MPs to ensure that there is a new vote on this issue in the near future.

D 62% of cartoon movies watched by young children on video or DVD contain images of injuries caused by violence and half of these are fatal injuries. Children are easily frightened by these images and there is a relationship between time spent watching television and sleep disturbances caused by nightmares. This shows that watching television contributes to sleep problems in young children.

OCR Unit 2, January 2007

REMEMBER

Identify the evidence and the reason or conclusion it is supporting. Consider the following.

■ *Relevance*: Is the evidence talking about precisely the same thing as the conclusion?

■ *Sufficiency*: Is there enough evidence to support the conclusion? Has the evidence been selected to omit evidence which would oppose the conclusion?

The median

As we learnt in Unit 1, the mean is a good way to work out the average. However, there are two other common ways. Let's look again at the nine students who took a test and gained the following results.

> Nine students took a test, and their results were as follows:
> 40%   99%   45%   49%   52%   45%   53%   59%   45%

The first of the two other ways to work out the average is the median mark. This is found by first putting the percentages in order.

> 40%   45%   45%   45%   **49%**   52%   53%   59%   99%
>
> *median*

The median is the middle value, which in this case is 49%.

If there were an even number of marks, as shown below, then you could find the median by calculating the value that is mid-way between the two middle values, as in the example below.

> 35%   40%   45%   45%   **45%**   **49%**   52%   53%   55%   99%
>
> *median*

Here the median is between the fifth and sixth values – that is, between 45% and 49%. In this case the median is 47%.

Finally, the 'average' could be found by identifying the mode. This is the value in the set of percentages that occurs most often.

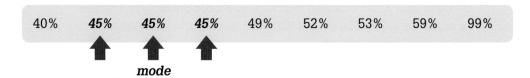

> 40%   **45%**   **45%**   **45%**   49%   52%   53%   59%   99%
>
> *mode*

As we have seen, starting from the same set or data but using different methods to calculate the average produces very different figures. The mean is 54%. The median (mid-point) is 49% and the mode (most commonly occurring value) is 45%. So why does this matter?

A local newspaper reporter could take the mean and gleefully pronounce that 78% of these students are below average. The teacher could use the mode and defiantly claim that 89% are average and above average. Both would be right in their own terms. We need to set the use of averages in context for evidence to be meaningful.

The use of averages in evidence

It is important to consider how averages are used in an argument to support reasons and conclusions. An average is often used to represent a whole group. However, the members of that group may be very different, and the average is a very rough tool. It will not be representative of everyone in the group. Let's take an example to illustrate this.

> Every student in a class of 20 writes down the number of CD albums they own. The person with the smallest number has 50, and the person with the most has 100. The average (mean) is 65. So it is not unreasonable to say that everyone in the class has around 65 CDs. The teacher, Mr Mackie, however, is a jazz and blues fanatic, and has 2500 albums. If we add him into the calculation, the average number of CDs owned by people in the room becomes 181. Yet everyone apart from Mr Mackie owns fewer albums than the average.

We need to remember that an average figure does not apply to everyone when we evaluate how averages are being used as evidence to support reasoning in Critical Thinking. Let's look at an example.

> A wedding is a very important day for a couple and their family. However, the average spend on a wedding day is now a whopping £20,000, so it is clear that things have got out of hand. New couples need every penny for mortgages and setting up home, not to mention the costs of bringing up children. This shows that the people who can least afford it are spending excessive money on weddings.

Answers may include the following. Each paragraph represents a strong AS answer.

- The evidence that the average spend on a wedding is £20,000 might give some support to the reason that 'it is clear that things have got out of hand'. If the average spend is this much, then the people at the top extreme of the group must be spending huge amounts of money, and the total amount spent on weddings must be vast.

- It could also be argued that a wedding is a sign of public commitment (possibly in the eyes of God), which can be arranged for as little as £150. Even a church wedding can be arranged for under £300. Any additional spending can therefore be seen as excessive – and an average of £20,000 would indicate that most people are spending more than a few hundred pounds.

- The author uses the average spend of £20,000 as if it were representative of what every couple spends on their wedding day. It may be that there is a small group of couples such as celebrities who spend millions on their wedding with the majority of couples spending a lot less than £12,000. The average is thus not very informative, and not sufficient to support the conclusion that 'the people who can least afford it are spending excessive money on weddings'.

- We cannot be sure which couples are spending the largest amounts of money on their weddings. It may be those who can least afford it, but it may also be celebrities and the wealthy who can afford it. Therefore, this evidence does not give strong support to the conclusion that 'the people who can least afford it are spending excessive money on weddings'.

ACTIVITY 16

Evaluate whether the use of the average is weak or strong in the following passage.

School leavers are having second thoughts about university, aware that an average graduate starting salary of £17,000 is hardly going to cover debts of up to £15,000 after three years at university. It is obvious that graduate salaries no longer match the crippling cost of getting a degree.

OCR, January 2006

Interpreting evidence from graphs, tables and charts

As in Unit 1, in Unit 2 you may come across evidence presented visually in the form of charts, tables or graphs rather than written data. In Unit 1 you might be asked about the source, reliability and representativeness of the data. In Unit 2 the focus is on interpreting and using the evidence from these visual sources of numerical data in an argument. You need to consider whether the evidence supports the author's reasons and conclusion by asking these questions.

■ Is this evidence precisely relevant to the reason or conclusion it is supporting?

■ Is this evidence sufficient to support the reason or conclusion?

■ Are there any alternative conclusions that could be supported by this evidence?

Let's look at an example.

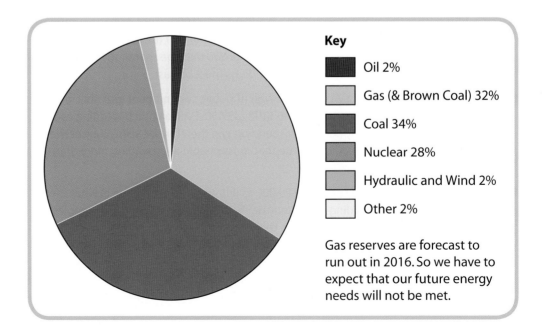

Key

- Oil 2%
- Gas (& Brown Coal) 32%
- Coal 34%
- Nuclear 28%
- Hydraulic and Wind 2%
- Other 2%

Gas reserves are forecast to run out in 2016. So we have to expect that our future energy needs will not be met.

▪ Energy currently generated by fuel used.

Here we have a short argument supported by visual evidence and a prediction about the gas supply, which is another form of evidence.

> **Ev** Gas reserves are forecast to run out in 2016.
> **Ev** Pie chart shows that 32% of our energy comes from gas.
> **C** We have to expect that our future energy needs will not be met.

We need to ask ourselves whether the evidence supports this conclusion.

- Is it relevant?
- Is it sufficient?
- Is there another conclusion that can be drawn from the evidence?

The evidence about the source of our energy is partly relevant to the conclusion. However, the evidence in the pie chart is referring to our current sources of energy, whereas the conclusion is referring to meeting our future energy needs. In future, we may have different sources of energy. We cannot assume that the information in the pie chart will remain the same between now and 2016. Past and current trends are not a reliable guide to the future.

The evidence is not sufficient because we do not have forecasts about future energy sources.

The evidence could be used to support the conclusion that, 'in future we will need to develop alternative energy sources'.

ACTIVITY

Look at the details below. Does the evidence support the caption?

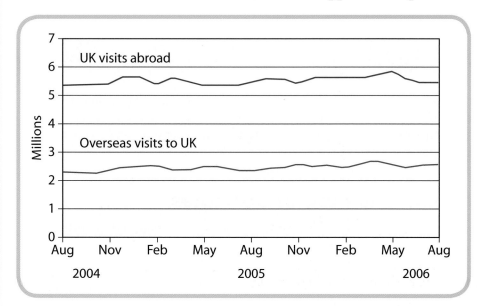

- Visits to the UK from overseas up by 5% in July 2006.

EXAM TIP

You should approach evidence that is displayed visually (i.e. in a chart, table or a graph) in exactly the same way as you would evaluate any other piece of evidence. Ask yourself the same sorts of questions.

EXAM TIP

Here are some questions you need to ask yourself when considering whether evidence is relevant to the reason or conclusion it supports.

- Does the evidence refer to one year, where this may not be representative of a trend or a reliable guide to past or future?

- If the evidence refers to an average, is this statistic being used (incorrectly) in a way which suggests it is representative of the whole group?

- Does it refer to the same group of people or subject as the reason it is meant to be supporting?

- Does it refer to the same timescale as the reason?

Additional evidence to strengthen or weaken an argument

Some multiple choice questions may ask you to identify which piece of evidence, if true, would most strengthen or weaken an argument.

If a piece of evidence supports one of the reasons or the reasoning, then it strengthens the argument. If it would counter a reason or show it to be wrong, or if a piece of evidence would support an opposing conclusion, then it would weaken an argument.

Once you have considered this, you need to consider whether the evidence is precisely focused and relevant to the conclusion. One of the possible answers in a multiple-choice question may seem to work well, but on closer examination may be focused on a different conclusion.

> New figures suggest that most children know whether they want to go to Sixth form college and university by the age of 11. Careers services, which cost a great deal of money, advise children based on a view that they do not know where they want to go after school. Clearly, children who do know where they are going are in no need of careers advice. This new evidence suggests that we may be wasting some of the money currently spent on careers work.
>
> Which of the following, if true, would most strengthen the above argument?
>
> **A** 80% of those who said that they would go on to college, did so.
> **B** The 33% who said that they would not go on, were often found to change their mind about this decision.
> **C** Some teenagers continue on to college even though they would prefer a more practical career.
> **D** The majority of teenagers do go on to college after leaving school.
>
> OCR, January 2007

In this example, A strengthens the argument, by showing that most children did know whether they wanted to go on to college. B and C would give us reason to believe that careers advice would be useful. D does not relate to whether young children know what they want to do after school.

Evaluating the use of examples

As well as using evidence, authors often use examples to illustrate or develop their reasoning. Examples do not support an argument in the same way as evidence supports reasons or reasons support conclusions. They do not provide logical grounds for us to accept a reason or conclusion, but give a specific situation in which the reason holds.

Examples can strengthen or weaken an argument. In order to strengthen an argument, an example should be typical or representative or precisely illustrate the situation at issue. If we are using an example to illustrate the effects of a change in policy or circumstances, we need to be sure that the example is precisely of that change and its effects, and does not include other circumstances which might confuse the issue. Weak use of examples will weaken an argument. Many people use the example of someone who has smoked all their life, is as fit as a fiddle and does not have lung cancer. However, this one isolated example does not (in any way) prove that smoking does not cause lung cancer. The scientific evidence overwhelmingly supports the claim that smoking causes cancer. As a general rule of thumb, approach examples with suspicion and look for problems, but be prepared also to identify and explain strength.

REMEMBER

An example is used to support a reason by giving a specific situation in which the reason holds to be true.

When evaluating examples, ask the following questions.

- Is the example illustrating the argument or is it being used to support a general conclusion?

- Is the example precisely the same as the situation being talked about?

- Is the specific example typical or representative of the group being talked about?

Let's look at an example.

> Firm rules and kindness are a great way of getting children to behave in an acceptable, sociable manner. This is because children respond to being understood and they like to understand what the limits are. Mrs Devi, for example, is extremely kind, but she makes sure the children in her class understand the rules. She only allows one person to talk at a time, and she enforces this by giving one child at a time a talking spoon, and they are only to talk when they are holding the spoon. She and everyone else listen carefully to the person holding the spoon. Even Jake, the most badly behaved boy in Year 6, listens when Mrs Devi gives someone else the talking spoon.

Let's identify the examples in this passage.

- Mrs Devi is used as an example of someone who is kind but who enforces firm rules.

- A talking spoon is used as an example of setting clear guidelines.

- Jake is used as an example of someone for whom Mrs Devi's approach works.

These examples are used to illustrate a very simple argument.

> **R** Children respond to being understood and they like to understand what the limits are.
>
> **C** Firm rules and kindness are a great way of getting children to behave in an acceptable, sociable manner.

We need to ask whether the examples strengthen the argument.

■ Does Mrs Devi represent precisely the situation at issue in the argument?

As far as we can tell, she does seem to embody the firm kindness advocated in the argument.

■ Does using a talking spoon represent precisely the situation at issue in the argument?

• Even Jake listens when Mrs Devi gives someone the talking spoon.

The talking spoon does seem to be a strong example of firm kindness: it emphasises the importance of listening to other people, sets a clear, simple rule and creates a feeling of calmness. It also makes it clear to the reader how someone can use firm rules and kindness to encourage acceptable behaviour – it gives us a concrete, real situation so that we can see how it might work.

■ Does Jake represent precisely the situation at issue in the argument?

Jake is not a typical boy – he is described as the worst behaved boy in Year 6. But he is not being used as an example of the typical boy. He is being used as an example of how firm kindness can be effective in modifying behaviour. The idea in the argument is that, if Mrs Devi's methods are effective even on Jake, they are likely to be effective in encouraging acceptable behaviour in other children too.

So, these examples do seem to strengthen the argument by illustrating exactly how the ideas in the argument might work in a real situation.

■ But the examples aren't sufficient to support the reason or the conclusion, are they?

No, the examples we have here of a single situation are not sufficient to support the reason that children generally respond to being understood and like to know what the limits are. Nor are they sufficient to show that firm rules and kindness are a great way to encourage acceptable behaviour. One example is not enough to support a general claim. However, these examples are not supporting the general claims. They are illustrating them, showing how the general ideas can work. Because the examples do seem to show how firm kindness can encourage good behaviour, they strengthen the argument.

Let's work through a weaker example.

> Harry sits really quietly in Mr Kumar's lessons. It is clearly good for boys to be taught by men.

The example used is of one boy's behaviour in one teacher's lessons. This single example is used to support a very general claim. But one example cannot be enough to support such a general claim. So the use of this example is poor.

■ Is the example illustrating precisely the situation being talked about?

The example is of a boy being taught by a man. However, we cannot be certain that Mr Kumar's teaching is good for Harry. Sitting quietly may be an important first step towards learning – but it may be that Mr Kumar is trying to get the boys to learn through active, boisterous play, or that Harry is so scared of Mr Kumar that he sits quietly, and therefore is not learning well.

■ Is Harry a typical boy?

We do not know what sort of boy Harry is. Is he normally lively, or mischievous or studious? Without this information, we cannot judge whether he can be used to represent other boys.

■ Is Mr Kumar a typical teacher?

Mr Kumar may be an outstanding teacher, and it may be this rather than his maleness which has a positive effect – if, indeed, there is a positive effect. We do not have enough information about him to be sure that he can be used to represent other male teachers.

PAUSE FOR THOUGHT

What qualities do you think make a good teacher? Why? What qualities do you think make a good learner? Why?

ACTIVITY 18

Evaluate the examples in the passages that follow.

A We should not reject modern fabrics out of hand. They have many advantages over traditional and natural fibres. Many modern fabrics are easy to wash and care for, and are not ruined as easily as, for example, silk. Furthermore, modern fabrics allow us to adapt to the weather conditions we find. For example, neoprene allows us to engage in water sports throughout the year. It is even possible to go surfing in Scotland in December in a modern wetsuit.

B Driving a car through London is unbearably slow. It is often quicker to go on foot. Jeremy Clarkson drove from the suburbs to central London in a race with a marathon runner, and lost. We should consider whether a car is really necessary for our journey.

C Television distorts important debates and ideas. Successive debates between American presidential candidates have been won, according to polls conducted after the broadcast, by the candidate with the best appearance and snappy one liners rather than the candidates with best arguments. Perhaps radio listeners are in a better position to evaluate important debates.

OCR Unit 2, January 2007

D Hospitals have been encouraged to introduce strict new guidelines on hand washing because it is thought that this can help to reduce serious infections in patients. Evidence from a number of hospitals indicates that poor hygiene is a key factor in spreading infections such as MRSA between patients. One example of a successful reduction in incidence of MRSA is Nowheresville Hospital. The hospital has recently enforced guidelines on hand washing. Everybody – doctor, nurse or visitor – must wash their hands before they see each patient. There are antiseptic hand wash dispensers at the entrance to each ward and by each bed with clear instructions reminding people to wash their hands. This is the only significant change which has been made at the hospital.

REMEMBER

Ask questions about examples, as you did with evidence.

- Is the example illustrating the argument or is it being used to support a general conclusion?

- Is the example precisely the same as the situation being talked about?

- Is the specific example typical or representative of the group being talked about?

- Hospitals have been encouraged to introduce strict new guidelines on hand washing.

Offering alternative explanations

Authors also often use explanations to support their reasoning (especially in a scientific or social scientific context). These explanations often affect the strength of support for the conclusion. If an author has used an explanation which is clearly wrong or implausible, this will weaken the support for their conclusion. You may need to identify such weakness and offer plausible alternative explanations. If you can offer a better, alternative explanation, you will really show the weakness in an author's argument. You may need to evaluate the effect on the conclusion of the author's weak explanation.

Let's look at an example.

> There has been a rise in the number of cases of measles in the UK since 1998. This can be explained by bugs which are resistant to antibiotics. So we need to work hard on developing new drugs to combat measles.

The author's explanation for the rise in the number of cases of measles since 1998 does not work, as measles is a virus which does not respond to antibiotics so, because the author's explanation of the evidence in terms of antibiotics is not adequate, we cannot accept their conclusion that we need to develop new drugs.

An alternative, more plausible explanation for the rise in the number of cases of measles would be that a prominent doctor claimed in 1998 that the measles, mumps and rubella vaccine caused autism. As a result of this, a significant proportion of parents stopped taking their children for the vaccination, and the percentage of the population which has been vaccinated dropped. This then allowed measles to spread.

When you are considering evidence and explanations in your other subjects, you should always look up real evidence and explanations as we have done in the worked example about measles. However, as this is not possible in an exam, you should consider whether an explanation is plausible and whether there are any other plausible or probable explanations. This is what you should do in Activity 19.

ACTIVITY 19

Read the passage below and suggest one alternative explanation for the incidence of diseases such as cancer.

Although we regard ourselves as much healthier than people a hundred years ago, we suffer from far higher rates of cancer, Alzheimer's, motor neurone disease and other such illnesses. This can be explained by our fast-paced, high-pressure, consumer-orientated urban lifestyle. To reduce the incidence of these illnesses we should revert to the calmer, more measured lifestyle of our great-grandparents.

ACTIVITY 20

Read the texts below and answer the questions that follow on page 163.

A

Many people argue that video games can be beneficial in terms of hand–eye coordination and problem-solving skills. Nevertheless, there is no way of getting around the problem that playing video games leads to aggressive, violent behaviour, so parents should not let their children use these games.

People who play violent video games are more aggressive, more likely to commit violent crimes and less likely to help others. This is supported by many studies which have found this link and also found that players are more likely to be tense, frustrated, suffer from stress-related illness and ADHD. This can be explained by the way violent video games activate the fight or flight mechanism, but provide no natural way to release it. A real fight, or a real flight, would release the body's adrenaline in a healthy way. Children would be better off boxing or running than playing video games.

One study has demonstrated that violent gamers show diminished brain responses to images of real-life violence, such as gun attacks. However, they show normal 'surprise' or 'disturbance' reactions when they see images of dead animals or sick children. This clearly demonstrates that they are normal human beings who have been made violent by games.

B   **Reader profile**
Janey says husband Harry spends up to 4 hours every evening at his games console in the shed, playing speed racing games and assassination scenarios. 'Often he is grumpy and bad tempered with me when I venture out to suggest that he comes to bed,' says Janey. 'Last week he even kicked the shed door. The games are having a really bad effect on his personality; he is so much more aggressive than the lovely man I married. I do sometimes worry where it will all end.'

a) **How effective is the explanation given in Text A, paragraph 2 for the link between violent video games and problems such as aggression?**

b) **Suggest one other explanation for the findings in the studies.**

c) **Explain one other weakness in the use of evidence in this paragraph to support the claim that, 'Parents should not let their children use video games.'**

d) **Explain one weakness in the use of evidence in paragraph 3 to show that violent gamers, 'are normal human beings who have been made violent by games'.**

e) **Evaluate the strength of the reader profile (Text B) as an example of video games causing violent behaviour.**

PAUSE FOR THOUGHT

'Animal testing is unnecessary.'

■ Research evidence that would support and challenge this claim.

■ Write an argument either to support or to challenge the claim.

■ Exchange arguments with another student.

■ Evaluate each other's use of evidence and look for ways to improve.

Summary

You should now be able to:

■ evaluate the use of evidence in an argument by asking:

– Is this evidence precisely relevant?

– Is this evidence sufficient?

– Is this evidence used in a strong way?

■ evaluate the use of examples in an argument by asking:

– Is the example illustrating the argument or is it being used to support a general conclusion?

– Is the example precisely the same as the situation being talked about?

– Is the specific example typical or representative of the group being talked about?

■ evaluate the use of explanations in an argument by:

– offering alternative, plausible explanations.

Learning objectives

● Understand the meaning of the term 'appeal'. Recognise appeals within arguments.
● Identify and evaluate:
  ● appeal to authority
  ● appeal to popularity
  ● appeal to tradition
  ● appeal to history
  ● appeal to emotion.
● Understand how to answer appeals questions in the exam.

Evaluating reasoning

In Unit 1 you evaluated the logical link between reasons and conclusion by checking whether the reasons really support the conclusion and whether they are precisely relevant. You may find it useful to revise this logical link, using pages 55–56 of Unit 1, Chapter 4.

In the next two chapters we are going to **evaluate** arguments. We will do this by considering some very specific patterns of argument which can weaken the logical link between the reasons and the conclusion. In this chapter we will consider irrelevant appeals, and will go on in the next chapter to look at flaws.

What are appeals?

An **appeal** is a reference to something or someone in order to persuade an audience to accept a conclusion. Many arguments refer to an authority to strengthen their claims, or use the popularity or traditional status of an idea, in order to support it. People may refer to past events to support a future action. Other arguments may try to persuade you by arousing strong emotions.

Arguments which use appeals can be weak because they tend to engage your emotions rather than using reason. An argument is defined as an attempt to persuade by giving reasons, so engaging your emotions isn't enough to make it strong. On the contrary, not every appeal is a weakness in an argument: as you learnt in Unit 1, someone's expertise or authority can make their evidence more credible, and it can therefore be used to support a claim. As we look at each kind of appeal, we will consider what might make it a strong or weak form of argument.

Appeal to authority

We often refer to an expert witness or look to a recognised authority in a field to help us make judgements about which claims to accept. This is particularly the case when the evidence is complex and we are not experts ourselves. For example, if you woke up one morning with a nasty rash, you would seek expert advice – you would go to the doctor.

> I was worried about having meningitis. But the doctor said that my rash was typical of a less serious virus, and she did a test with a cold glass. The spots faded under the glass, and they don't do that with meningitis. Also, she said that if I had meningitis, I would have a stiff neck and joint pain, rapid breathing and be confused. I don't have any of those symptoms. So I can stop worrying and enjoy being just ill enough to stay in bed, but not seriously ill.

Here, the doctor's authority is appealed to. We also hear the doctor's reasons for holding the opinion that the student does not have meningitis. So in this case, the appeal to the doctor's authority strengthens the student's conclusion that 'I can stop worrying'.

KEY TERMS

Evaluate
Judge whether the argument or reasoning is strong or weak.

Appeal
A reference to something or someone, in order to persuade an audience to accept a conclusion.

KEY TERM

Appeal to authority
Referring to an expert witness or recognised authority to support a claim.

However, doctors, like other experts, can be wrong and, as you learnt in Unit 1, experts and authorities can disagree, so an appeal to authority cannot finally end an argument. Let's look at a weaker example of an appeal to authority.

It is right to go to war. The Prime Minister says so.

The Prime Minister has authority, and should have considered all the evidence very carefully. But just because he says so is not a good reason to go to war. Just because someone is an authority does not mean that their opinion overrides all others. Arguments should be evaluated on the quality of the evidence and the reasons given, not just on the authority of the people who use them.

One further way in which an appeal to authority can be weak is if the authority appealed to is irrelevant to the case in question or has a vested interest to put forward a particular point of view. The doctor would be a poor authority on whether your tooth needed to be filled or extracted, for example. You can use the skills you practised in Unit 1 to evaluate the relevance and reliability of an appeal to authority.

Let's look at an exam-style question and answer it.

Smoking should be banned in all public places, not just some. It is not fair that some bar workers should be protected but not others. As the government's chief medical adviser says, it would be very negative if smoking were allowed in some public places.

- Smoking should be banned in all public places.

Name: Appeal to authority.

Description: The author has appealed to an authority to support their claim that 'smoking should be banned in all public places, not just some'.

Evaluation: The government's chief medical adviser is a relevant authority, who should have access to reliable evidence. However, this appeal does not present his evidence. It simply quotes him paraphrasing the conclusion, which cannot give logical support. So this appeal does not strengthen the conclusion and the argument is quite weak.

ACTIVITY 21

Name the appeal in the argument below. Explain why it does not support the conclusion.

There are psychological benefits to participating in the National Lottery. Knowing that they could win the jackpot gives hope to many participants who lead humdrum, boring lives. Moreover, smaller wins are quite common and, as the National Lottery organiser has said, these give a boost to those who receive them.

Appeal to popularity

An **appeal to popularity** justifies a conclusion by its popularity alone. For example, 'most people are in favour of capital punishment, so the government should bring it back'. However, just because something is popular does not mean it is right. Popularity is not a bad thing in itself, but it is not enough to support a conclusion.

As with an appeal to authority, an appeal to popularity need not be a weakness if it is used appropriately. Consider this example.

> Thousands of people read their horoscopes in newspapers and magazines. So we should include horoscopes in our magazine.

In this case the popularity of horoscopes probably is a good reason to include them in a magazine because including popular features sells magazines. If there was a good reason not to include horoscopes this should probably override their popularity.

ACTIVITY 22

Name the appeal in the argument below. Explain why it does not support the conclusion.

Hundreds of thousands of people read their horoscopes in newspapers or magazines. So there must be some truth in them.

Appeal to tradition

An **appeal to tradition** justifies a claim or an action on the basis that it is traditional, or has always been done this way. However, the fact that something has been done for a long time does not make it right. Such arguments are often attempts to persuade us to resist change, and appealing to tradition in this way avoids the real issues. Here are two examples.

> ■ We've always left weak infants on the mountainside to die. So we should carry on doing that. It's our tradition.
>
> ■ Our family has always donated one-fifth of its income to charity. It's what we do. So we should carry on giving money to the needy.

Exposing weak infants and giving money to charity are both supported in the same way here. So, on the basis of the argument in front of us, we should accept or reject both of them, even though we would consider killing small babies to be a wrong act, and donating money to charity to be a right act. So we can see that this pattern of reasoning is not enough to support a conclusion. If an action is wrong, a tradition of doing it cannot support its continuation.

- Even giving to charity should be justified on its own merits, not just by appeal to tradition.

However, we might want to take tradition into account in an argument. There may be good reasons to prefer something that has stood the test of time to something new and untried. We can also take our emotional attachment to old, familiar things into consideration in an argument. It will not necessarily outweigh good reasons for change, but an appeal to tradition is not *necessarily* a weakness. For example:

> My new boyfriend has asked me to go to Australia with him for two weeks over Christmas. I would really like to go, but my family always spend Christmas together. We have a lot of fun putting up the decorations, and singing silly songs at the tops of our voices, and playing games. And we get the biggest turkey and I always help Mum stuff it with apples. It makes us giggle. And we go for a long, cold walk to the pub on Boxing Day. I would be really sad to miss all that. It would feel odd being hot on the beach. So I'm going to have Christmas with my family and try to persuade John to go to Australia in January.

In this example, the speaker has appealed to tradition, but has also given reasons why she wants to stick with tradition – not just because it's traditional, but because the traditions are fun. So this is a fairly strong appeal to tradition.

PAUSE FOR THOUGHT

Consider the following appeal to tradition. Think of good reasons why it might be better to break with tradition and not have a 6-week summer holiday.

> Since state schooling began, there has always been a 6-week summer holiday. So we should carry on having long summer holidays from school – it's our country's tradition.

ACTIVITY 23

Name the appeal in the argument below. Explain why the appeal does not support the conclusion. (Consider any other reasons why the reasoning does not support the conclusion.)

We should not disapprove of smoking in public places. It is an important part of British culture. Something particularly English would be lost with the demise of the small, smoke-fugged pub, or the aroma of Cuban cigars mingling with leather in a gentleman's club. Pubs and clubs smelling of body odour or scented with manufactured 'baking bread' aroma will simply not have the same appeal.

Appeal to history

An **appeal to history** suggests that because something has happened before, it will happen again. That is, a reference to the past is used to predict the future. For example, a student might say, 'I've always passed exams without putting in much effort, so I'll breeze through my A Levels too.'

Of course, we often use the past as a guide to the future. If someone has lied to you or cheated on you ten times, it is not unreasonable to think that they might do so again. However, the past is not a reliable guide to the future. These predictions are only probable, not certain. There may be all sorts of changes in circumstance that mean that future events are different. In the case of the A Level student, it may be that A Levels are harder and need more work. It may be that the student develops an illness like glandular fever, which would make A Level studies much more difficult.

ACTIVITY 24

Name the appeal in the argument below. Explain why the appeal does not support the conclusion.

This train is due in at 6.30. It's never been late before, so I'll see you at 6.30.

Appeal to emotion

An **appeal to emotion** works by referring to things that make us feel very emotional, and attempts to persuade the audience to support the conclusion because they feel strongly about it, rather than by using good reasons. Look at the example below.

KEY TERM

Appeal to emotion ●
A form of argument that attempts to support a conclusion by engaging the audience's emotions rather than by giving reasons.

- Winston Churchill appealed to loyalty, pride and patriotism of wartime Britons.

> I have, myself, full confidence that if all do their duty, if nothing is neglected, and if the best arrangements are made, as they are being made, we shall prove ourselves once again able to defend our Island home, to ride out the storm of war, and to outlive the menace of tyranny, if necessary for years, if necessary alone. At any rate, that is what we are going to try to do. That is the resolve of His Majesty's Government – every man of them. That is the will of Parliament and the nation.
>
> Winston Churchill, 4 June 1940, http://www.presentationhelper.co.uk/winston_churchill_speech_fight_them_on_beaches.htm

In this rousing speech, Churchill gives little reason to support his claim that 'we shall prove ourselves once again able to defend our Island home', but appeals to the loyalty, pride, patriotism and other emotions of the audience. It is a beautifully pitched piece of rhetoric and gained the support of the British people in a way that no rational argument could have. All the same, most of the time we do not want advertisers or political leaders manipulating our emotions rather than giving us reasons to buy their product or accept their view.

ACTIVITY (25)

Name the appeal in the argument below. Explain why the appeal does not support the conclusion.

The government was wrong to spend more on the NHS. Billions have been squandered on pay rises and price increases, and good, honest, hard-working taxpayers have footed the bill.

Characteristics of a weak appeal

It is important to remember that finding an appeal in an argument does not necessarily mean that the conclusion is wrong. A conclusion cannot be supported by a weak or irrelevant appeal, but it may well be possible to support the conclusion in another way.

You also need to evaluate the appeal, and check that it is a weak one, before saying that the conclusion cannot be supported that way. Ask yourself whether the appeal is used:

■ to override or exclude other opinions and evidence

■ without any form of evaluation or convincing evidence

■ to take the place of logical reasons to support the conclusion.

TAKE IT FURTHER

Discussion: Should a democratic government do only what the people want? Why (not)?

■ Should we continue to listen to traditional folk music?

ACTIVITY 26

Read passages A–C, and answer the questions that follow each argument.

A The government should not tax aviation fuel. As the Prime Minister told senior MPs: 'You don't set out as Prime Minister or as a government to be deeply unpopular.'

Which of the following is an appeal in the argument?

1 Appeal to emotion.
2 Appeal to history.
3 Appeal to popularity.
4 Appeal to tradition.

B I need to get a Trendie. Trendies are the must-have items this Christmas. Everyone loves them.

Which of the following best expresses the appeal in the argument?

1 The fact that everyone loves Trendies is a good reason for you to hate them.
2 The fact that everyone loves Trendies means that they are a must-have item.
3 The fact that everyone loves Trendies does not mean that you need one.
4 The fact that everyone loves Trendies shows how shallow fashion is.

C Everyone should attend folk music festivals at least once a year. This kind of music is our heritage and it's really important to be aware of our heritage and give it all the support we can to stop it dying out.

Which of the following best expresses the appeal in the argument?

1 Folk music sounds dreadful so it would be torture to attend a folk festival every year.
2 If folk music is so unpopular people have to be forced to support it to stop it dying out, it might be better if it did die out.
3 Just because folk music has been typical English music in the past doesn't mean it always will be.
4 Just because folk music is traditional doesn't mean we should continue to support it.

REMEMBER

Appeals often give weak support to a conclusion, because an argument requires logical support and appeals arouse our feelings rather than engage us in logical thinking. But an appeal can be strong. Our feeling of concern for the survivors of a natural disaster can be a good reason to offer help.

ACTIVITY 27

Read the letter and answer the questions below.

Sir,

1 It has been proposed that the government should allow trials of longer, heavier lorries in the UK. This idiotic, imbecile proposal should be thrown out immediately before snorting monster-lorries kill our children and wreck our villages as they thunder through them, invading our lives and wrecking the peace.

2 Roger King of the Road Haulage Association asserts that: 'Longer, heavier lorries can be integrated into existing traffic patterns with little risk.' His opinion can be dismissed because he clearly has a vested interest in getting more lorries on our roads. Furthermore, lorries always have created risk on our roads and they always will. They create spray, sit on your tail and drive dangerously.

3 Lorries are simply dangerous, and bigger lorries would be more dangerous. As Philippa Edmunds of Freight on Rail says: 'HGVs are twice as likely to be involved in fatal accidents as cars. Because of their weight and length, the impact of LHVs (longer, heavier vehicles) in an accident will be proportionately greater. There are questions about braking distances, jack-knifing and blind spots.'

4 No one wants bigger, heavier lorries on the roads. The government should listen to the people.

a) **Name the appeal in paragraph 1. Explain why this appeal does not support the conclusion that, 'this proposal (to allow trials of longer, heavier lorries on UK roads) should be thrown out'.**

b) **Name an appeal in paragraph 2. Explain why this appeal does not support the conclusion.**

c) **Name the appeal in paragraph 3. Evaluate its strengths and weaknesses, and decide whether or not it supports the conclusion.**

d) **Name the appeal in paragraph 4. Evaluate its strengths and weaknesses and decide whether or not it supports the conclusion.**

- Should trials of longer, heavier lorries be allowed in the UK?

Summary

You should now be able to:

◼ understand what appeals are

◼ name, describe and evaluate:

    – appeal to authority

    – appeal to popularity

    – appeal to tradition

    – appeal to history

    – appeal to emotion

◼ understand how to answer appeals question in the exam.

Learning objectives

- Name common flaws in reasoning.
- Describe common flaws in reasoning.
- Explain why these flaws do not support a conclusion in a specific argument.

What are flaws?

In Chapter 10 you learnt about appeals to something outside of the argument, such as authority, and how this might either strengthen or weaken the argument. In this chapter, you will learn about **flaws** that are weaknesses within the argument. A flaw is a fault in the pattern of reasoning and it is always a weakness.

Reasoning from wrong actions

Reasoning from wrong actions is a flaw committed by everyone from children to international politicians. However, one wrong action cannot justify another wrong action. There are two subtly different forms of this flaw: the **'two wrongs don't make a right'** flaw, and the **'Tu quoque'** flaw.

Two wrongs don't make a right

The two wrongs don't make a right flaw is an attempt to justify one bad action on the basis that another, different, bad action is often or has been accepted. It is a version of: 'Why are you telling me off for texting during the lesson? You didn't tell Jake off for spitting.' However, two wrongs don't make a right. Jake's wrong action is not a reason for you to do something wrong.

Tu quoque

Tu quoque is a Latin phrase which literally means 'you too'. This pattern of reasoning is an attempt to justify an action on the basis that someone else is doing it too. It is a sophisticated version of: 'My friends are going; why can't I?'. The problem is that if it is wrong for your friends to go shoplifting in town, it is wrong for you too. Their wrong action is not a reason for you to do something wrong as well.

Even if they are not doing anything wrong, you should base your conclusions on what to do on good reasons, not on what other people are doing. This applies even when politicians justify policy decisions at an international level on the basis of what other countries are doing. Let's work through an example.

> Of course America should sign international agreements to reduce greenhouse gas emissions. Other countries have.

Name: Tu quoque.

Description: The fact that other countries have signed up to international agreements is used to support the conclusion that America should sign up to international agreements to reduce greenhouse gas emissions.

Evaluation: Other countries' actions cannot be used to justify the need for America to act in the same way, so this reasoning is weak and does not support the conclusion. America should make a decision based on good reasons, not on the actions of others.

Of course, we probably think that reducing emissions is a good thing. It may be that the measures to reduce emissions will only work if all the countries join in. In that case this, combined with the reason that other countries have signed up, would be reasons why (we think) America should sign up.

However, on its own, the fact that other countries are taking a particular measure is not enough reason for America to do so.

- Al Gore has given reasons for America to reduce emissions.

Remember, just because the reasoning does not support the conclusion does not mean that the conclusion is wrong, only that it cannot be supported in this way. You may well agree that America should sign up to international agreements to reduce greenhouse gas emissions. But you would need stronger reasoning to support this conclusion.

ACTIVITY 28

Look at the two arguments that follow.

a) **Name the flaw in argument A. Explain why the reasoning does not support the conclusion.**

b) **Name the flaw in argument B. Evaluate to what extent the reasoning supports the conclusion.**

A We cannot afford to pay all our workers the minimum wage. We will have to use illegal immigrants to pick our strawberries as we can pay them very much less than workers protected by British law. If we look around, we can see that other farmers and the catering industry are making similar decisions.

B The government should not try to stop us eating unhealthily. For one thing, they don't try to stop us breaking our legs skiing down mountains, or prevent people from jumping off cliffs without even thinking whether there might be rocks just under the surface of the water. Both of these activities are choices that can have a bad effect on our health. So it is inconsistent to try to stop us eating unhealthily. For another thing, the more they try to control what we eat, the more we are going to resist and eat exactly what we like.

Generalisation

Generalisation is drawing a general conclusion from specific evidence. There are two forms of unwarranted generalisation that you are likely to meet in your Critical Thinking AS exam: hasty and sweeping generalisation. Both these forms of generalisation are flaws that mean the conclusion cannot be supported.

Hasty generalisation

A **hasty generalisation** draws a general conclusion from insufficient evidence. Typically, this reasoning moves from one example to a general conclusion – for example: 'Refi is a good Critical Thinking student. Refi is a tall girl. So all good Critical Thinking students are tall girls.' However, one does not imply all, so we cannot move from Refi to all Critical Thinking students. Just because one Critical Thinking student has a particular quality, we cannot suppose that they all do. Let's look at a more complex example.

KEY TERM

Hasty generalisation
Draws a general conclusion from insufficient evidence.

- Are GM crops too dangerous for human consumption?

> Australian researchers have shown that genetically modified peas trigger allergic reactions in some people. Genetically modified crops are simply too dangerous for human consumption.

Name: Hasty generalisation.

Description: Generalises from insufficient evidence (about the effects of GM peas on some people) to a general conclusion (about GM crops on humans in general).

Evaluation: The author cannot use specific evidence about one crop to draw a conclusion about all GM crops. One does not imply all. So we cannot conclude that GM crops in general are too dangerous.

It is also insufficient to use evidence about 'some people' to draw a conclusion about human consumption in general. 'Some' does not mean 'all'. So we cannot conclude even that GM peas are too dangerous for all human consumption.

EXAM TIP

In the exam, remember to say what specific evidence the author is generalising from, and what general conclusion they are drawing. The author is generalising *from* one student to the whole class / the author is generalising *from* one GM crop to all GM crops.

KEY TERM

Sweeping generalisation

A generalisation that moves from some or many to all, creating a stereotype. It may sometimes move back to one individual again.

Sweeping generalisation

A **sweeping generalisation** is a form of stereotyping. The reasoning moves from some or many to all – for example: 'They're all single mothers on benefits in Brook Park'. It may be the case that there are a significant number of single mothers who depend on benefits living in Brook Park. However, this does not mean that everyone from Brook Park can be characterised in this way. There are probably single mothers who live in Brook Park and work; or married/cohabiting mothers, or women who are not mothers – there may even be some men! So we cannot generalise from some or many to the conclusion that 'they *all* are'.

The sweeping generalisation sometimes moves from the sweeping, stereotypical conclusion back to an individual. For example: 'They're all single mothers on benefits in Brook Park. Sara is from Brook Park. So Sara must be a single mother on benefits.' Because the argument is based on an unwarranted, sweeping generalisation, it does not support the conclusion. For all we know, Sara may be an A Level student doing a part-time job and applying for university. Or she may be working full time in a good job.

This kind of stereotyping generalisation is commonly found in the media, and informs prejudice, abuse, bullying and even government policy. It can be annoying, hurtful and even cruel – and it is poor reasoning that fails to support its conclusion.

- Kyle and his girlfriend prefer playing chess to going clubbing.

It is important not to confuse generalisation from one case with giving an example to support your reasoning. As you learnt in Chapter 9, it is perfectly acceptable to make a general point and give an example to illustrate it. It is not acceptable to take a specific example and draw a general conclusion from it. Let's consider the following example.

> Not all young people are attracted by the riotous partying we associate with modern teens. For example, Jaz prefers talking to her friends at home, and Kyle enjoys playing chess with his girlfriend more than going clubbing. So we should accept that young people are interesting and varied.

Here, Jaz and Kyle are given as examples to illustrate a general point. This argument is quite strong. Compare this with the following argument.

> Jaz prefers talking to her friends at home to going clubbing and Kyle would rather play chess with his girlfriend. This shows that stereotypical images of young people going to drunken parties are rubbish.

In this argument, a general conclusion is drawn from the examples of Jaz and Kyle. However, the two examples are not enough to support the conclusion so the generalisation does not support the conclusion.

ACTIVITY

Read the two arguments and answer the questions that follow.

A Two cars were involved in a crash. One was driven by Amir Hussein, a 19-year-old male, the other by Susan Lovegood, a 49-year-old woman. As young men drive more aggressively than middle-aged women, Amir must have been to blame for the accident.

B The GrubTastic! cafe has had good reviews. But the reviewers seem to have been to the wrong place. I went to GrubTastic! and it was terrible. The chips were half raw, the omelette was like leather on the bottom and runny on top, and it took half an hour to arrive. And the waitress was rude.

a) Name the flaw in argument A. Explain why the reasoning does not support the conclusion.

b) Name the flaw in argument B. Evaluate to what extent the reasoning supports the conclusion.

EXAM TIPS

When you identify a sweeping generalisation, you need to think about what is being generalised from, what is being generalised to, and explain why this does not work. Offering a counter-assertion, such as 'but some people from Brook Park might not be single mothers', is not sufficient evaluation to gain you the marks available.

When you identify a generalisation, you may not be sure whether it is a hasty or a sweeping generalisation. As long as you say that it is an 'unwarranted generalisation', explain what it generalises from and to, and explain why that does not support the conclusion, you will access the marks available. In the exam you do not need to specify whether the generalisation is hasty or sweeping.

Unwarranted assumption of a causal relationship

Reasoning can also be flawed if it assumes a causal connection without good reason to do so, or oversimplifies causal relationships, or confuses cause and effect. All these ways of getting a causal relationship wrong can be referred to as '**unwarranted assumption of a causal relationship**' or a **causal flaw**.

Confusing correlation and cause

One flawed pattern of causal reasoning is to assume that because one thing happens before another, or two things happen together, one causes the other. However, there may simply be a correlation – a relationship between two things which happen at the same time but where neither causes the other. For example:

> Every time the postman comes to our door, our dog barks. When the dog barks the postman goes away. The dog believes that her barking defends us from the postman.

The dog's belief is an example of a *post hoc* flaw. This name comes from the Latin, *post hoc ergo propter hoc*, which means, 'after this, therefore because of this'. The dog thinks that because the postman goes away after she has barked, the postman goes away *because* she has barked. However, the postman was going away anyway, so the dog is **confusing correlation and cause** in a *post hoc* flaw.

If the two things happen together, the problem with the reasoning is still a confusion of correlation and cause. Let's look at an example.

> My alarm clock goes off just as the sun rises. So my alarm clock beeping must cause the sun to come up.

In this example, it is clear that this is a case of correlation, not cause – my alarm clock just happens to go off at the same time as the sun comes up. The conclusion that it *causes* the sun to come up is obviously unfounded. In more complex examples, it is not so obvious that the conclusion that A causes B is wrong – but this pattern of reasoning is not enough to support the conclusion. We would need more evidence.

Let's consider two more complex examples.

> **Example 1** Since the early twentieth century the Earth's temperature has risen. During the same time period, women around the world have become increasingly represented in politics. It therefore seems likely that warmer weather causes women to be more politically active.

> **Example 2** Since the late nineteenth century great industrial nations have risen and polluted the atmosphere with a number of gases. During the same time period the average temperature around the Earth has risen. It therefore seems that industrial pollution causes global warming.

EXAM TIP

In the exam you may be expected to identify the special case of *post hoc*. For the other patterns of reasoning relating to cause, correlation and effect you can use the term 'causal flaw' or 'unwarranted assumption of causal relationship'. In all cases you need to explain exactly what is wrong with the reasoning and why it does not support the conclusion.

The conclusion in argument A is supported with exactly the same pattern of reasoning as the conclusion in argument B, and in neither case can we be sure that there is a causal relationship rather than just a correlation on the basis of this reasoning. There is no evidence (that I know of) to suggest that warmer weather really does cause women to be more politically active. However, climatologists and other scientists have provided a great deal of evidence in addition to the chronological correlation to show that industrial pollution probably causes global warming. We need this additional evidence to support the conclusion.

Oversimplifying cause and effect

Another flawed pattern of causal reasoning is to look at a complex situation and say that factor A causes factor B. In a complex situation, though, there may be several factors which together bring about an effect. Let's look at an example.

> If the school introduces a zero tolerance policy on poor behaviour, students will start to behave well.

Name: Oversimplifying causal relationship.

Description: The author oversimplifies the causes of poor behaviour in schools.

Evaluation: Poor behaviour can be caused by lots of things: trouble at home, a bad diet, drugs, drink, poor teaching … . So changing just one factor (the way the school responds to poor behaviour) is unlikely to be enough to make students 'start to behave well'. This reasoning therefore does not support the conclusion.

A slightly different version of this flaw of oversimplifying cause and effect comes when A is argued to cause B, but actually, C causes both A and B. For example:

> People with low educational attainment often have ill health throughout their lives. So we can see that a good education is necessary to ensure a healthy life.

In this example, a simple causal connection between A (education) and B (health) is inferred – poor education causes poor health and good education causes good health. However, the situation is not so simple. It may be that factor C (poverty) is at least a partial cause of poor educational attainment and poor health.

Confusing cause and effect

A third common, but flawed, pattern of causal reasoning is confusing cause and effect – that is, thinking that the effect is the cause. For example:

> The weather reporters should give us better weather. They can clearly influence the weather as it generally does what they say it will. We would like less winter in future.

Name: Causal flaw – confusing cause and effect.

Description: The author treats the weather report as the cause of the weather, which is confused (the wrong way round).

Evaluation: In this case, the author has confused cause and effect. The weather reporters look at weather patterns and predict how they will develop over the next few hours or days. So the weather is the cause and the report is the effect. This means that the author's further conclusion that the weather reporters should give us better weather is unsupported.

Of course, nobody would really think that the weather forecast caused the weather, but people often do make similarly weak causal connections. For example:

> Having more police patrolling the streets is not very effective. Every year they put more police on the streets, and every year there are more crimes. It's probably because the sight of the police winds people up so much that they feel the urge to commit crimes. It's like when they have so many riot police that they start a riot.

In this example, the writer believes that the increasingly visible presence of police on the street is *causing* an increase in crime. This is not entirely unreasonable – there are situations, as the writer points out, when highly visible police can aggravate a tense situation and cause the riot that they were hoping to prevent. However, in this case:

Name and description: The author has confused cause and effect by suggesting that the increasing numbers of police are causing an increase in crime.

Evaluation: It is more likely that there are increasing numbers of police on the streets because there is increasing crime. The crime is probably caused by something else altogether – perhaps by resentment of the 'us-and-them' celebrity society – and the increase in crime is likely to be the cause of the decision to use more police.

So, whenever you read that one thing leads to another, or that doing something will have a certain effect, think about the causal relationships and ask these questions.

- Is the author suggesting (or assuming) a causal relationship?

- What does the author think is the cause? And the effect?

- Is it any of the following?
  – Correlation not cause (and if so, is it *post hoc*?).
  – Oversimplifying cause and effect.
  – Confusing cause and effect.

ACTIVITY 30

Read the arguments and answer the questions that follow.

A   I had a bad cold last week. I took a new remedy, and it worked. The cold has gone.

B   Public perception of GM crops will soon improve. We have been unhappy about GM crops until now because they only benefit farmers. A major GM seed producer has recently developed a soya bean with massive health benefits for consumers. Further similar products are in production.

a)   **Name the flaw in argument A. Explain why the reasoning does not support the conclusion.**

b)   **Name the flaw in argument B. Evaluate to what extent the reasoning supports the conclusion.**

Other logical flaws

In this section you will learn to identify and evaluate the following flaws: restricting the options, slippery slope, circular argument and confusing necessary and sufficient conditions. These four flaws are problematic because they do not give strong, logical support to the conclusion.

Restricting the options

This flaw in reasoning presents a limited picture of choices available in a situation. It is also known as false dilemma, false dichotomy or an 'either or' flaw. It often tries to support a particular course of action on the basis that there is only one, unpleasant alternative. We can show that it does not support the conclusion by mentioning the middle ground: the other alternatives. For example:

> We must either increase the number of speed cameras on the roads or accept increasing road deaths. So we must increase the number of speed cameras.

Name: Restricting the options/false dilemma.

Description: The author supports an increase in the use of speed cameras by suggesting that the only alternative is increasing road deaths and ignores other options.

Evaluation: The author ignores the possibilities that road deaths will not increase or that other methods, such as more police, lower speed limits or graphic advertising campaigns, might be used to reduce road deaths, so we cannot accept the conclusion on the basis of this reasoning.

Slippery slope

A **slippery slope** flaw reasons from one possibility, through a series of events that are not properly or logically linked, to an extreme consequence. It is called a slippery slope flaw because it is like putting one foot on a slippery slope and slithering uncontrollably to the bottom. Such reasoning is often negative – but the pattern of weak links leading to an extreme consequence also fails to support an extreme positive conclusion. This positive version may be known as the flaw of wishful thinking. Look at these examples.

> **Example 1** 'If I don't do my homework tonight I'll fail all my exams, lose my place at university, be unemployed, get addicted to drugs and die in the gutter. So I'd better do my homework.'
>
> **Example 2** 'If I do my homework tonight, I'll pass my exams with excellent grades, get to a good university, earn loads of money in a satisfying job and win a Nobel prize for my contributions to humanity. So I'd better do my homework.'

Name: Example 1: Slippery slope flaw.
　　　Example 2: Wishful thinking.

Description: Both statements start from a simple event and move through a series of weak links to an extreme consequence.

Evaluation: It is unlikely that failing to do your homework once will lead to such dire consequences. It is equally unlikely that doing your homework just once will lead to such positive consequences. In both cases, the links are too extreme and are unjustified. In both cases we would want to accept the conclusion: but in neither case does the reasoning support the conclusion.

REMEMBER !

If we find a flaw in the argument, it does not necessarily mean that the conclusion is wrong. We may just need to find another way of supporting the conclusion. But we do need to be careful not to accept conclusions that are only supported by flawed reasoning.

Circular argument

In a **circular argument** one of the reasons is the same as the conclusion, so the argument goes round and round in circles rather than getting anywhere – for example: 'You've got blue eyes because your eyes are blue.'

One special kind of circular reasoning is 'begging the question'. In this pattern of reasoning, the reasons only work if the conclusion is true. For example: 'We know the Pope is infallible because God says so. We know that God says so because the Pope has told us. The Pope must be right because he's infallible.'

Confusing necessary and sufficient conditions

As we discussed in Chapter 8, some reasons are necessary to support a conclusion, and some are sufficient. If an argument confuses these, and assumes that because something is necessary it is also sufficient, it is flawed and does not support the conclusion. Similarly, if an argument assumes that because something is sufficient it is also necessary, it does not support the conclusion. Let's look at two examples overleaf.

KEY TERMS

Circular argument
An argument in which one of the reasons is the same as the conclusion, *or* an argument in which you have to assume that the conclusion is right in order for the reasons to make sense.

Confusing necessary and sufficient conditions
An argument that assumes that a necessary condition is also sufficient, or that assumes a sufficient condition must also be necessary.

Example 1 Jamal is really talented. He is an extremely fast runner. He's bound to run in the sprint races at the Olympics.

Name: Confusing necessary and sufficient conditions.

Description: The author assumes that because being an extremely fast runner is necessary to run in the sprints at the Olympics, it is sufficient/enough.

Evaluation: The reasoning does not support the conclusion because the necessary condition of being a fast runner is not enough/sufficient to mean that Jamal is 'bound' to run in the Olympics. He will also need hard work, good luck and lots of support from friends and family, for example.

Example 2 Murdering someone means you definitely go to prison. But Annie didn't murder anyone, she only supplied crack. So she won't go to prison.

Name: Confusing necessary and sufficient conditions.

Description: The author takes a condition which is sufficient to send someone to prison (murder) and assumes that it is necessary.

Evaluation: Murder is not a necessary condition of going to prison. Other things, such as selling crack cocaine, can get you sent to prison too. So this confusion of necessary and sufficient conditions means that the conclusion that Annie won't go to prison is completely unsupported.

ACTIVITY 31

Read the arguments below. Name the flaws and explain why they do not support the conclusions.

A   Kofi is bound to get the job. He has all the qualifications for it, and plenty of relevant experience.

B   I have to dye my hair green today, otherwise I'll never know what it felt like to express my true personality.

C   Of course there are wizards who hide from muggles. Otherwise we'd know they were there, wouldn't we?

> **Read the arguments below. Name the flaws and evaluate to what extent the reasoning supports the conclusion in each case.**

D   Environmentalists plan to reintroduce wolves to fairly heavily populated parts of America and Europe, despite fears of attacks on humans. We should support this plan unless we are happy for wolves to become extinct.

E   Christmas present crisis! Father Christmas only has enough toys for half the good boys and girls. We must all go to Lapland and help make more toys. If we don't, our children won't get any presents. Not only that, Father Christmas will go out of business, the elves and reindeer will be unemployed, homeless and starving, we'll all have the most miserable Christmas ever and there will be an end to peace and joy on earth.

F   Photonic make-up is truly beautiful. It will undoubtedly be a huge success for the cosmetic companies. The shimmering, ever-changing colours are inspired by the morpho butterfly and peacocks' tails. It is not pigments, but multiple reflections of light within the material that create the iridescent effect of this material.

Misleading language

Finally, we come to a group of flaws that weaken reasoning in a slightly different way. Rather than involving problems with logic, these flaws all use language, one way or another, to mislead or to shift the focus away from the argument.

Attacking the arguer

Attacking the arguer, or *ad hominem*, is a form of reasoning that dismisses an opposing view by attacking the person putting forward that view, rather than by addressing the reasoning used to support that opposing view. This kind of reasoning does not give us a good reason to dismiss a counter-argument. For example:

> We can't accept Dr Jones' point about hereditary aspects of criminal behaviour. Look at her – she's a blonde woman.

KEY TERM

Attacking the arguer (*ad hominem*)

A form of reasoning that dismisses an opposing view, by attacking the person putting forward that view rather than by addressing their reasoning.

Name: Attacking the arguer (*ad hominem*).

Description: The author's only reason for not accepting Dr Jones' point is that she is a blonde woman, which attacks the woman rather than her reasoning.

Evaluation: The author has given us no reason not to accept Dr Jones' point. Attacking her does not mean that her argument is weak. Blonde women are as likely to be intelligent and make good points as anyone else. Her expertise as a doctor ought to be more significant than her hair colour or gender. So the author has not supported their conclusion at all.

- Dr Jones has done considerable research into hereditary criminality.

Straw person

A **straw person** flaw misrepresents or distorts an opposing view in order to dismiss it. Sometimes this means picking on a weak part of the argument and misrepresenting the whole argument as weak. A straw person flaw often misses the point and attacks something which does not exist. For example:

> Situation: The school won't let the SU organise a Christmas party in college. They say there are no teachers to supervise it, and there are building works going on.
>
> SU rep: 'The school won't let us have a party because they just don't want us to have fun. This is unfair. We should refuse to go to lessons until they change their minds!'

Name: Straw person.

Description: Misrepresenting the position of someone who opposes your view.

Evaluation: The SU rep has misrepresented the argument of the school and ignored the health and safety concerns. This distorts the school's concerns and makes their decision seem unfair. As this is distorted, the student has not given a good reason to support their conclusion.

┌─ **PAUSE FOR THOUGHT** ─────────────────────────────────

How often do you use this form of reasoning? Many of us use it almost without realising it in arguments with our families and partners. 'You're only saying that because you don't love me!' 'You're saying I'm a bad person!' It is worth pausing for thought to consider whether this is really what the other person is saying or whether you are distorting their view. This sort of distortion doesn't support a conclusion because it is weak reasoning. It also contributes to huge rows.

Conflation

Conflation is bringing two or more different concepts together and treating them as the same thing. This can fail to support a conclusion because of the confusion between terms. For example:

> Obesity is a growing problem in western societies. The increasing number of obese people is causing tremendous problems for health provision and insurance. If we want to avoid an obesity crisis we must encourage these people to get fit.

Name: Conflation.

Description: The author treats obese and unfit as the same thing.

Evaluation: The author conflates obese and unfit. However, although many obese people are unfit, a significant minority are fat but fit. Conversely, many thin people are not fit. So the conclusion that these (obese) people should be encouraged to get fit is not fully supported.

Arguing from one thing to another

Sometimes an author might make a point about one thing and use it to support a conclusion about something different. This is a special case of using reasons which are not relevant to a conclusion, and which therefore do not support the conclusion. We can call this **arguing from one thing to another**. For example:

> A survey indicated that 11% of graduates in employment were working in sales and marketing. This clearly indicates that supermarket checkouts will soon all be operated by graduates. So it is not worth getting a degree.
>
> Adapted from OCR Unit 2, January 2006

KEY TERM

Conflation ●

Bringing together two or more different concepts and treating them as the same thing.

KEY TERM

Arguing from one ●
thing to another

A form of reasoning which uses a reason about one thing to support a conclusion about something different.

Name: Arguing from one thing to another.

Description: The author is arguing from the percentage of employed graduates working in sales and marketing, to a conclusion about supermarket checkouts being operated by graduates.

Evaluation: It does not follow from 11% of employed graduates working in sales and marketing that all checkouts will soon be operated by graduates. You cannot move from one to the other because there is no logical connection. Even if 100% of graduates worked in sales there may not be enough of them to operate all the supermarket checkouts – and that ignores the conflation between sales and checkouts.

ACTIVITY 32

Name the flaws in arguments A and B. Explain why the reasoning does not support the conclusions.

A Mathilda Plume of the Tobacco Manufacturer's Confederation argued that figures relating to deaths caused by smoking are distorted. She claims that health professionals count all cases of lung cancer as a smoking-related disease, whether or not the person smoked. However, her vested interest renders her opinion totally unreliable, so we can be sure that the smoking death figures are accurate.

B There is a pressing reason to take happiness seriously: unhappiness is an expensive business. Mental ill health costs the country about £9bn in lost productivity and benefits.

 Name the flaw(s) in argument C. Evaluate to what extent the reasoning supports the conclusion.

C Some scientists have suggested that computer games are actually good for children. This is no doubt because scientists live in a world where social skills are a rarity and moral values are insignificant. Those of us who value the truly important things in life should continue to encourage children away from computer games.

ACTIVITY 33

Read the letter, then answer the questions that follow.

Sir,

1   As a matter of urgency the retirement age must be extended with immediate effect to 85. My reasons are as follows.

2   If we do not extend the retirement age, the British state will collapse under the weight of greybeards. Pension payments are essentially state hand-outs funded by the tax of the young.

3   People who defend the current system of early retirement are simply looking forward to 30 years of luxurious idleness. We should not listen to these selfish silvers.

4   Old people now live for longer than ever before. If they were able to work they would have an interest in life and not get so ill. They would thus not be such a burden on the health service.

5   Surely any intelligent person can see that my arguments cannot be refuted.

Yours,
D. I. M. White

a) **Name the flaw in paragraph 2. Explain why this reasoning does not support the author's conclusion.**

b) **Name the appeal in paragraph 5. Explain why this reasoning does not support the author's conclusion.**

c) **Name the flaws in paragraph 3. Explain why this reasoning does not support the conclusion.**

d) **Name the flaw in paragraph 4. Evaluate to what extent the reasoning supports the conclusion.**

EXAM TIP

In the Unit 2 exam you will come across multiple choice questions in Section A that ask about flaws. You will find some examples of these questions on the CD-ROM and there are some in the Teacher Resource File that accompanies this book.

In Section B you will come across questions which ask you to identify flaws and explain why they do not support the conclusion.

Summary

You should now be able to:

■ name and describe common flaws in reasoning and explain why these patterns of reasoning do not support a conclusion.

12 Evaluating reasoning: analogies, hypothetical reasoning and principles

Learning objectives

- Evaluate analogies.
- Evaluate hypothetical reasoning.
- Evaluate the use of principles in argument.

Analogies

In the last chapter, you looked at flaws – patterns of reasoning that weaken the support given to a conclusion. In this chapter, you will learn to evaluate three patterns of reasoning that can provide strong support to a conclusion, but which are sometimes weak. These are:

- analogies

- hypothetical reasoning

- the use of principles in argument.

As you read in Chapter 8, **analogies** are a form of argument that use parallels between similar situations to persuade the audience to accept a conclusion. The analogy is a special form of comparison which suggests that the situations are significantly similar and work in the same way. So, if we accept a claim about one situation, we should accept the claim about the other situation.

KEY TERM

Analogy
A form of argument that uses parallels between similar situations to persuade the audience to accept a conclusion.

> **REMEMBER**
>
> When you identify an analogy, you need to identify:
>
> - precisely the situations being compared
> - the conclusion being supported by the analogy.

For example:

> It is unfair to keep teenagers in school. It deprives them of freedom, self-esteem and purpose in life. We may as well send them straight to prison.

- Is it unfair to keep teenagers in school?

Step 1: This analogy compares the restrictive situation of sending teenagers to prison with the restrictive situation of keeping them in school.

Step 2: This analogy is used to support the conclusion that it is unfair to keep teenagers in schools.

REMEMBER

Remember that analogies do not always state both situations clearly, or may leave the conclusion being supported unstated. It is important in your analysis to establish exactly what is being compared.

The analogy works by suggesting that these two situations are significantly similar and tries to persuade us that, because we wouldn't send teenagers to prison, we shouldn't keep them in the similar situation, school. Our next step is the evaluative question: 'How well does this analogy work?'

Evaluating analogy

When you evaluate an analogy, you are asking whether it works well. This means:

■ Is it a good comparison between the situations?

■ Does this comparison give strong support to the conclusion being drawn?

In order to answer these questions you need to identify the two situations and the conclusion being supported (see Steps 1 and 2 above) and work through the remaining steps.

Step 3: Consider significant similarities between the situations.

Step 4: Consider significant differences between the situations.

Step 5: Evaluate whether the differences outweigh the similarities.

Step 6: Decide whether the analogy helps support the conclusion.

Let's work through an evaluation of the analogy between keeping teenagers in school and sending them to prison.

Step 3: Significant similarities between keeping teenagers in school and sending them to prison.

Both situations are restrictive. The teenagers have to be in a certain place at a certain time, so they do not have the freedom to do what they want. As the argument states, both situations can reduce a teenager's self-esteem and purpose in life.

Step 4: Significant differences between keeping teenagers in school and sending them to prison.

Education is a benefit which can improve the rest of your life, whereas prison is a punishment for wrongdoing and often has a negative impact on the rest of your life.

School ends during the afternoon, allowing teenagers the freedom to do as they wish during the evening, whereas prison does not.

Step 5: Do the differences outweigh the similarities?

Yes. The differences are fundamental, especially the difference between education as a benefit and prison as a punishment. This means that the comparison between the situations is not very good.

Step 6: Does the analogy support the conclusion?

No. Because the differences between the two situations are fundamental and outweigh the apparent similarities, we cannot conclude that it is unfair to keep teenagers in school on the basis of a comparison between the restrictions of school and the restrictions of prison.

Evaluating analogy as counter-argument

Sometimes an analogy is used as a form of counter-argument to show that a conclusion would be silly and that we should therefore accept the opposite conclusion. The idea is the same – in both cases, the situations are held to be so similar that a conclusion that holds for one of them should also hold for the other. Let's work through an example that uses analogy as counter-argument.

> Many people would argue that boxing should be banned because participants may sustain serious injury. This is like saying we should ban motor sport because drivers may be hurt in a crash. This would clearly be ridiculous, so we shouldn't ban boxing either.

Step 1: Identify precisely the situations being compared.

The situation of boxing possibly leading to participants sustaining serious injury is compared with the situation of motor sports possibly leading to drivers being hurt in a crash.

Step 2: Identify the conclusion being supported by the analogy.

The analogy is used to counter the idea that boxing should be banned because of the possibility of injury to boxers. It is used to support the opposing conclusion that we should not ban boxing.

Step 3: Consider significant similarities between the situations.

> Fatal injuries are possible in both activities.
> Injuries happen quite often in both activities.
> Both boxing and motor racing have strict rules to ensure safety.
> Participants know that both sports can be dangerous.

Step 4: Consider significant differences between the situations.

> In boxing, the aim of the sport is to injure the opponent – a blow to the head causing unconsciousness or a dazed inability to stand up is a winning blow. However, in motor sport, the aim is to win a race or rally, and injury is an unfortunate side effect of unplanned crashes.

Step 5: Evaluate whether the differences outweigh the similarities.

Although we have listed four similarities and only one difference, the difference is a very important one. The difference in intention (hitting someone in the head vs winning a race) is probably so significant that it outweighs the similarities and seriously weakens the analogy.

Step 6: Decide whether the analogy helps to support the conclusion.

Because one significant difference makes this a weak analogy, it does not provide strong support for the conclusion. Our belief that banning motor sport would be ridiculous does not provide grounds for a belief that banning boxing would be similarly ridiculous.

Further problems

There is a further problem with this analogy. Let us suppose that boxing and motor racing were so similar that a conclusion drawn about motor racing could be applied to boxing. Would this analogy support the conclusion that we should not ban boxing?

The simple statement that banning motor racing would clearly be ridiculous does not provide any grounds for us to accept that. It is a just a statement of opinion. So even if this was a strong analogy, it would not support the conclusion that we should not ban boxing, because it has not supported the first conclusion, that we should not ban motor racing.

> ### REMEMBER   ❗
>
> Remember that an analogy is saying: A is to B as C is to D. In the exam, the analogies will often be in a specific pattern: A leads to B is like C leads to D. A (boxing) may lead to B (injury) is like C (motor sports) may lead to D (being hurt in a crash). You will need to make sure that you mention all the parts of the analogy.

How do I tell if a difference is significant?

When evaluating analogies, we put quite a lot of emphasis on *significant* similarity and *significant* difference. A significant similarity or difference is one that is important and affects whether the pattern of the two situations is the same or not. One of the key mistakes students make in exams is to mention differences that are not very important and do not affect whether the two situations work in the same way.

Let's look at the boxing and motor sports example. Working through the example, we said that the different intentions of these sports – hitting someone in the head vs winning a race – was a significant difference, because it makes a real difference to the situations. Let us consider another possible answer.

> Boxing happens between two people in a ring, whereas motor sports involve lots of drivers on a track.

This is a difference, but it is not relevant to the situation of the activity possibly leading to injury.

ACTIVITY 34

Evaluate the analogies in arguments A–E.

> **REMEMBER**
>
> Remember to use all six steps.
>
> *Step 1*: Identify precisely the situations being compared.
> *Step 2*: Identify the conclusion being supported by the analogy.
> *Step 3*: Consider significant similarities between the situations.
> *Step 4*: Consider significant differences between the situations.
> *Step 5*: Evaluate whether the differences outweigh the similarities.
> *Step 6*: Decide whether the analogy helps to support the conclusion.

A It has been suggested that darts should be an Olympic sport. This proposal should not be taken seriously. Darts involves no physical exertion at all. We may as well introduce competitive reading as an Olympic sport.

B We need greater research into GM crops before deciding whether to allow their use in Britain. However, the very process of research involves growing and eating them and evaluating how much damage they do. It is like setting off a nuclear bomb to see what happens. By the time we know what happens, it will be too late to undo the damage.

C Students have been using their mobile phones to video teachers losing it or other children being bullied. Head teachers should require students to check mobile phones into lockers before they go into class, and pick them up at the end of the day. This works perfectly well with rabid journalists at film screenings; it would work perfectly well with 14-year-olds. No one has the right to be perpetually contactable.

Natalie Haynes, The Times, 6 August 2007

D New road building can have a negative social impact. Feeding our addiction to cars (which everyone knows are bad for us) by building new roads must be wrong in the same way that it has been proven that giving alcohol to an alcoholic causes health problems.

E Because music accesses our deepest emotions, playing an instrument can also provide a valuable emotional outlet. People who are stressed, sad or excited can play through their emotions, turning them into something beautiful, rather than repressing their feelings or taking them out on friends and family. Depriving people of a musical outlet for their feelings would be as bad for their health as depriving them of medication to treat illness.

Hypothetical reasoning

In Unit 1 you learnt how to identify hypothetical reasoning in an argument as a pattern of reasoning that takes the form, 'If … then …'. In this unit we will consider how to evaluate this form of reasoning.

> **REMEMBER**
>
> A hypothetical claim is a claim in the form 'If … then …'.
>
> A hypothetical claim within an argument may be a reason or conclusion.
>
> Hypothetical claim indicator words and phrases include:
> *If, provided that, on condition that, given that … then …*
>
> Hypothetical reasoning looks at the consequences that might occur if something were the case.
>
> You may wish to have another look at Unit 1, Chapter 2, page 24 to remind yourself about hypothetical reasoning.

Evaluating hypothetical reasoning

Hypothetical reasoning suggests a condition = *if* X happens,
looks at the consequences = *then* Y will happen,
and uses this to support a conclusion.

When we evaluate hypothetical reasoning, we have to consider these questions.

■ Is the condition likely?

■ Do the consequences follow?

■ Does the reasoning support the conclusion?

Let's work through an example.

> If it rains, we will get wet. The children don't like getting wet, so we should stay at home.

Step 1: Is the condition likely?

'*If* it rains …'. It is certainly plausible that it might rain, especially if we are in the UK. Whether it is likely depends on the weather forecast, and perhaps on the view from the window.

> **REMEMBER**
>
> 'Plausible' means that something could happen, and is not far-fetched.

Step 2: Does the consequence follow from the condition?

'… *then* we will get wet.' It does follow that people outside in the rain without suitable protective clothing will get wet. However, we don't know what the plan was. Were these people planning a walk in the country or a trip to the covered shopping centre? Even in the rain it is unlikely that indoor shopping will make you very wet.

REMEMBER

'Follow' means to come as a logical consequence of.

Step 3: Does the hypothetical reasoning support the conclusion?

This hypothetical reasoning gives some support to the conclusion. The condition is plausible, the consequence does follow from the condition, so it is reasonable to use this hypothetical reasoning in an argument about what to do. If the weather forecast suggests that it is likely to rain, and if the planned activity involves being outdoors, then there is some support for the conclusion that we should stay at home.

This does not mean that the conclusion is fully supported. If the weather forecast suggests glorious sunshine for the next week, this reasoning would give us no grounds at all for staying at home today just in case of rain.

- Go out or stay at home?

The hypothetical reasoning is also only part of the argument. We might question whether the children not liking getting wet is enough reason not to take them for some healthy exercise, or we might suggest that the family should wear suitable protective clothing, or that a dry activity such as shopping or visiting the free local art gallery could be substituted for the proposed wet activity.

Plausible, real and slippery

Once you have evaluated how reasonable the hypothetical claim is, don't forget to check whether the condition *is* the case. For example:

> If I win the lottery I'll be able to buy a Maserati. I'll have a look in the showroom, and maybe go for a test drive.

It is plausible that I might win the lottery, assuming that I have bought a ticket. And the consequence that I would be able to buy an expensive car would follow from winning the lottery. But this hypothetical reasoning depends on an extremely unlikely condition (the odds of winning the lottery are about 1:14 million). So it would be rash to rush to the Maserati showroom.

TAKE IT FURTHER

It is possible to conduct thought experiments using hypothetical reasoning to try to support or limit principles or find the limits of acceptable behaviour. For example, if I knew my neighbour's baby was the next murderous dictator, it might be right for me to kill the baby to prevent its dreadful actions. So I can put limits on the principle that 'it is wrong to kill'. You may need to use this sort of reasoning in Section C of Unit 2 when you develop your own reasoning to support or challenge a principle, and in Unit 3. In everyday life, and for the purposes of evaluating hypothetical reasoning in Unit 2, we will always come back to the fundamental point that I *cannot* know that my neighbour's baby will be a murderous dictator, so I cannot work on the basis that it might be.

Much slippery slope reasoning comes from sloppy hypothetical reasoning such as the above example. Let's remind ourselves of the definition of a slippery slope flaw from Chapter 11.

REMEMBER

A slippery slope flaw reasons from one possibility, through a series of events that are not properly or logically linked, to an extreme consequence.

The possibility in a slippery slope flaw is often a hypothetical condition: 'If we do not limit the number of migrants entering the UK …', followed by a series of extreme consequences that do not logically follow from the condition: '… *then* the population will explode, the strain on housing and public services will be enormous and the welfare state system will collapse and there will be civil war.' In this case, each possible consequence is used as a condition for the next possible consequence.

ACTIVITY 35

Evaluate the hypothetical reasoning in arguments A–D.

A If you have unprotected sex, you will get a sexually transmitted infection and she will have a baby. So you should use a condom.

B If we stopped paying a licence fee, the BBC would either have to have adverts and become a commercial channel, or would cease to exist. Public service broadcasting is really important, and the BBC is part of our national identity. So we should support the licence fee.

C The British are extremely negative about their sports people. Tim Henman made four Wimbledon semi-finals in a five-year span, yet we regard him as a failure because he didn't win. In one week in 2007, the English rugby team came second in the World Cup, narrowly missing being the first team ever to win twice in a row, Lewis Hamilton missed being World Champion by one point in his first ever season in Formula 1 racing, and the English football team failed to qualify for the World Cup quarter finals. Newspapers talked of 'a hat trick of defeat'. Yet surely, only the poor performance of the football team was a defeat. Coming second in the world is quite a success. If we want talented British youngsters to work hard to excel in sport, we should praise their successes rather than slamming everything except absolute victory. We don't want to put them off, especially with the 2012 Olympics being held in London. So we should be more positive about sporting achievements.

D Asteroid 2004 MN4 is predicted to come within 20,000 miles of earth and may even collide with us on Friday 13 April 2029. If the lump of rock and metal, which is 380m across, hits us, it would have an impact equivalent to 50 1-megaton hydrogen bombs exploding simultaneously. It could devastate an area the size of a large American state and cause tsunamis around the world. We must act now to prevent this collision. If we fire missiles at the asteroid we might deflect its orbit; if we cover it with aluminium foil, the sun will thrust it into a different orbit. If we develop space tugs, these could either tug the asteroid away from us, or bring it into orbit around Earth as a metal rich second moon. We should start preparing space tug development.

- We should praise the successes of talented young people.

Principles

In Chapter 8 you learnt how to identify principles. Now we will consider how to evaluate the use of principles in an argument.

REMEMBER !

A principle is a general, rule-like statement that applies beyond the immediate circumstances and acts as a guide to action.

A principle can be a reason, intermediate or main conclusion in an argument.

Evaluating the use of principles in argument

In order to evaluate the use of a principle in an argument you will need to consider the following questions.

- ■ How generally does this principle apply?
  - – Does the principle apply to the situation in question?
  - – In what other situations does the principle apply?
  - – Are there any situations in which the principle doesn't apply?
- ■ Does this principle support the author's conclusion?

Let's look at an example.

> I am in a sweetshop and there is no one watching me. I could easily take some sweets. But we should not steal, so I should buy some when the shopkeeper comes back.

In this argument, the principle, 'we should not steal', is used as a reason in an argument to support the conclusion that, 'I should buy some when the shopkeeper comes back'. It is clearly a guide to action. It may be appealing to get something we want without paying, but the principle guides our action towards socially acceptable behaviour.

- ▪ It would be wrong to steal sweets.

Step 1: How generally does the principle apply?

The principle that 'we should not steal' clearly does apply to the situation of being in a sweetshop. It is a very general principle that applies in almost all situations. For example, taking your friend's mobile, or even using it to make an hour-long call to Australia without asking, would be stealing, and therefore something we should not do.

- It would be wrong to steal your friend's mobile!

Are there any situations in which the principle that 'we should not steal' does not apply? We might wonder whether it is OK to steal from people or organisations which are so rich that they wouldn't notice. Well, it's still stealing, and apart from being against the law, it still feels wrong to gain things we want by stealing them. It seems unfair for someone else to pay for things we want.

What about if they are rich and won't notice and my family will die if I don't steal food for them? This is a different situation from stealing someone's car because you are bored and want some excitement. It is certainly unfair that some people have so much while others have so little. But this does not necessarily make it acceptable to steal from them. You may like to discuss this in class.

So, there may be exceptions to the principle that we shouldn't steal. But that doesn't mean that we have to abandon the principle. It is a useful principle and it applies in most situations.

Step 2: Does the principle support the author's conclusion?

The principle that we should not steal, combined with the assumption that I want some sweets, does give support to the conclusion that I should buy some sweets later (rather than stealing them now).

Evaluating more complex examples of principles

It was fairly easy to decide that the principle 'we should not steal' was very general and applied in almost all situations, including being unattended in a sweetshop. However, there are principles which seem to be very general, but need to be carefully restricted. Let's look at an example.

> Killing is wrong. You are just about to kill Emmi. You must stop.

'Killing is wrong' is a very general principle, and it seems to be a good guide to action. In the argument above, the general principle that killing is wrong is used to support the conclusion that you should stop before you kill Emmi. The principle seems to apply in this situation. But it is actually not clear that it does. Let's consider some situations in which the principle would not necessarily apply as clearly as it seems on first sight.

Emmi is a carrot plant.

This may seem extreme – after all, most of us would not name our vegetables. But it raises an interesting question that would limit the principle that 'killing is wrong'. Most of us would accept that killing a vegetable plant in order to eat its roots is not wrong. We might need to rephrase the principle, saying that, 'killing is wrong except for killing plants'.

Emmi is a cow.

Do we want the general principle to apply in this situation if Emmi is a cow? If we do, the consequence would be that everyone should become a vegetarian. People disagree on this matter, so it becomes important to be able to justify your opinion with argument. If you do not want the principle to apply if Emmi is a cow, we might try to refine the principle to 'killing humans is wrong'.

- Principles don't always apply to every situation.

TAKE IT FURTHER

When you are developing your own arguments in Section C of the exam, you may be asked to write an argument to support or challenge a general principle. This will be covered in Chapter 15 of this book.

Emmi is a convicted serial child murderer and you are the executioner.

Is it wrong for an executioner to kill a convicted, serious criminal? Do we want this to be an exception to the general principle that killing is wrong? This is an open question and there is considerable debate about this issue. If we do want this to be an exception, we would have to limit the principle as follows: 'It is wrong to kill innocent humans.'

> **PAUSE FOR THOUGHT**
>
> Do your emotions sway your thoughts about when killing is wrong? Should they? Are principles there to give us rules that stop us acting in accordance with strong emotions? Does it make any difference in any of these situations that Emmi is a woman?

Emmi is an enemy soldier in a battle.

Many of us would accept that killing enemy soldiers in battle is necessary, even if we don't like it. However, most soldiers on the other side are probably just normal, innocent human beings like us. So we would have to refine the principle again: 'It is wrong to kill innocent humans except in war.'

Emmi is just about to kill you.

Again, we would normally accept that killing someone else as a last resort in self-defence was OK, even if it is not desirable. And this would mean another restriction to our general principle: 'It is wrong to kill innocent humans except in war or in self-defence.'

Emmi has just dumped you.

This seems to be a clear example of a situation in which the general principle, that killing is wrong, does apply. In British society we agree that it is wrong to kill someone just because they have ended a relationship with you. This is not the case around the world, though. Revenge killings do happen and are sometimes thought to be acceptable.

> **PAUSE FOR THOUGHT**
>
> Are there any situations in which revenge killing might be acceptable?
>
> Does it make any difference whether a society agrees that something is wrong? Or is killing someone wrong whatever we think about it? We will deal with many more questions like this in Unit 3.

Emmi is your gran.

It would be particularly wrong to kill your gran, wouldn't it? Older members of the family should be respected, not killed. This seems to be another situation in which it is clear that the general principle that killing is wrong does apply. However, let's consider a complication of this situation.

Emmi is your gran and she has an advanced, terminal and painful illness and she has asked you to provide her with the means to give her a peaceful end.

We might want to accept that euthanasia is another exception to the general principle that 'killing is wrong' and revise the principle to 'killing innocent humans is wrong except in war, self-defence or in the case of euthanasia'. We would, however, have to be careful. The line between mercy killing and murder is very, very fine.

PAUSE FOR THOUGHT

If you were in government, how would you ensure that euthanasia was not used as a cover for murdering (rich) elderly relatives?

Does the principle support the author's conclusion?

So we can see that our answer to the question 'Does the principle support the author's conclusion?' will depend on exactly who or what Emmi is. In some of these cases, the principle that it is wrong to kill would support the conclusion that you should stop before you kill her. In others, we would feel that the principle should be limited or restricted and that it would not support the conclusion that we should stop before we kill Emmi.

ACTIVITY **36**

Work in groups. Think of situations in which the following principles apply, and situations in which they do not apply.

A   People shouldn't be given treatment on the NHS for self-inflicted injuries.

B   People who break the law should not be given treatment on the NHS.

C   We should provide aid to those who need it.

D   People who do not contribute to society should not benefit from it.

E   Everyone has a right to education.

ACTIVITY 37

Evaluate the use of principles in the following arguments.

A Our lifestyle is not sustainable. We are destroying the world with our emissions, our rubbish and our exploitation of natural resources. We should put the future of the world before our selfish desires. So we should moderate our lifestyle.

B Every year thousands of people inflict damage on themselves. It is not fair that genuinely ill people have to wait for treatment, so people who cause their own problems should not be treated in hospital.

C We absolutely must attend the meeting tonight to protest about the proposal to build 345 new homes on the common. Common land is really important as wide open space in city centres. It is our only contact with nature, and provides peace, greenery and somewhere for children to play. We should protect our common land.

- African nations need to develop their own capacity in science, engineering, medicine and technology.

ACTIVITY 38

Read the passage and then answer the questions that follow it.

1 African nations need to provide their own solutions to African problems. So Africa needs help to develop its own capacity in science, engineering, medicine and technology. Most research is carried out in developed countries and focuses on their own interests. Just 10% of the global budget for health research is spent on the diseases that affect 90% of the world's population. If Africa had its own science and technology base, this balance would be redressed.

2 If Africa can develop centres of excellence in science and technology, it will be able to close the scientific gap with the rest of the world. It will be able to provide a skills base right across the educational system. From this will come the capacity to provide, for example, clean water and hygienic living conditions. Basic services like this are desperately needed. We have a duty to provide aid which really aids.

3 We do not encourage mature, independent adults by continuing to spoon feed them beyond babyhood. Neither will we encourage the poorest countries in the world to develop to maturity unless we allow them access to the spoon. Aid for developing nations must focus on the development of science and technology.

a) **'If Africa had its own science and technology base, this balance would be redressed.' How effectively does this reasoning support the conclusion that, 'Aid for developing nations must focus on the development of science and technology'?**

b) **Evaluate the hypothetical reasoning in paragraph 2.**

c) **To what extent does the principle in paragraph 2 support the conclusion that, 'Aid for developing nations must focus on the development of science and technology'?**

d) **Identify the situations being compared in the analogy in paragraph 3.**

e) **How effectively does this analogy support the conclusion that, 'Aid for developing nations must focus on the development of science and technology'?**

Summary

You should now be able to:

■ evaluate analogies

■ evaluate hypothetical reasoning

■ evaluate the use of principles in argument.

Section 5   Developing Your Own Argument
Basic reasoning skills

13

Learning objectives

● Be able to give a simple explanation or reason for why something might have happened.

● Be able to give an explanation that would fit in with the author's argument.

● Be able to suggest an alternative explanation to that presented by the author in the passage.

● Write a developed explanation.

● Know how to include evidence and examples to support your explanation.

● Be able to give a principle that would support the author's argument.

Developing your skills

So far, Unit 2 has been concerned with looking at other people's arguments and developing the strategies needed to analyse and evaluate them. We will now change the focus to help you to develop your own writing skills in terms of Critical Thinking. A significant part of this is developing your own arguments. But as well as writing a structured, developed argument (covered in the next chapter) your basic reasoning skills will be tested.

As part of developing your own Critical Thinking skills, you will be asked to give reasons and explanations. Sometimes you will be asked to give simple suggestions, other than those that the author may have given, as an explanation in the passage for a certain course of events. You may be asked to offer a simple explanation or give alternative reasons to what the author has written. Other times you will be asked to develop this further and include examples and evidence to support your own explanation. You might also be asked to suggest a general principle that supports what the author is arguing.

Giving reasons and simple explanations

In both Units 1 (Chapter 4) and 2 (Chapter 7) you were asked to identify various elements of argument (e.g. reason, conclusion) that an author has used in an argument. To help us start to think about developing our own argument, we are going to look at giving reasons and offering simple explanations that would support a claim.

REMEMBER

An explanation tells how or why something happens but does not persuade listeners or readers to agree with anything.

Let's try to think of a reason or simple explanation for why something might be the case or might have happened by looking at the example below.

> In the last election 61% of people who were eligible chose to vote. This is only just over half of the population so the government doesn't really represent everyone.

Here, we need to think of reasons why nearly 40% of the population chose not to vote in the last election, even though they were eligible. You are not being asked for the main reason or the most likely, just to suggest possible explanations.

There will be many reasons, both political and practical, why people chose not to vote, as the examples overleaf show.

- Does the government really represent everyone?

Reasons to do with politics.

■ They didn't like any of the candidates standing in their area.

■ They don't think their vote will make a difference, as another party to the one they support won by a landslide last time.

■ There is no point in voting as they don't think politicians listen to their constituents.

Practical reasons.

■ They forgot to go to the polling station.

■ They lost their postal vote.

■ They ended up having to do overtime at work and so couldn't get to the polling station before it shut.

PAUSE FOR THOUGHT

How many other reasons can you think of?

As you can see from the example, there isn't one answer to these type of questions. Anything that is reasonable and could explain what has happened will be accepted.

ACTIVITY 39

Read the following claims. For each give two possible explanations for why this might be the case.

A Families rarely sit down together at the table and eat a meal together.

B More students are choosing to go to university in their home town rather than a university further away.

C There has been an increase in the number of European holidays British people take each year.

Offering alternative explanations

When you looked at flaws of causation in Chapter 11, you realised that causality is often complex. It is rare that there is a clear connection between one thing and another. Often there are many reasons for why something has happened. In Critical Thinking passages authors will often give one reason or explanation for why they think something is the case, when in actual fact there may be many other possibilities for what has occurred.

Let's look at an example.

> In recent years there has been a huge increase in the number of people using the Internet to do their weekly grocery shop. This is because many people found the whole experience of going to the supermarket and pushing a trolley up and down aisles packed with other shoppers far too stressful.

In this example the author is supporting the claim that 'there has been a huge increase in the number of people using the Internet to do their weekly grocery shop' with an explanation that many people find shopping at a supermarket a 'far too stressful' experience.

This may well be one explanation for why there has been an increase in the number of people ordering their groceries over the Internet rather than going to the supermarket, but there could be many other possible explanations as well, including:

- people have greater access to the Internet
- supermarket websites have become more user friendly
- the supermarkets offer discounts for shopping online
- there is a greater variety of products offered online than in the local supermarket
- people like having their groceries delivered to the front door.

- Lots of people do their weekly grocery shop via the Internet.

PAUSE FOR THOUGHT

What other explanations can you think of?

You can see from the examples (and from the ideas you yourselves came up with) that there are many alternative explanations for this increase. It is quite likely the increase is down to a combination of some or all of these suggestions, but this doesn't matter. You are being asked to suggest possible alternative explanations, not make a judgement about which you think is the most likely. So long as what you write in response to these questions in the exam is relevant and reasonable you will get credit.

For example, you would still get credit for writing 'the closest supermarket has closed down and it is too far to walk to the next nearest' as it is relevant, even though it is a quite specific example and probably wouldn't be the main contributing factor to a national increase in online supermarket shopping. Whereas anything concerned with the stressful nature of shopping – for example, supermarkets being too busy – is too close to the explanation that the author gives to gain credit.

ACTIVITY 40

Read the following and suggest alternative explanations for what is claimed in each.

A Most electronic stores no longer sell VHS video recorders. This is because it is very difficult to buy films on media other than DVD.

B Despite Nottingham having an excellent public transport system with regular bus services and an efficient tram service, many people still prefer to drive into the city. This is because at the end of the day we prefer the privacy of our own car to sharing transport with others.

Let's look at the type of question that you might come across in the exam.

Recently, 16,000 university students were interviewed and only one-third expected to get, or look for, a graduate-level job after university. Also 26% of graduates go on to take further qualifications. This suggests that getting a degree does not lead to better employment prospects.

a) Give one explanation that would support the claim that getting a degree does not lead to better employment prospects.

b) Give two other possible explanations for the increase of students going on to take further qualifications.

OCR, January 2006

- In a recent survey only one third of students expected to get or look for a graduate-level job when they left university.

What we have on page 217 is an example of the two types of questions you might come across.

- Giving an explanation that would fit in with the author's argument.

- Giving alternative explanations to those the author presents in the passage.

First, let's analyse the passage. The author uses two pieces of evidence to support the claim that 'getting a degree does not lead to better employment prospects'.

- Only one-third of 16,000 university students interviewed expected to get, or look for, a graduate-level job after university.

- 26% of graduates go on to take further qualifications.

Let's look in more detail at how you might answer these questions.

Giving an explanation that would fit in with the author's argument

Question a) asks you to consider why the author might think that there are an increasing number of students staying on at university to study for additional qualifications. Your answer to this part needs to be consistent with the author's reasoning that 'getting a degree does not lead to better employment prospects', so your response should be about the possible benefits of gaining further qualifications, or suggestions of why this might be of benefit to getting a better job.

Possible answers could include:

- the author seems to think that the reason for the increase is that students know (or think) that they are not able to get a job when they graduate from university

- having a postgraduate degree would give them a competitive advantage over other job seekers, who only have a first degree

- having a postgraduate degree means that they are more likely to get a job with a higher income.

Giving alternative explanations to those the author presents in the passage

Now let's look at part b). Give two other possible explanations for this increase.

We have already suggested explanations that fit in with the author's argument, and now we need to think of other reasonable suggestions why there may have been an increase in graduates staying on at university to take additional qualifications, other than the fact that it may lead to better job prospects.

They are many possible answers, including:

- the funding for postgraduate courses has increased so more people are able to take these courses

- there are more postgraduate courses on offer

- more people are going to university and this has had a knock-on effect of more people doing postgraduate courses.

ACTIVITY 41

- More people are prepared to pay higher prices for organic food.

Read the following passage, then answer the questions below.

Despite higher prices there has been a year-on-year increase in the sale of organic food. There have been several health scares in recent years caused by intensive farming methods. People are prepared to pay higher prices as organic food is produced using strict guidelines, which means that organic vegetables do not contain high residues of damaging pesticide, and organic meat is unlikely to be affected by outbreaks of diseases such as BSE.

a) **Give one explanation that would support the claim that the increased sales of organic food is a result of people's concern about food scares, which may be caused by intensive farming methods.**

b) **Give two other possible explanations for the increase in the sales of organic food.**

Writing a developed explanation

As well as being asked to give simple explanations, you may be asked to give a more detailed explanation for something. This is not the same as writing an argument, and you are not being asked to give reasons in support of a conclusion. Instead, what you should be seeking to do is to give a developed explanation that is supported by examples and/or evidence.

Often people base an argument on the similarities between two situations, saying that as something is the case in one situation, it should be the case in the other.

Let us look at the following example.

> In 2005 the licensing laws were changed to allow all-day drinking in pubs and bars.
>
> In some countries in mainland Europe there have been extended drinking hours for many years and they do not have the problems with 'binge drinking' and disorder at closing time that there are in England. It was argued that the situation was sufficiently similar in England and countries like France for what had worked in Italy to work in England.

However, many people feel that the change has not led to a decrease in binge drinking or a reduction in drink-related violence in town centres. They would argue that there are too many differences between the two countries for us to draw conclusions about the UK based on what had worked in France. A developed explanation supporting this view might read as follows.

> Café culture is well established in these countries. People in France appear to have a more relaxed attitude towards drinking alcohol. They drink differently, seated at a table, having a meal while talking to friends, whereas many people in England go out to the pub with the aim of getting drunk.

PAUSE FOR THOUGHT

What other similarities and differences between England and other European countries relevant to the extension of licensing hours can you think of?

In the exam, you will be asked to consider how similar or different two situations are and whether we can make a judgement that they are sufficiently alike for us to draw conclusions about one based on the other.

It doesn't matter whether you decide that they are similar or not. You are being asked to justify your decision by explaining your choice and supporting this with relevant examples and/or evidence.

> When the Olympics was hosted in Sydney in 2000, it was a huge success. Based on this example, decide whether you think that the Olympics in London in 2012 will be equally successful.

We could decide that there are sufficient similarities between the Sydney and London Olympics and how they are being organised to say that the London Olympics will be a success, and so suggest a developed explanation, such as the following.

- The investment in the public transport system in Sydney continues to have benefits for the local residents; this could be the same case for London.

- The building of the stadium provided Sydney with an excellent sports centre, which can be used to host major sporting events after the Olympics.

- The Sydney Olympics regenerated a site and the London Olympics could lead to the urban regeneration of the East End of London.

Alternatively, we could decide that there are too many differences between the two situations for us to draw conclusions about London based on what happened in Sydney.

We could give a developed explanation like one of the following.

- Australia is more supportive of sport as a nation so more people will want the Olympics to be a success and get behind it.

- The Australian government puts more funding into sport than the UK.

- Australia has a better track record of completing large building projects on time.

- Much of the public transport system was already in place before the Olympic stadium was built.

- The 2000 Sydney Olympics stadium.

Including evidence and examples to support your explanation

When you are asked to give a developed reason, you may need to support what you have written with examples and/or evidence. In the OCR AS Unit 2 exam, questions will be quite broad, and will not require specialist knowledge, or knowledge of specific facts such as which Rugby competition was held in which former Olympics stadium. In the exam you will be tested on your understanding of what sort of examples might support or illustrate a reason. Let's take one developed reason supporting the statement and one opposing and offer some evidence and examples.

> The building of the stadium provided Sydney with an excellent sports centre which can be used to host major sporting events after the Olympics.

This could be supported by following examples.

- The stadium (now known as the Telstra Dome) was used for the 2003 Rugby World Cup Final.

- The Olympic Stadium in the UK is planned to be used as the home ground for one of the London Football Clubs.

- It could also be used as part of a bid to host future major sporting events, e.g. Champions League Final or the Football World Cup.

> Australia is more supportive of sport as a nation so more people will want the Olympics to be a success and get behind it.

This could be supported by the following evidence.

- A higher percentage of Australians regularly attend sports matches than in the UK.

- A higher percentage of Australians play sport on a regular basis than in the UK.

- When Australia is involved in international sporting competitions a higher percentage of Australians follow their national team's performance and watch the event.

PAUSE FOR THOUGHT

In pairs, suggest evidence and examples that could be used to support the other developed reasons suggested above.

ACTIVITY

Read the passage below, then answer the questions that follow.

It may be possible to reduce the amount of traffic in the future. Congestion charging in London, where motorists have to pay to drive into the centre of London at peak times, has reduced the amount of congestion at the busiest times by 18%. We should introduce a national road charging scheme as this would reduce congestion across the country by a similar amount.

a) **Based on the evidence of the successful charging scheme in London, which has reduced congestion, decide whether a national road-charging scheme would OR would not reduce congestion.**

b) **Explain your decision by giving a developed reason. You can include relevant examples or evidence to support your answer.**

Adapted from OCR Unit 2, June 2007

EXAM TIP ●

If the question refers to a specific example or piece of evidence, make sure you refer to it in your answer.

REMEMBER ───────────

Remember that you are not being asked to write an argument with reasons supporting a conclusion, *but to give* a developed explanation with examples and/or evidence in support.

Give a principle that would support the author's argument

In Chapter 8 you learnt how to identify principles that the author had used as part of their argument. In questions on longer passages you might also be asked to suggest principles that, while not used by the author, could be used to support the author's argument.

REMEMBER ───────────

A principle is a general, rule-like statement which applies beyond the immediate circumstances and acts as a guide to action. A principle can act as a reason, intermediate conclusion, assumption or conclusion in an argument.

PAUSE FOR THOUGHT ───────────

Can you think of some general principles?

A general principle is a moral guideline which has wider relevance. It isn't just relevant to the situation that the author is writing about but can be applied to many, if not every, situation. You will remember that many principles are moral guidelines concerned with right and wrong – e.g. 'It is wrong to murder'; 'You should help people less fortunate than yourself' – and are often phrased as recommendations: 'The government should pass laws to prevent us from harming ourselves.'

Let's look at an example. Read the passage below.

> The NHS does not have an infinite source of funding. The government allocates money to NHS trusts and the trust managers have to decide how best to spend the money. There are many thousands of people waiting for operations and medication who have become ill through no fault of their own. People who take illegal drugs shouldn't be given NHS treatment.

As with any passage, the first thing you should do is analyse it and identify the argument components.

EXAM TIP

It is a good idea to phrase general principles as 'we should...', 'the government should ...'. This will remind you of their general nature, that they apply to many situations not just the context of the passage you are evaluating.

	The NHS does not have an infinite source of funding.
R1	The government allocates money to NHS trusts ...
R2	... the trust managers have to decide how best to spend the money.
R3	There are many thousands of people waiting for operations and medication who have become ill through no fault of their own.
C	People who take illegal drugs shouldn't be given NHS treatment.

The conclusion, 'People who take illegal drugs shouldn't be given NHS treatment', could be supported by the following general principles.

■ People shouldn't be given free treatment for self-inflicted problems.

■ People who break the law shouldn't be given free treatment.

■ The government shouldn't help people who break the law.

You might also want to say that there is general principle working as an assumption in this passage, that 'NHS trusts should allocate resources to ensure that the greatest number of people can be treated'.

In fact this idea – 'that we should do whatever will lead to the greatest good for the greatest number of people' – often called the principle of utility (which you will learn more about in Unit 3 if you continue Critical Thinking onto A2 Level), is a very common general principle. It is often used to decide spending or allocation of resources for many and different contexts, not just government funding, but whether your school or college decides to refurbish the sixth-form common room or invest in a new computer suite for use by the whole school. The decision will often be made on the basis of what is going to provide the most benefit for the greatest number of students.

ACTIVITY

a) **Read statements A and B and suggest a general principle that, if accepted, would support each claim.**

A Parents who earn more than £60,000 a year shouldn't receive child benefit.

B It was wrong for the police to plant evidence on the Great Train Robbers.

b) **Read the following passage and suggest a general principle, not used by the author, that would support the author's argument.**

REMEMBER

Analyse the argument first.

C With the new Eurostar station open at St Pancras in London, reaching parts of Europe by train is now much easier from parts of England than before. You don't have to take the tube across London. The check-in time for flying to Europe is longer than for travelling by train. Travelling by train will have less of an impact on the environment. I think it is better to take the train from Birmingham to Paris rather than to fly.

▪ The new Eurostar station at St Pancras, London.

Summary

You should now be able to:

◾ give a simple explanation or reason for why something has happened

◾ offer an explanation that is consistent with the author's reasoning in the passage

◾ suggest alternative explanations for why something might have happened

◾ write an explanation, giving a developed reason, why something might be the case

◾ know how to include evidence and examples to support your explanation

◾ give a principle that would support the author's argument.

Learning objectives

- Appreciate that writing your own arguments is just as important as criticising others.
- Understand the importance of clearly stating the conclusion of your argument.
- Be able to include several reasons to support your chosen conclusion.
- Be able to include an intermediate conclusion as part of writing a more developed argument.
- Be able to work to some common argument structures.
- Know how to include evidence and examples in your arguments.
- Know how to use counter-arguments and assertions in your own arguments.

The process of writing your own arguments

> ## PAUSE FOR THOUGHT
>
> Before we start, from what you have learnt in Critical Thinking so far, what do you think makes a good, persuasive argument? Make a list of what you as a class decide then come back to the list at the end of this chapter and compare it with what you have learnt.

- A speaker at Hyde Park Speakers' corner.

Developing your own arguments is an important Critical Thinking skill. A key point to remember is that you cannot 'win' an argument by merely criticising others. You also have to be able to put forward your own case in a reasoned and disciplined way.

The following sections will outline strategies that you can use to make sure your arguments are both persuasive and well-structured.

Clearly stating the conclusion

The first step in forming your own argument is being clear about the conclusion that you are heading for. That may sound obvious, but you might be surprised by the number of students who forget to write down their conclusion. Make sure that your own arguments always contain a clearly stated conclusion. You may find it helpful if you put the conclusion either first or last. Look at the two examples on the next page.

Example 1 (conclusion first)

C	Cats are excellent pets.
R1	They are affectionate.
R2	They are full of fun.
R3	They do not take too much looking after.

Example 2 (conclusion last)

R1	Cats are affectionate.
R2	They are full of fun.
R3	They do not take too much looking after.
C	Therefore, cats are excellent pets.

It is not wrong to put the conclusion in other places in your argument, but it is often clearer if it is at the beginning or end. Many students find it easiest to put the conclusion at the end of their arguments.

Other students prefer to write the conclusion as the first sentence of their argument. Having the conclusion clearly stated at the beginning means that you can refer back and make sure that what you are writing remains relevant. It also means that you are less likely to forget the conclusion if you run out of time.

Keeping a close link between reasons and conclusions

The second step in forming your own argument is to think of some reasons that support the conclusion. Strong, persuasive arguments contain reasons that give good support to the conclusion. In Unit 1, Chapter 4, you learnt the importance of reasons being relevant and giving strong support to a conclusion. You need to apply this when you write your own arguments. To make sure that you write a strong argument there needs to be a close link between the reasons and the conclusion. Thinking of reasons that give good support to the conclusion is vital to forming a strong argument.

We can illustrate this by showing some arguments where the reasons do give strong support to the conclusion and others where the reasons do not support the conclusion so well. Imagine that you are trying to argue that digital cameras are better than conventional film cameras.

Digital cameras are smaller than film cameras. Therefore digital cameras are better.

As it stands, the reason gives very little support to the conclusion, because size may or may not be related to the issue of whether the digital camera is better. If we accept the idea that the size of the camera is related to the relative merits of the two cameras, we need to do something with the argument to show this. So we can improve the argument by including a second reason.

EXAM TIPS

Make sure that you always write down the conclusion of your argument. You are more likely to get a better mark if you have two reasons and a conclusion, than two reasons and an example, providing what you have written is relevant, of course!

Make sure that the reasons you give are closely linked to the conclusion.

- Are digital cameras better than film cameras?

> Digital cameras are smaller than film cameras. Size is a key factor in choosing a camera. Therefore digital cameras are better.

This is better than our first version, but it is still not very persuasive as it seems unlikely that size *alone* would make a digital camera *better*, given the many things that cameras do.

We can make a closer link between the reason and the conclusion by making sure that the argument addresses the important things that cameras do. After all, if a camera is better, it must be *better* at something related to the things that cameras do. For instance:

> Taking pictures with a digital camera is easier than with a film camera. The picture quality of digital cameras is equal to that of film cameras. Therefore digital cameras are better.

The argument establishes that digital cameras are easier to use *and* that the picture quality is similar. Both these reasons support the conclusion independently, but neither supports it fully on its own. Taken together they give us good reason to believe that digital cameras are, in fact, better than film cameras.

You will not be asked to identify whether reasons are working jointly or independently in Unit 2. This is a skill you will learn in Unit 4, but it is helpful to think of how reasons support the conclusion when developing your own arguments. When two reasons support a conclusion jointly, both are needed to give the conclusion support, and when two reasons support a conclusion independently, either on its own would support the conclusion. Often two reasons working independently can give stronger support to the conclusion than two reasons acting jointly.

Including a third reason about digital cameras – that they are more flexible to use – would give even more support to our conclusion.

PAUSE FOR THOUGHT

Can you think of other reasons that make digital cameras better than film cameras?

EXAM TIP

Your argument should have two reasons that support an intermediate conclusion and at least one further reason that supports the main conclusion in a different way.

Include several reasons in your argument

The arguments that we have used demonstrate that a strong, coherent argument often has several reasons to support the conclusion. When you are writing an argument, you will need to think of several reasons that develop your idea and give good support to your conclusion. In the exam, you will specifically be asked to write arguments that contain several reasons. There is no target number, but there must be at *least* three to make a strong argument.

ACTIVITY **44**

Write at least three reasons that would support each of the following conclusions.

A You should buy me a drink.

B You should give me a pay rise.

C My mobile phone is one of the best on the market.

D Teaching is a very good career.

■ Teaching is a good career.

Strong and weak conclusions

Another way that a close link can be made between reasons and a conclusion is to make the conclusion 'weaker'. By this we mean make it a little less specific or less definite. Consider the following two versions.

> **Version 1** Everyone wanting to buy a new car should buy an estate car rather than a hatchback.
>
> **Version 2** Everyone wanting to buy a new car should consider the advantages that estate cars have over hatchbacks.

The first version is a very **strong conclusion** because the outcome it suggests is very specific and would apply in all situations. We would have a very hard job to successfully argue that *everyone* should buy an estate car. However, we are more likely to be successful in arguing that everyone should at least consider the advantages of an estate car, without suggesting that they go on to buy one. The second conclusion is therefore a **weaker conclusion**, as it suggests a less tightly defined outcome.

We will finish this section by considering a very poor argument in which the conclusion is not supported by the reasons because it is far too strong.

> **R**   Drinking too much coffee may lead to headaches.
> **R**   Drinking too much coffee may lead to disturbed sleep.
> **R**   You can become addicted to caffeine.
> **C**   Coffee should be banned.

The three reasons given suggest that there are problems with drinking coffee, which might lead us to think that we need to take some action. The conclusion given goes much further than that and suggests the most extreme action. The conclusion is far too strong. It would be better to give a *weaker* conclusion in order to make a *stronger* argument. Concluding that we should cut down our intake of coffee would be a much more reasonable conclusion from the reasons given.

KEY TERMS

Strong conclusion ●
A conclusion that is very specific and tightly defined.

Weak conclusion ●
A conclusion that is not so specific or tightly defined.

▪ Should coffee be banned?

ACTIVITY 45

Explain whether the following are strong or weak conclusions.

A   Clam shell mobile phones are much better than other types of phone.

B   Moving to a bungalow might have advantages for an elderly person.

C   Reducing the amount of fat in our diet is part of a healthy approach to eating.

D   Reducing the amount of fat in our diet prevents heart disease.

PAUSE FOR THOUGHT

Do you think it would be easier to write a convincing argument to support a strong or a weak conclusion?

Structured arguments

The previous section showed us that we need to think of several reasons to make an argument persuasive. We now need to consider how to structure the argument to ensure that various parts of that argument work well together.

Writing a long list of reasons will certainly make an argument, but it is generally considered to be a very simple way of arguing.

> Smoking causes lung cancer. Smoking creates unpleasant smells. Smoking causes heart disease. Smoking creates a nuisance for non-smokers. Smoking is very expensive. Therefore you should stop smoking.

It is not that this approach is wrong, but it does not resemble the more sophisticated and persuasive arguments that we are trying to write. The following sections will show you how to write a more developed and well-structured argument.

Including an intermediate conclusion

The first step in writing a well-structured argument is to make sure that it contains an intermediate conclusion, drawn along the way to the main conclusion. Including an intermediate conclusion is a key skill in writing arguments. We can re-work the previous argument about the dangers of smoking, beginning as follows.

R	Smoking causes lung cancer.
R	Smoking causes heart disease.
IC	Therefore, smoking is likely to lead to premature death.

This first part of the argument ends with the intermediate conclusion.

> **REMEMBER**
>
> An intermediate conclusion is a conclusion that is drawn on the way to the main conclusion. It is supported by reasons and then acts as a reason for the main conclusion.

The great thing about establishing an intermediate conclusion is that it then gives you many more choices about how to continue the argument – it allows you to go on to *develop* your argument. So far we have established that the dangers of smoking are likely to lead to a premature death. Most of us would consider this a bad thing. We might continue the argument as follows.

- Smoking can lead to a premature death.

> **R1** Smoking causes lung cancer.
> **R2** Smoking causes heart disease.
> **IC** Therefore, smoking is likely to lead to premature death.
> **R3** Everybody wants to live longer.
> **C** Therefore, you should give up smoking.

This is not perfect, but we now have a structured argument that we can work with. The structure is:

R1 and R2 support IC.

IC and R3 support C.

This is a very useful structure to use as a starting point for writing your own arguments. It is a relatively simple structure that contains all the vital elements. It includes reasons acting independently and jointly to support the conclusion. It can be used as a base from which to form more complex, sophisticated arguments.

Here is another argument about digital cameras that fits this structure.

> **R1** Digital cameras do not require different types of film for different lighting conditions.
> **R2** Pictures that are no longer wanted can be easily deleted from a digital camera and do not have to be developed.
> **IC** Therefore, digital cameras are more practical to use.
> **R3** They are also smaller than film cameras.
> **C** Therefore, digital cameras are better.

It is important to note that this is a suggested argument structure. It is not the only one nor the best one. However, it is useful to have a simple structure in mind when beginning to practise the skill of writing your own arguments.

ACTIVITY

Write structured arguments, following the above pattern, for these conclusions.

A Sixth-form students should have better facilities in school.

B We should consider banning the sport of fishing.

C Newly qualified drivers should not be allowed to drive on motorways.

D Buying designer clothes is a waste of money.

Including examples and evidence in a structured argument

The other great advantage of fitting your argument into a structure is that it is then much easier to include the evidence or examples that start to make an argument 'real'. They then begin to resemble the arguments that we might read in the press, for example. Every reason can have a piece of evidence or an example to go with it.

The following argument illustrates this technique. The argument is aiming to convince us that a car made by company X is better than a car made by company Y.

R1	X's cars have a greater range of safety features than Y's cars.
R2	X's cars have better suspensions for improved road-holding compared with Y's cars.
IC	Therefore, you are less likely to be involved in an accident in X's cars.
R3	X's cars are also more fuel efficient, so that they are better for the environment.
C	Therefore, cars made by company X are better than those made by company Y.

Adding in some evidence and examples, the argument is extended to:

X's cars have a greater range of safety features than Y's cars. They have electronic stability programmes and more airbags which are not available on cars made by Y. A recent report in the leading car magazine also showed that X's cars have better suspension for improved road-holding. Therefore, you are less likely to be involved in an accident in X's cars.

X's cars are also more fuel efficient, so they are better for the environment. Government figures show that the comparable models from X do up to 5 miles more to the gallon than Y's cars.

Therefore, cars made by company X are better than those made by company Y.

■ Car companies go to great lengths to persuade us that their cars are the best.

This may look much more complicated, but it is still the same structure, with some added extras. The first reason is now supported by some examples of the safety features available. The second reason is extended by reference to a report in a magazine, and the final reason is now supported by evidence from government testing of the cars. We can show this more clearly as follows:

> **R1** X's cars have a greater range of safety features than Y's cars.
>
> **Ex** They have electronic stability programmes and more airbags.
>
> **R2** X's cars have better suspension for improved road-holding compared with Y's cars.
>
> **Ev** As shown by a recent report in the leading car magazine.
>
> **IC** Therefore, you are less likely to be involved in an accident in X's cars.
>
> **R3** X's cars are also more fuel efficient, so that they are better for the environment.
>
> **Ev** Government figures show that the comparable models from X do up to 5 miles more to the gallon than Y's cars.
>
> **C** Therefore, cars made by company X are better than those made by company Y.

The result is a more realistic argument that contains the necessary elements of a strong argument in an organised and structured form. The structure chosen here is only an example – the important point is to have a structure, rather than just writing down reasons as they come to you.

ACTIVITY

Go back to the arguments that you wrote in the previous activity and include some evidence and examples.

Other common argument structures

The argument structure that we have used so far is an easy one and gives you a good basis to work from. Although a strong argument will be structured, structures vary from argument to argument, as we have seen earlier in the book. (Another common structure involves using a counter-argument or counter-assertion; see below.) While it is important to ensure that your arguments are structured and clear, there is no need to fit them into any particular structure.

Responding to other arguments

Using counter-arguments

In many cases, arguments arise because there is a difference of opinion on a particular topic. In such cases, we may want to argue against a particular point of view by showing how that view is in some way incorrect or flawed. Authors often do this by describing the counter-argument and then trying to show that it is wrong, ultimately supporting their own point of view. A counter-argument is often introduced by an author in order to show that it is weak or flawed and hence to support their own argument.

You learnt how to identify counter-arguments and counter-assertions in other people's writing in Unit 1, Chapter 2, and Unit 2, Chapter 7. Here we are going to learn how to use these argument components in writing our own arguments.

> ## REMEMBER
>
> A counter-argument is an additional argument that is against, or counter to, what the conclusion seeks to establish. The writer normally presents the counter-argument in order to dismiss it.

EXAM TIP

Keep your argument clear and simple. The limited time in an exam means you will not have time to produce anything too complicated. Work towards simple structures for your arguments that include several reasons, an intermediate conclusion and a conclusion. Examples, evidence and counter-arguments can be added as required.

Here is an example.

- Could scenes like this be avoided by the introduction of GM crops?

It has been suggested that GM crops should be welcomed. They will help feed the world because of the increased yield that they produce and because they are resistant to many common pests, reducing the need for harmful pesticides.

However, the improved yields have yet to be proven in the weather conditions of Africa and some pesticides would still be needed as the crops may not be resistant to all pests. The greater costs of the seeds could mean that the poorest countries will not be able to afford them. It must also be remembered that long-term research has yet to conclusively prove that they are safe for human consumption.

It is a dangerous road to travel, because once the crops are grown, the genetic composition of the crops will be spread by pollination and we will not be able to revert to non-GM crops. It is wrong to suggest that GM crops should be welcomed.

This probably looks far more complicated than it is. The author is clearly against the adoption of GM crops, but they start with the counter-argument which is as follows.

> **R** [GM crops] will help feed the world because of the increased yield that they produce …
>
> **R** GM crops reduce the need for harmful pesticides, as they are resistant to many common pests.
>
> **C** GM crops should be welcomed.

The author then goes on to show why this argument is wrong. First they point out problems with the original reasons. (Note how the word 'however' signals the change to the author's point of view and shows that what came before was the counter-argument.)

> **R** The improved yield is not proven in the weather conditions of Africa.
>
> **R** There will still be a need for some pesticides.

The author then goes on to set out their own argument by raising the issues of cost and safety for human consumption.

> **R** The greater cost of the seeds could mean that the poorest countries will not be able to afford them.
>
> **R** Long-term research has yet to conclusively prove that they are safe for human consumption.
>
> **R** The genetic composition of the [GM] crops will be spread by pollination.
>
> **C** It is wrong to suggest that GM crops should be welcomed.

This gives us a very common pattern of argument: showing why the opposition might be wrong, followed up by your own argument. To make a sporting analogy, the best form of defence is sometimes attack.

REMEMBER

'However' may be a sign that a counter-argument is being given so that the author can argue against it or dismiss it. It is worth looking out for this word in exam passages.

Using counter-assertions

A more straightforward variation of this type of approach is to start your argument with a counter-assertion (using CA as the notation). The counter-assertion can be introduced by phrases such as 'although', 'some may argue that', 'it is sometimes claimed that', because this is the idea that is about to be argued against. Here is a simplified version of the argument about GM crops using a counter-assertion.

CA	Although GM crops are thought to give greater yields.
R	The greater yield has yet to be proven in the weather conditions of Africa.
R	There are many other problems associated with the crops.
Ex	For instance, the high cost of the seeds.
Ex	We are not sure if they are safe to eat.
IC	GM crops are not as beneficial as has been suggested.
C	GM crops should not be welcomed.

- A GM crop.

REMEMBER

A counter-assertion is an assertion that supports an opponent's argument. An author often includes a counter-assertion in order to show a weakness in the opponent's argument.

EXAM TIP

Exam questions may ask you to challenge or support the conclusion of a passage. Starting with a counter-assertion can help focus your mind on where you want to go with the argument, because you know that you will begin by challenging the counter-assertion in some way.

As a further example, suppose you have read a passage suggesting hamsters are the best pets for a younger child, because they are so easy to look after. You might argue against this as follows.

CA	Although hamsters are very easy to look after …
R	… they offer little interest for a younger child, as they are only active at night time.
R	They also do not really like to be handled.
IC	Therefore, a younger child is unlikely to enjoy owning a hamster.
R	There are several other small animals that are easy to look after and are more entertaining …
Ex	… such as rabbits and guinea pigs.
C	Therefore, hamsters are not the best pets for a younger child.

ACTIVITY 48

Use the following as counter-arguments to introduce your new argument. Remember to include at least three reasons and an intermediate conclusion, and don't forget to clearly state your conclusion.

A People from many different religions and none celebrate Christmas. For many people this festival has nothing to do with the birth of Jesus. It should be renamed Winterfest.

B Pilates and Yoga are good forms of exercise. They involve gentle movements and require no special equipment. Everyone would benefit from these forms of exercise.

Writing your own arguments in the exam

In the time available to you in an exam, it is unlikely that you will be able to write an argument, evaluate it and then make major changes. The best approach is to have a few simple guidelines in mind as you think of the argument so that you do not need to make too many changes later on. The points below could usefully form a checklist.

- Make sure that you have a clearly stated conclusion.

- Make sure that you have an intermediate conclusion.

- Make sure that you have several reasons that support an intermediate conclusion and a further reason that supports the main conclusion independently. There should be at least three reasons overall.

- Make sure all of these support the main conclusion.

- Make sure that you have a clear structure.

- Make sure that you include examples or evidence to illustrate the reasons.

You might also want to try to include the following.

- A counter-assertion or counter-argument that you are responding to.

To help with writing your own arguments, you may find it useful to look at an argument written by someone who has *not* followed the guidelines above. Suggestions for improving it are given at the end of the discussion.

▪ Crowds go wild …

Your letters

Football is a fantastic game. Crowds go wild when a goal is scored, showing what an exciting game it is. When the national team play, everyone is glued to the television, willing them to win. Some killjoys talk about the violence at matches, but there were no arrests at any of the premiership matches last weekend.

Tara, Sunderland

The first sentence is the main conclusion – football is a fantastic game. However, it is not clear how some of the reasons give support to this conclusion. The lack of violence does not really affect the game's interest or excitement. Support for the national team does nothing to show the qualities of the game itself (but may support another conclusion about the importance of national teams). The excitement described would support the conclusion as long as we assume that most games involve goals, which is not always the case.

Equally, it is clear that not 'everyone' is glued to the television – this is overstating the case. 'Everyone' is often used on news or sports broadcasts when they really mean 'a lot of people'. This sort of sloppiness has no place in Critical Thinking arguments.

The argument seems to want us to assume (or generalise) that because there was no violence last weekend, there is in general little violence at football matches. However, there is nothing to suggest that this is the case, and we cannot rely on this assumption/ generalisation. Finally, there is no obvious structure to the argument, or intermediate conclusion present.

Now that we know what is wrong with this argument, what could we do to improve it? The most important way would be to include reasons that more closely support the conclusion. These reasons need to be connected to the game itself. Perhaps:

> **R** Football is a fast paced, skilful game.

or

> **R** Football can be played and enjoyed by all ages and all skill levels.

We can also remove some obvious problems from the original. Rather than using 'everyone' we could say that a 'significant number' of people enjoy watching the national team.

The last sentence could be improved by including a more general comment about decreases in violence that would offer more support to the conclusion than selecting just one weekend.

> **R** Some will say that it is not a fantastic game because of the violence at big matches, but evidence shows that violence at matches has reduced considerably over recent seasons.

Fitting in an intermediate conclusion would also help. We could have something like this.

> **R** Crowds go wild when a goal is scored.
> **R** Goals are scored in the vast majority of games.
> **IC** Football is a very exciting game.

Combining this intermediate conclusion with the two reasons given about the game itself would give much better support to the final conclusion. As a result, we now have a more persuasive argument that would receive a higher mark in the exam than the original version.

REMEMBER

An argument should always have a clearly stated conclusion, so make sure you have included it.

ACTIVITY 49

Write an argument to persuade someone that a sport (or pastime) that you enjoy is fantastic.

Hint: first of all make sure you have clearly stated the conclusion: e.g. *Therefore, it is clear that (your choice) is a fantastic sport.*

EXAM TIP

If you are being asked to write an argument that supports or challenges the conclusion in the main passage, make sure that you have accurately copied down the author's conclusion in your own argument.

▪ Dhana is very enthusiastic about skiing, and is persauding her friends to join her.

Summary

You should now be able to:

■ appreciate that writing your own arguments is just as important as criticising others

■ understand the importance of clearly stating the conclusion of your argument

■ include several reasons to support your chosen conclusion

■ include an intermediate conclusion as part of writing a more developed argument

■ work to some common argument structures

■ know how to include evidence and examples in your arguments

■ know how to use counter-arguments and assertions in your arguments

■ use the strategies outlined in this chapter as a method of planning your own arguments before you write them down.

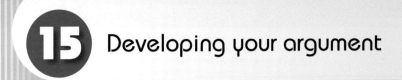

15 Developing your argument

Learning objectives

- Avoiding weakness in your argument.
- Using counter-argument in your own arguments.
- Using hypothetical reasoning in your own arguments.
- Using principles in your own arguments.

Constructing stronger, more complex arguments

In Chapter 13 you worked on basic reasoning skills, and in Chapter 14 you learnt how to write your own arguments. In this chapter you will learn how to strengthen your argument by making sure that you avoid flaws or glaring assumptions in your reasoning, and how to develop it by using more complex structures and patterns of reasoning. This chapter will extend your skills further towards A2, if you have mastered the basic and core skills covered in Chapters 13 and 14.

Avoiding weakness in your argument

Before you consider adding complexity to your arguments, you should check for weakness – and correct it. The most common forms of weakness seen in students' further arguments are:

- not supporting a precise conclusion
- flaws and irrelevant appeals
- assumptions.

Supporting a precise conclusion

Precision in Critical Thinking is extremely important. This applies to your own arguments too. Too often, students in an exam seem to grasp the topic, but not the precise conclusion they are supposed to be supporting. A piece of writing on a similar topic will not access marks, and even an argument which supports the wrong conclusion will not access high marks. Let's look at an example.

> **'We should stop building new roads.' Challenge this claim.**
>
> Although cars burn fossil fuel which is harmful to the environment, they are extremely useful in many ways. First of all, cars allow us to travel to work. This means that we can work further from home and have a better choice of jobs. So we might be able to work as a chef in a good restaurant ten miles from home, for example, rather than having to work in the local café. This freedom is good for us and good for the economy.
>
> Second, cars have some health benefits. If I drive to work in my car, rather than walking through the rain, I do not get wet, and do not have to stay wet at work. Driving your own car is also healthier than using public transport because we do not have to sit in a crowded environment with other people's cold and flu bugs.
>
> Third, cars allow us to visit family and see our country, thus aiding national culture.
>
> Without roads we cannot do any of these things. So we should not stop building new roads.

This student's argument does have some structure; they have attempted to use reasons, examples and intermediate conclusions. However, they have written an argument about the benefits of cars, not really about whether we should stop building new roads. At the end, the student includes, 'without roads we cannot do any of these things'. However, this does not make their writing about the benefits of cars relevant to the building of 'new roads'. We already have roads.

The most important aspects of writing a strong argument are producing reasons which support a conclusion, and using an argument structure with examples which support reasons which support intermediate conclusions which support the main conclusion. It is essential that you master these skills first, before trying to extend your reasoning skills. Adding complex patterns of reasoning to your argument will not improve it if you do not produce reasons which give logical support to a conclusion.

ACTIVITY 50

a) In groups, consider what would really count as reasons for building 'new' roads, rather than just keeping the ones we have already got. Use the Internet and library resources to find evidence to support your claims.

b) Write an argument to challenge the claim: 'We should stop building new roads.' Make sure that you focus precisely on the conclusion.

Avoiding flaws and irrelevant appeals

Once you have written your argument, read it through and check for flaws, irrelevant appeals and other rhetorical tricks. You may use some of these because you have been taught to use them in persuasive writing in English lessons. However, what is appropriate to a journalistic, persuasive piece is not always appropriate in a reasoned argument.

Common weaknesses which occur in students' arguments include:

- generalisations
- appeal to authority
- appeal to popularity
- slippery slope
- rhetorical questions
- rhetorical, oratory tone.

Let's look at an example.

Support the claim: 'Cars are bad for us.'

Although we all love our cars, they are bad for us for a number of reasons. As everyone knows, cars have a devastating effect on our health. The first reason for this is that cars encourage laziness – for example, faced with the choice between walking a mile to college on a wet morning, or driving, most of us would drive. It is therefore a woeful fact that we never exercise, which leads inevitably and unavoidably to obesity, heart disease and the regrettable demise of our generation at an earlier age than our parents.

The second reason for cars having a disastrous effect on our health is that they pollute, toxify and foul the atmosphere that is essential as our life breath. As Professor Blackman says in research from 2007, 'Juggernauts hurtling along the A27 at high speeds produce emissions equivalent to an aircraft in flight.' Who, then, could not believe that cars are bad for us?

- Do cars encourage laziness?

This student has attempted to include a counter-assertion, a conclusion ('cars are bad for us'), and an intermediate conclusion supported by two reasons, each of which is supported by evidence and examples. The basic structural framework is along the right lines. However, the support provided is weak for a number of reasons.

The first paragraph moves from a single and perhaps exceptional example of choosing to drive rather than walk to 'we never exercise', which is a logically unfounded step. It progresses from this to obesity, heart disease and early death. This is a form of slippery slope argument. There is, of course, a risk that if we overuse our cars and do not exercise sufficiently, we may become obese or suffer heart disease. It is not unreasonable to suggest that an increase in obesity, unfitness and heart disease may well lead to people dying earlier. However, it is dramatically overstating the case to say that these health problems come 'inevitably and inexorably' from a lack of exercise. This student has weakened their argument by their flamboyant overuse of rhetorical language. While this may be rewarded in some English courses, it tends to have a negative effect on the quality of argument in Critical Thinking.

In the second paragraph, the student has again used flamboyant, rhetorical language at the expense of the strength of their argument. The student has invented or approximated some research. While quoting a relevant authority's evidence would be acceptable, there is nothing to indicate that Professor Blackman is a relevant authority. The student also generalises from 'evidence' about juggernauts to cars being bad for us, which weakens their argument. The final, rhetorical question would be better phrased as a statement rather than a question.

ACTIVITY 51

Rewrite the argument in the previous example as a strong argument.

Avoiding assumptions

As you learnt in Unit 1, assumptions are missing steps in an argument which have to be accepted if the conclusion is to be accepted. Almost all arguments have unstated parts of the reasoning, but strong arguments do not have big gaps in the reasoning. Let's look at an example.

> Cars have a negative effect on the environment. They contribute to the greenhouse gases which are thought to be warming the Earth. The effects of global warming are thought to be very worrying – polar ice caps might melt and raise the sea level, for example. So cars are bad for us.

In this argument, we have to accept that having a negative effect on the environment means having a negative effect on us. This is a reasonable assumption to make, but to strengthen their argument, the student needs to show in their reasoning how having a negative effect on the environment means that cars are bad for us.

In general, you should read your arguments and look for the gaps in the reasoning – the things that are necessary to your argument but which you have not written down. Once you have identified these assumptions, you may simply need to write them down. However, you may find that you have assumed too much and need to rethink your argument.

Let's look at one more example.

> Evidence indicates that children whose parents spend time with them are less likely to develop behavioural difficulties. It is clear that mothers should not go to work while their children are small.
>
> OCR Unit 4 Multiple-Choice question, June 2006

This argument makes many, glaring assumptions to the extent that it does not support the conclusion. Assumptions that must be made include:

- fathers spending their time with children is not equally beneficial
- mothers who work do not/cannot spend time with their children
- mothers who do not work do spend time with their children
- the beneficial effects of parents spending time with children are reduced when they are no longer small.

- Should mothers work while their children are small?

We could challenge all of these assumptions. There is no reason to suppose that it should not be a father who spends time with a child, or that this effect is evident only when children are small. There is, however, evidence to suggest that fathers who spend time with their teenage sons can have a significant, beneficial effect on their sons' behaviour.

So – you have written all or part of an argument and realise that it has assumptions which can easily be challenged. What can you do? Well, in this case, writing the assumptions down as part of the argument won't help much, because they are so easy to challenge that your argument will be weak even if you do write them down. In this case, it would be better to draw a different conclusion. Let's suppose that you have been asked to support or challenge the claim: 'Mothers should not go to work while their children are small.'

Although some people claim that mothers should not go to work while their children are small, evidence indicates only that children whose parents spend time with them are less likely to develop behavioural difficulties. Children have two parents, a mother and a father, and both have a role in raising the child, even when parents are divorced. Schools are increasingly encouraging dads' and lads' nights because research indicates that fathers' involvement in their sons' education can be really beneficial.

Furthermore, mothers who do not work may be unfulfilled and unhappy, and may pass this unhappiness to their children. They may therefore be better working, and sharing the childcare with the father or grandparents or other loving carers. In addition, working parents do not necessarily have to work such long hours that they spend no time with their children. It is possible to work and spend time with children.

A further consideration is that if mothers work, the whole family may be better off, and evidence indicates that children from better-off families are healthier and have fewer behavioural problems than those from families which really struggle for money. This would be a good reason for mothers to work.

So, while parents should ensure that they spend time with their children, we cannot conclude that mothers should not go to work while their children are small.

This is not a perfect argument by any means, but you are not required to produce a perfect argument. This argument deals with the problem of glaring, problematic assumptions by starting again and challenging the conclusion instead. You do not have to agree with what you write – you have to provide logical support for a conclusion.

ACTIVITY 52

Identify the assumptions necessary in the following argument, challenge these assumptions, then write an argument to challenge the conclusion of the argument.

Children in wheelchairs have significant special needs. So such children cannot cope in mainstream schools and should therefore not attend them.

Using counter-argument to strengthen your own reasoning

In Chapter 14 you learnt how to include a counter-assertion or counter-argument in your own reasoning and dismiss it. Now we will consider ways of developing and strengthening this form of reasoning. A simple use of counter-argument might be to include a counter-assertion which is the direct opposite of your own conclusion.

Although many people argue that children should not watch television, this is not the case for many reasons. Television can be very educational …

In this argument, the counter-assertion is there, but it is only disagreed with rather than shown to be wrong. The line of reasoning that is introduced to do with television being educational would be a reason for children to watch educational forms of television. But it does not address the reasons why children should not watch television and show them to be wrong.

To show that the counter-argument is wrong or misguided, include one or more reasons to support the counter-conclusion. Then refute the counter-argument by showing that these reasons do not (completely) support that counter-conclusion. Then you can give your own reasons to support your own conclusion. Let's look at an example.

> Many people argue that children should not watch television because they believe that watching TV violence and violent behaviour are linked. However, this reason shows only that children should avoid violent programmes. There are many good reasons for children to watch television …

REMEMBER

'Refute' means demonstrate to be wrong. So if you refute someone's arguments, you show that their arguments do not work – you highlight the weakness in their arguments, perhaps by showing them to be inconsistent.

- Should children be allowed to watch violent TV programmes?

Now the counter-argument is a little more developed, and there is a response to the counter-argument, which picks up on a weakness in the counter-argument. This is a strong form of counter-argument, and leaves you free to argue that children could/should watch all forms of TV other than violent programmes.

You may wish to refute the counter-argument by arguing that children should even be able to watch violent programmes. You could do this in one of two ways.

1 Dispute the link between TV violence and violent behaviour.
2 Argue that there are benefits even to watching violence on TV.

Let's have a look at how you might construct these counter-arguments and responses.

1 Many people argue that watching TV violence and violent behaviour are linked, and TV programmes are very violent, so children should not watch TV. However, the link between watching TV violence and behaving in a violent way is not necessarily a causal link. It may be that people who tend to behave violently tend to watch more violent programmes. So a peaceful sort of child watching violent programmes will probably just enjoy the excitement of the action. Thus we can see that worries about violence are not sufficient to support the claim that children should not watch television. There are many good reasons why children should watch television, however …

2 Many people argue that children should not watch television because there is so much violence on television. However, for many children it is precisely because there is violence on the television that they should watch it. We evolved as hunters and warriors and retain the brutal instincts of hunters and warriors. Violent but unreal television programmes allow us to work through the impulses we feel without actually acting on them. It is quite possible for a child to benefit in this way from imagined violence, and to see the consequences of violence, without ever having to actually live through them. As there are many other reasons for children to watch television, we should not allow scruples about violence to prevent them from doing so …

When you are including counter-arguments in your reasoning you do need to remember that you are writing an argument, which is essentially one-sided. You are not writing a discursive essay which looks at both sides of an issue and comes to a conclusion. Nor are you, generally, considering claim and counter-claim as you might in a history essay. In Critical Thinking you are being asked to argue for or against a particular claim. So the only reason you include any information that might disagree with your own conclusion is in order to show that it is weak, and thus to strengthen your own, one-sided argument.

ACTIVITY 53

a) **Think of two other reasons why people might think that children should not watch television.**

b) **Refute this reasoning by showing why the reasons do not really support the conclusion.**

c) **Write an argument to challenge the claim: 'Children should not watch television.' Include your counter-argument and response.**

REMEMBER

Your argument should have at least two reasons which support one or more intermediate conclusions and at least one further reason which supports the main conclusion in a different way.

ACTIVITY 54

Choose one of the claims below.

a) **Research evidence on the Internet.**

b) **Write an argument to support or challenge the claim.**

Include:

- **a counter-argument**

- **a response to the counter-argument**

- **several reasons, intermediate conclusions, evidence/examples and your main conclusion.**

A   The government should promote the building of new nuclear power stations.

B   The state should not interfere with personal choices.

C   We should encourage the development of cars that drive themselves.

REMEMBER

- Support or challenge the claim precisely.
- Check for and avoid weakness such as flaws, poor use of evidence or irrelevance.
- Check for and avoid glaring assumptions.

Using hypothetical reasoning in your own arguments

REMEMBER

- A hypothetical claim is a claim in the form 'If … then …'

- A hypothetical claim has a condition (the 'if …' part of the sentence) and a consequence (the 'then …' part of the sentence).

- A hypothetical claim within an argument may be a reason or conclusion.

- Hypothetical claim indicator words and phrases include: *if, provided that, on condition that, given that … then …*

- Hypothetical reasoning looks at the consequences that might occur if something were the case.

Using hypothetical reasoning can increase the complexity and sophistication of your arguments, and help you to structure them, if you use it well. Remember to use your evaluative skills from Chapter 12 to check that:

- the condition is likely

- the consequence follows from the conditions

- the hypothetical reasoning supports your conclusion.

Hypothetical reasoning is particularly useful when you are considering consequences in order to make a decision about what to do. Let's consider how we might support the conclusion 'We should stop building new roads' with hypothetical reasoning. One way of approaching this decision is to consider the consequences if we *do* take this action and to consider the consequences if we *do not* take this action. We can then show that the consequences of continuing to build new roads are worse than the consequences of stopping road building.

> If we don't stop building new roads, we will struggle to address the problems of pollution and global warming. This is because, if we keep building more roads, it will be easier to keep driving everywhere.
>
> On the contrary, if we stop building new roads, congestion will get so bad that people start to think about alternative ways of travelling, such as walking or using public transport. People who walk to work become generally healthier and happier, so this would be very positive. Alternatively people might choose public transport. Studies suggest that if people used public transport more, the government would be more likely to invest in it properly, so public transport ought to improve.
>
> So the consequences of continuing to build new roads are significantly worse than the consequences of stopping building new roads. Therefore we should stop building new roads.

EXAM TIP

Practise writing arguments that are about 100–150 words long. In the exam you won't have time to write much more than this (although you shouldn't spend time in the exam counting words – you'd be better to spend any spare time thinking!). It is best to practise getting a strong structure into a concise argument so that you are really well prepared for what you need to do in the exam.

- If more people used public transport, it might improve.

If we look at the structure of this argument, we will see that considering the consequences of stopping building new roads and continuing building new roads has given the argument two clear lines (or strands) of reasoning. This argument would get a good mark at AS, and takes you some of the way towards the level of reasoning required in Units 3 and 4 of A2.

HR	If we keep building more roads, it will be easier to keep driving everywhere.
IC1 (HR)	If we don't stop building new roads, we will struggle to address the problems of pollution and global warming.
HR	If we stop building new roads, congestion will get so bad that people start to think about alternative ways of travelling …
Ex	… such as walking or using public transport.
R1	People who walk to work become generally healthier and happier.
R2	Alternatively people might choose public transport.
Ev	Studies suggest that if people used public transport more, the government would be more likely to invest in it properly,
IC2	so public transport ought to improve.
IC3	So the consequences of continuing to build new roads are significantly worse than the consequences of stopping building new roads.
C	Therefore we should stop building new roads.

EXAM TIP

Remember, in this chapter we are considering how to access the highest marks at AS, and preparing for A2. You must have developed the basic ability to support a conclusion, as discussed in Chapters 13 and 14 *before* you attempt to write arguments this complex. If you aim for complexity before you can write a simple, clear argument with strong links of support, you may gain a lower mark than if you try to write a clear, simple argument.

In this argument, we can see that IC4 is supported by ICs 1, 2 and 3. IC4 supports C. If you forgot to write IC4 down, you would be leaving a big hole in the argument – a glaring assumption. Strong arguments which gain many marks do not leave large, unstated steps in the reasoning.

ACTIVITY 55

Write arguments to support or challenge conclusions A–D. Use hypothetical reasoning to consider the consequences. Use the Internet to find real evidence to support your arguments.

A   We should all recycle all our plastic, glass, paper and Tetra Paks.

B   We should only buy toiletries which are not tested on animals.

C   We should all donate one-tenth of our income to charity.

D   We should not overuse our credit cards.

Using principles in your own arguments

In Chapter 8 you learnt how to identify general principles in an argument and in Chapter 12 you learnt how to evaluate the use of principles in an argument. In this chapter we will consider how you can best use principles in your own arguments.

REMEMBER

A principle is a general, rule-like statement which applies beyond the immediate circumstances and acts as a guide to action. A principle can be a reason, intermediate or main conclusion in an argument.

Writing an argument including principles

In the Unit 2 exam you will probably have to write an argument to support or challenge the main conclusion of the passage. You have covered the main skills needed to do this in Chapter 14. You could develop your basic argument structure by including a principle. Including a principle – a general, rule-like guide to action – should strengthen your argument if your conclusion is making a recommendation for action. Let's look at an example of how you might include a principle in a simple argument.

Basic argument
Context: You have to travel from Southampton to Manchester tonight.

R1   You are very tired.
R2   You tend to lose concentration driving when you are tired.
IC   So it would be better not to drive such a long way tonight.
R3   There is a direct train which only takes about four hours.
C   You should take the train from Southampton to Manchester.

> **_Developed argument with principle_**
> **Context: You have to travel from Southampton to Manchester tonight.**
>
> **R1** You are very tired.
> **R2** You tend to lose concentration driving when you are tired.
> **IC** So it would be better not to drive such a long way tonight.
> **R3** There is a direct train which only takes about 4 hours.
> **R4** (Principle) We should use the train whenever possible to protect the environment.
> **C** You should take the train from Southampton to Manchester tonight.

The first argument is quite strong. It gives us reasons why it would be better not to drive and shows that there is an acceptable alternative to driving. However, there is nothing compelling about the conclusion, which is a fairly weak recommendation. It would be easy to answer this argument by saying that there is a flight which is quicker and cheaper.

The second argument is stronger, though, because the principle supports the idea that you really *ought* to take the train. It is no longer just a recommendation, but implies that this is morally the right thing to do. Because the principle is a guide to action rather than a factual claim, it strengthens the conclusion. It is now no longer so easy to answer this argument by saying that there is a flight which is quicker and cheaper, because flying would conflict with the principle that we should use the train whenever possible to protect the environment.

REMEMBER

Remember when you are writing your own arguments that you should include evidence or examples. These arguments have been written without evidence and examples to highlight the role of principles.

When you use a principle in your own argument, remember to apply your evaluative skills.

- How generally does this principle apply?
- Does the principle apply to the situation in question?
- In what other situations does the principle apply?
- Are there any situations in which the principle doesn't apply?
- Does this principle support my conclusion?

Let's ask these questions about the argument above. We used the principle, 'We should use the train whenever possible to protect the environment.'

How generally does this principle apply? Well, it certainly applies to my journey to Manchester. It is possible to travel fairly quickly by train. The principle would apply in most situations where train travel was a reasonable, quick and affordable option. If there were no station, or I had a child, boat, tent and dog with me, we would probably think that the principle didn't apply, that this was not within the bounds of 'whenever possible.'

Does the principle support the conclusion? In this case, the principle supports the conclusion very clearly, because the conclusion is a specific instance of the principle's general recommendation.

ACTIVITY 56

a) Strengthen the following argument by adding a principle.

R The Fairtrade bananas come from co-operatives in Guatemala.

R The co-operatives ensure that the workers are paid a wage that allows them to feed and educate their children.

IC Buying Fairtrade bananas will help workers.

R In my supermarket, Fairtrade bananas cost me very little more than other bananas.

C I should buy Fairtrade bananas.

b) 'I should save my money.' Write an argument to support or challenge this claim. Include at least one principle.

Writing an argument to support a principle

It is possible that you may have to write an argument in the Unit 2 exam to support or challenge a principle. One of the best ways to do this is to consider various situations in which the principle might apply. We can also consider other principles which might be used to support the principle we are taking as our conclusion.

Consider situations in which a principle might apply

By working through two or three situations in which a principle might apply, we can discover whether we really do think that it should apply to all situations, or whether it should be limited. Let's look at an example.

> The government should restrict all potentially harmful activities.

Let's consider a number of situations to which this principle might apply.

1 Driving

Driving is potentially harmful. The government does and should restrict driving. Only those who have passed a driving test are allowed to drive. This is a basic safety measure. People who are regarded as too young to control a car responsibly are not allowed driving licences, and nor are those who have repeatedly driven in a reckless or criminal manner. The government also restricts the speed at which we can drive. As accidents are most harmful at high speeds, this also seems to be a reasonable restriction.

2 Drinking to excess

Drinking to excess is harmful. In the short term it can be harmful in terms of alcoholic blood poisoning, or damage inflicted on others in drunken brawls. Long term, excessive drinking can lead to memory loss, depression, heart and circulatory problems and liver cirrhosis. It does seem unreasonable that the government should restrict how much individuals drink, as that is a matter of personal choice. However, most of us do not want other people to be able to fight, break our windows or breach the peace on the way past our houses between pubs. Nor do we want to be the victims of drunken violence, or to pay through our taxes for hospital treatment for others who choose to drink excessively. Surely the government has a duty to protect us from people who abuse alcohol? And this means restricting their freedom to drink to excess.

Have I supported the conclusion?

This argument is already longer than you are likely to be able to write in the exam. It will clearly be impossible for you to consider all the possibilities. The claim you were given, 'The government should restrict all harmful activities', is a very strong claim. The reasoning above has supported the conclusion that 'The government should restrict some harmful activities'. You may find that, in order to fully support this strong conclusion, you need to include more principles in your argument.

Using more principles to support a principle

■ Should the government restrict all harmful activities?

It is often possible to support a principle by using more principles as follows.

> Although many people argue that the government should not restrict all harmful activities because many of these activities are a matter of individual choice, all harmful activities should be restricted in some way. The government has a duty to protect children, who are regarded as too young to make informed decisions about whether to engage in harmful activities. This means that all harmful activities should be restricted as far as children are concerned. The government also has a duty to protect people from the harmful activities of others. This means that, if an activity would be harmful to someone other than the person choosing to do it, the government must restrict it. Therefore the government should restrict all harmful activities.

This argument has provided some support for the conclusion that *all* harmful activities should be restricted by the government.

ACTIVITY 57

a) **Consider whether the principle that 'The government should restrict all harmful activities' should apply in the following potentially harmful circumstances:**

A   poor diet

B   extreme sports

C   smoking

D   crossing the road.

b) **Think of two more principles which would help you to support *or challenge* the conclusion that 'The government should restrict all harmful activities'.**

c) **Write your own argument to support or challenge the principle that 'The government should restrict all harmful activities'. Refer to situations and more principles.**

REMEMBER

In an exam you should not re-use the reasoning from the passage. Treat this exercise as exam practice, and develop your own reasoning which does not reuse the ideas from the examples above. Do use your ideas from parts a) and b).

ACTIVITY 58

a) **Consider two or three situations in which the principle below might apply.**

We should treat others the way we would like to be treated.

b) **Think of two more principles which would help you to support or challenge this claim.**

c) **Write your own argument to support or challenge the principle that 'We should treat others the way we would like to be treated'. Use your thoughts from parts a and b.**

Structure of argument

When you are writing an argument to support a principle, you must remember that it is an argument and not get distracted by interesting thoughts. An argument *must* have a conclusion and a structure to support that conclusion. That structure should include reasons, examples and intermediate conclusions. Let's go back to a part of the argument we used earlier (page 258) and analyse it into its component parts. This will give you an idea of how to access the higher marks.

R1	Driving is potentially harmful.
R2	Only those who have passed a driving test are allowed to drive.
R3	This [requirement to pass a driving test] is not interference, but a basic safety measure.
Ex1	People who are regarded as too young to control a car responsibly are not allowed driving licences, and
Ex2	nor are those who have repeatedly driven in a reckless or criminal manner.
Ex3	The government also restricts the speed at which we can drive.
R4	As accidents are most harmful at high speeds,
IC1	this also seems to be a reasonable restriction.
IC2	The government does and should restrict driving.
C	The government should restrict harmful activities.

ACTIVITY

Go back to one of your arguments from Activity 51 or 52 and analyse it. Consider how you might improve your argument.

ACTIVITY

Write your own argument to support or challenge the claim below. Focus on the structure of your argument.

'All people should be treated as equal.'

Writing an argument from principle

We have looked at using principles to support an argument, and writing an argument to support a principle. It is also possible to write an argument from a principle, using a principle as the starting point. This form of reasoning is extremely useful in decision making. It forms the bulk of Unit 3, so we will not cover it in detail now, but let's look at one example.

> I am unexpectedly pregnant after a contraceptive failure. I need to decide whether to keep the baby or to have an abortion.

> **I might argue as follows.**
>
> Life is sacred. Life begins at conception. I have a duty to take effective contraceptive measures if I don't want to create life. These principles mean that I should have my baby.

> **Or I might argue as follows.**
>
> A woman's right to control what happens to her body overrides all other considerations. An embryo only becomes a living person when it could survive outside the mother's body. Children also deserve the best home life possible, and I could not offer this child a good home life. So, it would be best to have an abortion.

Neither of these arguments is 'right' in any absolute sense. It might be necessary to support the principles used to strengthen the arguments.

PAUSE FOR THOUGHT

Should abortion be available as a choice for women? How is this consideration different from deliberations about whether I should have an abortion?

What role should men have in considerations about whether a child should be born?

ACTIVITY 61

Write short arguments from principle which would help to make a decision in the following situations.

A I really enjoy my partner's company, but there is someone else I find really attractive. The problem is, I don't know if I would have such a comfortable relationship with the other person. I don't know what I should do.

B My grandmother often sends me really expensive but truly hideous presents. Would I be justified in asking her to send the money instead?

Summary

You should now be able to:

- avoid weakness in your own arguments
- use counter-argument in your own arguments
- use hypothetical reasoning in your own arguments
- use principles in your own arguments.

Exam Café
Relax, refresh, result!

Relax and prepare

Getting started in Critical Thinking

Focus your skills effectively

You can help yourself to succeed in AS Critical Thinking by reading lots and lots of different articles in newspapers and magazines – not just articles on serious topics, but also reports of court cases, readers' letters in the local newspaper, and articles in lifestyle, fashion or music magazines. As you read, try to:

- take time to understand **what** the writer is trying to persuade you to accept
- think about **how** the writer is trying to persuade you of their point of view
- work out **how** the article succeeds – or does not succeed – in persuading you
- think about the **meaning** of key words that the writer uses
- think about whether the evidence or examples used support the point the writer is making
- compose a short argument to **counter** what you read.

You can also practise the skills you will learn in Critical Thinking when you talk to friends and relatives, or when you prepare essays or reports for other subjects. You should try to focus on **precision** and **accuracy** whenever you produce written work.

Refresh your memory

Revision tips

Critical Thinking is a skills-based subject without a large body of knowledge so you cannot revise for the exam in the same way as for other subjects. So you should try the following.

- Use the key terms and the glossary to learn the meaning of important Critical Thinking terms.
- Go back and practise the activities in this book or those given to you by your teacher. Your teacher may also give you past papers to practise on.
- Apply Critical Thinking skills to passages that you read elsewhere (the letter pages and comments sections of newspapers are ideal for this). You can try to:
  - analyse argument structure
  - look out for flaws
  - think about whether the evidence and examples used actually support the reasoning
  - consider what other explanation there might be other than what the author is saying
  - think about how you could counter the argument.

Read each question carefully, and **highlight** or **underline** key words – **what** are you being asked to identify or explain? Watch out for phrases like '**more/less** likely' – you are being asked to compare – make sure your answers include **both** parts of the comparison.

Key terms guidance

Identify: Quote the argument component, e.g. conclusion, exactly from the passage. Make sure you don't include any extra information, e.g. examples, evidence, explanations.

Hypothetical reason: Remember that hypothetical reasons are usually expressed in the form 'If ... then ...'.

Flaws: If you are asked, state clearly the name of the flaw, or if you cannot remember the name **describe** clearly why the reasoning is flawed. Explain clearly how the flaw weakens the reasoning and relate it directly to the passage. You might find quoting part of the text helpful.

Strengths/Weaknesses in the use of evidence: Ask yourself whether the evidence is sufficiently representative or relevant to support the reasoning. In your mind work through the questions on page 69, Chapter 5. You will need to explain how the use of evidence is strong or weak.

Strengths/Weaknesses in the use of examples: Ask yourself whether the example provides good or poor support for the reasoning. In your mind work through the questions on page 94, Chapter 6.

Inconsistency: If you are asked to find an inconsistency within the passage, look for evidence, examples that do not quite agree with the author's overall conclusion or one of the reasons, or reasons that cannot both be true.

Contradiction: If you are asked to find a contradiction, look for evidence, examples that say completely the opposite to the author's overall conclusion or one of the reasons.

Inference: If you are asked what can be inferred from the passage, you are being asked what conclusion/reason the author would like us to think that isn't stated in the text. You should aim to state this clearly and accurately (what can be inferred about whom/compared with what).

Analogy: Many students find analogies tricky. Remember that analogies always have five parts (the unlikeliness/likeliness of A – B is like C – D) even if they are not explicitly stated in the text.

Evaluating analogies: When you are asked to evaluate an analogy, you need to think about the ways in which what is being compared is similar enough for the comparison to be made, or whether it is too different for the analogy to work. Asking yourself the following questions may help you decide.

- Are they both caused by similar/comparable things?
- Is the timescale similar enough to be comparable?
- Do they use/need the same sort of skills?
- Do they actually have the same effects?

You will get no marks for simply saying that they are different.

Principle: You will either be asked for a general principle used by the author, or for one not stated in the passage but that would support the author's argument – read the question carefully.

If you are asked for a general principle, these should be phrased using 'should', and you should be able to apply them in situations other than that which is being described in the passage.

Further arguments: You will be asked to write two further arguments. The type of question you will get asked will vary.

- You may be given the conclusion you are arguing for – highlight this. You might want to copy the conclusion out as the first line of your argument. Make sure that what you write *does* argue for the conclusion you are asked to support, and not against it.

- You may be asked to write an argument that either supports or challenges a general principle. You should think of different situations in which the general principle would apply and use these to support your reasoning.

- You may be asked to argue in support of or against the main conclusion of the passage. A good tip is to turn to your answer for question 16 and copy it out.

Make sure you don't just repeat reasons or evidence from the passage. Yours needs to be a 'new' and different argument.

You are allowed to re-use information in a different way – e.g. use a reason as a counter-assertion. Make sure you:

- remember to write the conclusion clearly; it doesn't matter whether this is at the beginning or end of the argument

- remember that further arguments are marked according to levels of response. Your argument needs to be relevant and support your conclusion as well as having the correct structure, for example, to gain top band marks.

'A relevant argument is one with a clear structure that includes at least three reasons and at least one properly supported intermediate conclusion. The argument is persuasive and relies on only one or two reasonable assumptions. The argument will also contain a further reason or reasons/examples/evidence/counter-examples that support the argument. The main conclusion is precisely stated.'

Get the result !

What is in the exam?

The Unit 2 exam lasts for 1 hour and is split into three distinct **sections**.

Section A: 15 multiple-choice questions.

Section B: a series of questions that require you to analyse and evaluate a passage of text.

Section C: a chance to show your skills at writing your own arguments.

Section A – Multiple choice

1. Which one of the following is an argument?   [1]

   a) Great scientific advances open up whole new areas of knowledge. This is illustrated by the award of the Nobel prize for medicine to the researchers who discovered and used stem cells.

   b) Stem cell research can help scientists create new cures for diseases. A stem cell can develop into any kind of cell. This means that they can replace damaged cells in people who are ill.

   c) Thousands of scientists have studied the molecular biology of the cell during the last half century. They have made discoveries about DNA and RNA which have enabled great advances in medical science.

   d) Using stem cells from embryos for research is morally worrying. Some techniques involve creating embryos and removing stem cells. This kills the embryo. It seems wrong to create life in order to kill it.

2. Satire – that form of humour which uses sarcasm and ridicule to expose negative aspects of society – is as necessary in the twenty-first century as it was in the mid-twentieth century when Ned Sherrin and David Frost presented, *That Was the Week That Was*. That show was condemned as destroying 'all that Britain holds dear'. In October 2007, U Pa Pa Lay, the star of the Moustache Brothers, was arrested in Myanmar. He had organised a troupe of performers to take part in protest marches. In Kenya in 2007, the comedy group Redykyulass lampooned President Kibaki to persuade Kenyans to vote.

Is this:

   a) Examples explaining a point?
   b) Opinion and examples?
   c) Reasons to support a conclusion?
   d) Unconnected sentences?   [1]

3. Food companies that claim that they do not use chemicals in their products are talking complete nonsense. Some may argue that it is a sensible advertising ploy, as people believe that chemicals are bad additives. However, food is made of chemicals. Water is a chemical. Lemon juice is mostly the chemical citric acid.

Which of the following is the main conclusion of the argument?   [1]

   a) Claiming not to use chemicals in their products is a sensible advertising ploy.
   b) Food companies that claim that they do not use chemicals in their products are talking complete nonsense.
   c) Food is made of chemicals. Water is a chemical. Lemon juice is mostly the chemical citric acid.
   d) People believe that chemicals are bad additives.

4. Striking can never be justified. When workers go on strike they damage the economy and inconvenience thousands if not millions of people. These workers also lose pay, which threatens their own families' well-being.

Which one of the following is a principle which would weaken the argument? [1]

   a) If workers do not strike, the managers can easily reduce their pay.
   b) If workers strike, they make the public aware of how badly they are being treated.
   c) People should fight for what is right.
   d) Workers should put the convenience of customers above their own needs.

Questions 5, 6 and 7 refer to the following passage.

It has been argued that the tax and benefit system should be changed to encourage couples to stay together, because children living with single parents are more likely to experience serious illness than those living with married parents. However, tweaking the tax and benefit system is unlikely to affect the number of lone parent families. The proportion of families headed by a lone parent has barely changed over the past ten years. So there is no evidence that the existing tax and benefit system is encouraging people to live apart. Furthermore, most lone parents have been married, and their average age is 36. Nearly 60% are in paid work.

5. 'The tax and benefit system should be changed to encourage couples to stay together.' Is this: [1]

   a) Conclusion of counter-argument?
   b) Counter-argument?
   c) Counter-assertion?
   d) Reason of counter-argument?

6. 'There is no evidence that the existing tax and benefit system is encouraging people to live apart.' Is this: [1]

   a) Evidence?
   b) Intermediate conclusion?
   c) Main conclusion?
   d) Reason?

7. 'In the nineteenth century lone parents headed around the same proportion of families as today.' If true, does this additional evidence: [1]

   a) Have little relevance to the argument?
   b) Neither strengthen nor weaken the argument?
   c) Slightly weaken the argument?
   d) Strengthen the argument?

Questions 8 and 9 refer to the following passage.

Although the festival of Halloween has a long history, dating back to Celtic Druids, we should fight against it in a modern world. First of all, it encourages superstition in a modern, scientific world, which cannot be a good thing. Second, it is commercial theft, an occasion hyped up to take our money from us. Also not a good thing. Third, it glorifies criminal behaviour. We must either encourage children to beg with menaces or cower in our darkened homes all evening. This is unacceptable.

8. Which of the following best expresses the conclusion of the argument? [1]

   a) It is wrong to celebrate an occasion which marks superstition, theft and unlawful behaviour.
   b) People today should combat celebrations of Halloween.
   c) The Festival of Halloween dates back to pagan times.
   d) Trick or treating is unacceptable.

9. The text about Halloween contains a flaw. This flaw is: [1]

   a) Conflation.
   b) Confusing cause and effect.
   c) Restricting the options.
   d) Slippery slope.

10. Pacific crows have been filmed making tools to help them catch grubs and other insects. Eighteen different crows were filmed making tools from leaves, twigs and grass stems. One crow used a stiff strand of grass to poke the ground looking for ants. It carried the tool with it when it flew from one patch of ground to another. Sometimes the crows used twigs to probe the trees for large grubs, or stripped the serrated edge of a tree leaf to use the barbs as hooks for fish. This is truly amazing. Birds are clearly much more intelligent than we previously believed.

Which one of the following best expresses the flaw in the argument? [1]

   a) Evidence about crows cannot be used to infer a conclusion about birds in general.
   b) Information about eighteen crows is not enough to show that crows make tools.
   c) Just because the crows were seen to use tools does not imply a relationship of cause and effect.
   d) The argument unreasonably assumes that the crows knew that they were making tools.

Questions 11 and 12 refer to the following passage.

For a long time science has held that humans were the only mammal females which do not show signs of coming into heat, or 'oestrus' when they are at their most fertile. That there are signs when women are fertile. Research indicates that women put more effort into their appearance when they are fertile, choosing more revealing tops and more seductive perfumes. New studies show that lap dancers earn bigger tips when they are in the fertile part of their cycle.

11. Which of the following is the main conclusion of the argument? [1]

    a) For a long time science has held that humans were the only mammal females which do not show signs of coming into heat.
    b) Lap dancers earn bigger tips when they are in the fertile part of their cycle.
    c) Research indicates that women put more effort into their appearance when they are fertile.
    d) There are signs when women are fertile.

12. Which of the following most strengthens the claim that women experience 'oestrus'? [1]

    a) Women are often mistaken about when they are fertile, which causes problems both becoming pregnant and avoiding becoming pregnant.
    b) Women become bad tempered and snappy just before their period.
    c) Women experience heightened desire and unexpected thoughts of babies halfway through their monthly cycle.
    d) Women notice changes in their body odour and have greasier hair and skin just before their period.

13.

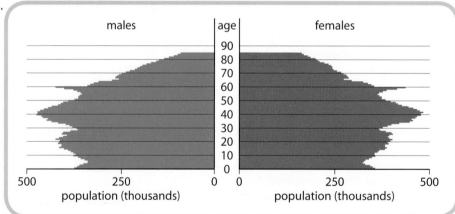

Which of the following can reliably be concluded from the chart above? [1]

    a) More boys are born than girls.
    b) Most immigrants are between 37–48 years old.
    c) The birth rate increased from 1995–2005.
    d) Women tend to live longer than men.

Questions 14 and 15 refer to the following passage.

We should rejoice in the beer, burgers and bonking which make it likely that we will all die naturally within a normal life span. If we all lived healthy lives for two hundred or more years, there would be a population explosion which the planet could not sustain. We might have to face moral questions about which elderly people to terminate to make way for the young. If the population were vastly too large, we might have to consider whether some genetically inferior young people should be sterilised. These dilemmas would be unbearably difficult. It is much easier for nature to make these decisions for us.

14. Which of the following best expresses the main conclusion of the argument? [1]

    a) We should be glad that nature makes difficult decisions for us.
    b) We should enjoy our bad habits.
    c) We should hope that the average life expectancy drops.
    d) We should not have to face difficult moral decisions.

15. Which of the following best expresses a weakness in the reasoning? [1]

    a) Eating burgers may be a sufficient cause of low life expectancy but it is not necessary.
    b) It may be that we should put our own personal interests before the interests of the species.
    c) It uses hypothetical reasoning with implausible consequences.
    d) The reasoning moves through several steps which are logically unconnected to an extreme conclusion.

Section A Total [15]

Worrying increase in the use of health supplements

1 The use of health supplements such as multivitamin tablets has increased greatly in the western world. People take these supplements because advertising suggests that they prevent a range of medical conditions from developing. However, there is concern that people are consuming worryingly high doses of these supplements and the European Union has issued a directive that will ban the sale of a wide range of them. This EU directive should be supported.

2 Research suggests that people who take Vitamin C supplements of over 5000 milligrams a day are more likely to develop cancer. This shows how much damage these health supplements do to people's health. A spokesman for the health supplement industry has argued that other research shows that Vitamin C supplements help prevent heart disease, but we can dismiss this evidence as it is from a biased source.

3 Science fiction of the 1960s and 1970s predicted that pills would replace meals as the way in which people would get the fuel they needed. This, it was argued, would mean a more efficient use of time as people wouldn't have to waste it preparing or eating meals. The EU directive would help prevent this nightmare of pills replacing food becoming a reality.

4 People already take too many pills instead of adopting a healthier lifestyle. For example, the consumption of painkillers in Britain in 1998 was 21 tablets per year for every man, woman and child in the country. People do not need all these pills.

5 Some might argue that the EU directive is an infringement to the right to freedom of choice. However, there are many legal precedents for such intervention when it is in the individual's best interests. We now make people wear seatbelts rather than allowing them to choose to do so. Opposing the EU directive would mean beneficial measures like this would be threatened.

6 If people cannot buy these banned health supplements then the sales of fruit and vegetables will increase. This will be good for the British economy and good for the people. After all, one cannot get too much of the vitamins and minerals that fruit and vegetables have to offer, which is why health professionals encourage us to eat at least five portions of fruit or vegetables per day.

Adapted from OCR Critical Thinking Paper, 2 January 2005

Analysing and evaluating argument

1. Identify the **main conclusion** of the argument presented in
    the passage.   [2]

2. Identify a **counter-assertion** within the passage.   [2]

3. In **paragraph 2** the author uses evidence about people taking high
    doses of Vitamin C being more likely to develop cancer. Explain how
    this does not support the reasoning in this passage.   [2]

4. In **paragraph 2** the author dismisses research presented by the
    Health Supplement Industry spokesman.

    a) Name or describe the flaw behind the author's dismissal.   [1]

    b) With reference to the text explain why the author's reasoning
        is flawed. You must explain clearly why there is a problem with
        the reasoning.   [3]

5. In **paragraph 3** the author uses evidence from the 1960s and 1970s
    that predicted pills would replace meals.

    a) Give a possible **weakness** in the use of this evidence.   [2]

    b) Give a possible **explanation** for why this hasn't happened. [2]

6. In **paragraph 4** the author states that 'People already take too many
    pills instead of adopting a healthier lifestyle'.

    a) Name or describe the flaw within the author's reasoning.   [1]

    b) With reference to the text explain why the author's reasoning
        is flawed. You must explain clearly why there is a problem with
        the reasoning.   [3]

7. In **paragraph 4**, the author uses evidence about painkillers. Give a
    possible **weakness** in the use of this evidence.   [2]

8. In **paragraph 5**, the author uses an analogy involving the law on
    wearing seatbelts in a car to persuade us to support the EU directive.

    a) Identify precisely what is being compared in this analogy. [2]

    b) Give one way, relevant to the author's argument, in which the
        things being compared in this analogy are similar.   [2]

    c) Give one way, relevant to the author's argument, in which the
        things being compared in this analogy are dissimilar (i.e. different). [2]

9. Identify a possible **contradiction** between the reasoning in
    paragraph 6 and the rest of the passage.   [2]

Total [28]

Developing your own arguments

10. In paragraph 6 the author argues that the ban on health supplements will lead to an increase in the sales of fruit and vegetables.

    Explain whether you think this will be the case. You should refer to examples or evidence to support your answer. [4]

11. Consider the following general principle:
    'Governments should legislate to prevent us from harming ourselves.'

    This is a general principle that would support the author's argument. Consider the way in which this principle might be applied to a wide variety of situations and construct a further argument that either supports this principle or challenges it.

    Marks will be given for a well-structured and developed argument that contains at least three reasons, intermediate conclusions and an overall conclusion. Your argument should also contain examples and/or evidence. [12]

12. Construct one further argument that challenges or supports the main conclusion of 'The worrying increase in the use of health supplements'.

    Marks will be given for a well-structured and developed argument that contains at least three reasons, intermediate conclusions and an overall conclusion. Your argument should also contain examples and/or evidence.

    You may use information and ideas from the original passage, but you must use them to form a new argument. No credit will be given for repeating the original arguments in Document 1. [12]

Total [28]

Total Sections B and C [56]

Glossary

Ability to perceive
A source's ability to use any of their five senses to assess an event or situation.

Ambiguous
A word or phrase is ambiguous if it can have more than one meaning and it is not clear which meaning is intended in a particular context.

Analogy
A form of argument that uses parallels between similar situations to persuade the audience to accept a conclusion.

Appeal
A reference to something or someone, in order to persuade an audience to accept a conclusion.

Appeal to authority
Referring to an expert witness or recognised authority to support a claim.

Appeal to emotion
A form of argument that attempts to support a conclusion by engaging the audience's emotions rather than by giving reasons.

Appeal to history
A form of argument that supports a prediction about the future with a reference to the past.

Appeal to popularity
A form of argument which justifies a conclusion by its popularity.

Appeal to tradition
A form of argument that supports a conclusion by saying it is traditional, or has always been done this way.

Arguing from one thing to another
A form of reasoning that uses a reason about one thing to support a conclusion about something different.

Argument
An attempt to persuade a reader (or listener) to accept something. An argument must have a conclusion and at least one reason.

Argument indicator
A word or short phrase that helps the reader to identify the elements of an argument.

Assumption
This is a missing reason in an argument. The writer accepts the assumption, but has not stated it. The assumption is essential for the conclusion to be drawn.

Attacking the arguer (*ad hominem*)
A form of reasoning that dismisses an opposing view, by attacking the person putting forward that view rather than by addressing their reasoning.

Bias
Tendency to be prejudiced against, or in favour of, certain beliefs, or people who engage in particular activities. This gives a motive or subconscious reason to lie, misrepresent or distort information or evidence, e.g. by being selective in what is reported in order to blame someone else or support strongly held beliefs.

Circular argument

An argument in which one of the reasons is the same as the conclusion, *or* an argument in which you have to assume that the conclusion is right in order for the reasons to make sense.

Claim

A statement or judgement that can be challenged.

Conclusion

The *conclusion of an argument* is a statement of something that the writer (or speaker) wants the reader (or listener) to accept based on the reasons given.

Conflation

Bringing together two or more different concepts and treating them as the same thing.

Confusing correlation and cause

Assuming that because one thing happens before another, or two things happen together, one causes the other. However, there may simply be a correlation – a relationship between two things which happen at the same time but where neither causes the other.

Confusing necessary and sufficient conditions

An argument that assumes a necessary condition is also sufficient, or that assumes a sufficient condition must also be necessary.

Contradiction

This is a special form of inconsistency. Ideas or facts which are contradictory say exactly the opposite things.

Corroboration

Confirmation of, or support for, evidence given by one source by another source.

Counter-argument

An additional argument that is against, or counter to, what the conclusion seeks to establish. The writer normally presents the counter-argument in order to dismiss it.

Counter-assertion

If the writer presents a reason that would support an opponent's argument, rather than a counter-argument, then the writer is making a counter-assertion/claim.

Credibility

Whether someone's claims or evidence can be believed.

Criteria

Standards, measures, or benchmarks, against which something can be measured.

Evaluate

Judge whether the argument or reasoning is strong or weak.

Evidence

Evidence is often in the form of numerical data, an estimate or a factual claim. It is used to develop or support a reason.

Example

Something which is used as evidence because it is characteristic of the same kind of things or because it can serve to illustrate a principle.

Expertise

Skills, experience and training that give someone specialist knowledge and judgement.

Eye-witness

Someone who provides evidence based on first-hand experience.

Fact
Information that can be verified and that is held to be true.

Factual claim
A statement or judgement based on information that can be verified and that is held to be true.

Flaw
A fault in the pattern of reasoning that weakens the support given to the conclusion of an argument.

Hasty generalisation
Draws a general conclusion from insufficient evidence.

Hearsay
Evidence based on secondhand information from another source, who may have interpreted it.

HR
This stands for hypothetical reason.

Hypothetical claim
A claim in the form 'If this … then that …' Hypothetical claim indicator words and phrases include: *if, provided that, on condition that, given that … then …*

Hypothetical reasoning
This looks at the consequences that might occur if something were the case.

Inconsistency
Inconsistent parts of the argument cannot both be the case at the same time, or they would support different conclusions.

Infer
To draw a conclusion; to consider what is implied by evidence. To decide what the next step is; what can be supported by the evidence or reasons.

Intermediate conclusion
A conclusion that is formed on the way to the main conclusion. The intermediate conclusion is supported by reasons and gives support to/acts as a reason for the main conclusion.

Main (or overall) conclusion
The conclusion of an argument that logically follows from the reasoning. There may be one or more intermediate conclusions providing support for the main conclusion of an argument. There will be one or more intermediate conclusions before a main conclusion.

Motive
Factor that may cause a person to act in a particular way.

Neutrality
Being impartial; having no reason to favour either side in a dispute or difference of opinion.

Plausibility
Whether or not a claim or piece of evidence is reasonable.

Principle
A general principle (or rule) is a guide to action which can be applied in a range of circumstances, beyond the immediate context of the argument. There are different kinds of principles, e.g. ethical principles, legal rules, medical ethical guidelines, business or working practices. Principles can be used in an argument as reasons, conclusions or assumptions.

Reason
A statement that aims to persuade the reader to accept a conclusion.

Reputation
What is generally said or believed about the character of a person or an organisation.

Restricting the options
Presents a limited picture of choices available in a situation in order to support one particular option.

Reverse test
A strategy for checking whether an assumption is needed by an argument, by asking yourself if the argument would work with the assumption reversed.

Slippery slope
Reasons from one possibility, through a series of events that are not properly or logically linked, to an extreme consequence.

Source
A person, organization or document providing information or evidence.

Straw person
This flaw misrepresents or distorts an opposing view in order to dismiss it.

Strong conclusion
A conclusion that is very specific and tightly defined.

Sweeping generalisation
A generalisation that moves from some or many to all, creating a stereotype. It may sometimes move back to one individual again.

Tu quoque
An attempt to justify an action on the basis that someone else is doing it.

'Two wrongs don't make a right'
A flaw that attempts to justify one harmful thing on the basis of another, different harmful thing.

Unwarranted assumption of a causal relationship/causal flaw
Reasoning that assumes a causal connection without good reason, oversimplifies causal relationships or confuses cause and effect.

Verify
To confirm if something is true, accurate or real.

Vested interest
Personal interest, usually financial, in a state of affairs or in an organization leading to the expectation of personal gain from a favourable outcome.

Weak conclusion
A conclusion that is not very specific or tightly defined.

Witness
A person who saw (or heard) an event.

Witness statement
A report by someone who has actually seen (or heard) an event.

Heinemann is an imprint of Pearson Education Limited, a company incorporated in England and Wales, having its registered office at Edinburgh Gate, Harlow, Essex, CM20 2JE. Registered company number: 872828

www.heinemann.co.uk

Heinemann is a registered trademark of Pearson Education Ltd

Text © Pearson Education Limited, 2008

First published 2008

12 11 10 09

10 9 8 7 6 5 4 3

British Library Cataloguing in Publication Data is available from the British Library on request.

13-digit ISBN 978 0 435467357

Typeset by Geoff Ward, Tower Designs UK Ltd, Barnet, Hertfordshire

Original illustrations © Pearson Education Limited 2008

Illustrated by Sam Thompson, Calow Craddock Ltd

Cover photo: M.C. Escher's 'Symmetry Drawing E69' © 2007 The M.C. Escher Company-Holland. All rights reserved. www.mcescher.com

Picture research by Zooid Pictures

Printed in Spain by Graficas Estella

Acknowledgements

The author and publisher would like to thank the following individuals and organisations for permission to reproduce photographs:

Carson Ganci/Design Pics/Corbis UK Ltd p6. Anwar Hussein/Getty Images p7. Zooid Pictures p16. Ellen McKnight/Alamy p23. Picturebox-uk.com/Alamy p25. A. Williams/Robert Harding Picture Library Ltd/Alamy p29. Jo Hale/Getty Images p33. Image Source/Corbis UK Ltd p38. David Hoffman Photo Library/Alamy p41. Jenny E. Ross/Corbis UK Ltd p43. Picturesbyrob/Alamy p46. [apply pictures]/Alamy pp52, 249. Schlegelmilch/Corbis UK Ltd p60. Bryan & Cherry Alexander Photography/Alamy p64. PA Photos pp67, 100, 167, 178, 226, 241. Richard Sheppard/Alamy p75. Kerry Ghais/Rex Features p79. Eddie Mulholland/Rex Features p80. Adrian Sherratt/Alamy p82. Liquid Light/Alamy p86. Getty Images/PhotoDisc p88. Dennis Degnan/Corbis UK Ltd p110. Cristina Lombardo p112. Ken Welsh/Alamy p114. Electrolux p117. Medical-on-Line p118. Photofusion Picture Library/Alamy p121. PCL/Alamy p122. Patrice Latron/Corbis UK Ltd p125. Mike Powel/Getty Images p129. Gabe Palmer/Corbis UK Ltd p130. Corbis UK Ltd p131. PA Archive/PA Photos p136. Photofusion Picture Library p136. Mike McGill/Corbis UK Ltd p138. White Cross Productions/Getty Images p140. Zooid Pictures p145. Science Photo Library p146. Corbis UK Ltd p149. PA Wire/PA Photos p160. Patrick Durand Sygma/Corbis UK Ltd p164. Dominic Burke/Alamy p169. Hulton-Deutsch Collection/Corbis UK Ltd p171. Ian Miles Flashpoint Pictures/Alamy p175. Moritz von Hacht/iStockphoto p176. David Hoffman Photo Library/Alamy p179. Lwa-Dann Tardif/Zefa/Corbis UK Ltd p190. Visuals Unlimited/Corbis UK Ltd p194. Ian Shaw/Alamy p195. Andrew Fox/Alamy p201. Dimaggio/Kalish/Corbis UK Ltd p204. Tim Gainey/Alamy p205. George Osodi/Associated Press/PA Photos p210. Jim Craigmyle/Corbis UK Ltd p212. Mark Sykes/Alamy p214. Image100/Corbis UK Ltd p217. Organic Picture Lib/Rex Features p219. William Taufic/Corbis UK Ltd p221. Rex Features pp225, 255. Liam White/Alamy p227. Fujifilm UK Limited p229. Elena Moiseeva/iStockphoto p231. Zooid Pictures p233. BMW p235. Louise Gubb Saba/Corbis UK Ltd p237. Roger Coulam/Alamy p239. Linographic p244. Yellow Dog Productions/Getty Images p247. Photolibrary Group p259.

We would like to thank the following people for permission to reproduce copyrighted material: Page 10 Reproduced with permission of Curtis Brown Ltd, London on behalf of The Estate of Winston Churchill. Copyright Winston S. Churchill. Page15 Copyright Guardian News & Media Ltd, 2003. Reprinted with permission. Page 24 Reprinted with permission of Solo Syndication. Page 45 Wolverhampton Express and Star. Reprinted with permission. Use of a short adapted extract from www.birdguides.com. Reprinted with their kind permission. Pages 47, 48 The Parliamentary Office of Science and Technology (Reproduced under the terms of the Click-Use Licence). Pages 56, 70 Reproduced with permission of Telford & Wrekin Council. Page 61 Extracts from article on F1 by Nik Berg, from BBC Focus Magazine, no 152 July 2005. Copyright © Nik Berg. Reprinted with the kind permission of the author. Page 70 Four headlines from The Times. Copyright NI Syndication Limited, 2007. Reprinted with permission. Page 84 Roger Boyes, Moose with wind are worse than gas guzzlers, The Times/NI Syndication. Reprinted with permission. Page 90 Copyrighht © Michael Portillo. Reprinted with the kind permission of the author. Page 93 Reprinted with permission of Trinity Mirror. Page 94 Reprinted with permission of Solo Syndication. Pages 96¬–99 TWAS ref: T433/153. Reprinted with permission of TWAS. Pages 100–101 Reprinted with permission of Solo Syndication. Page 107 Crown Copyright material reproduced with permission of the controller of the HMSO. Page 153 Crown Copyright. Page 154 Crown Copyright. Page 171 Quote from a speech by Winston Churchill, House of Commons Speech, 11 November 1947. Reproduced with permission of Curtis Brown Ltd, London on behalf of The Estate of Winston Churchill. Copyright Winston S. Churchill. Page 199 © NI Syndication Limited 2007. Reprinted with permission. Page 270 Crown Copyright.

All OCR questions contained in these components are printed with the permission of OCR. Pages 29, 32, 39, 49, 59, 62, 63, 115, 116, 124, 126, 131, 151, 153, 155, 159, 191, 217, 222 © OCR, www.ocr.org.uk.

Every effort has been made to contact copyright holders of material reproduced in this book. Any omissions will be rectified in subsequent printings if notice is given to the publishers.

Websites

The websites used in this material were correct and up-to-date at the time of publication. It is essential for tutors to preview each website before using it in class so as to ensure that the URL is still accurate, relevant and appropriate. We suggest that tutors bookmark useful websites and consider enabling students to access them through the school/college intranet.

Your AS Critical Thinking CD-ROM

Opposite you will find the AS Critical Thinking CD-ROM. Open up the CD, explore its contents and develop your Critical Thinking skills further.

LiveText

On the CD you will find an electronic version of the Student Book, powered by LiveText. As well as the Student Book and the LiveText tools there are:

- guidance to the activities – indicated by this icon

- interactive activities to help develop your Critical Thinking skills further – indicated by this icon.

Within the electronic version of the Student Book, you will also find the interactive Exam Café.

Exam Café

Immerse yourself in our contemporary interactive Exam Café environment! With a click of your mouse you can visit three separate areas in the café to **Relax**, **Refresh your Memory** or **Get the Result**. You'll find a wealth of material including the following.

- Revision Tips from students, Key Concepts, Common Mistakes and Examiner's Tips.

- Language of the Exam (an interactive activity).

- Revision Flashcards, Revision Checklists and The Basics.

- Sample Exam Questions (which you can try) with student answers and examiner comments.

Minimum system requirements

- Windows 2000, XP Pro or Vista

- Internet Explorer 6 (and above) or Firefox 2.0

- Flash Player 8 or higher plug-in

- Pentium III 1GHz with 512 Mb RAM

To run your LiveText CD, insert it into the CD drive of your computer. It should start automatically; if not, please go to My Computer (Computer on Vista), click on the CD drive and double-click on 'LiveText.exe'.

If you have difficulties running the CD, or if your copy is not there, please contact the helpdesk number given below.

Software support
For further software support between the hours of 8.30–5.00 (Mon–Fri), please contact:
Tel: 01865 888108
Fax: 01865 314091
Email: software.enquiries@pearson.com